D0881196

Springer Series in Agent Technology

Series Editors: T. Ishida N. Jennings K. Sycara

Marco Mamei · Franco Zambonelli

Field-Based Coordination for Pervasive Multiagent Systems

With 127 Figures

 Springer

Authors

Marco Mamei
Dipartimento di Scienze
e Metodi dell'Ingegneria
Università di Modena e Reggio Emilia
Via Allegri 13
42100 Reggio Emilia, Italy

marco.mamei@unimore.it

Franco Zambonelli
Dipartimento di Scienze
e Metodi dell'Ingegneria
Università di Modena e Reggio Emilia
Via Allegri 13
42100 Reggio Emilia, Italy

franco.zambonelli@unimore.it

Series Editors

Professor Toru Ishida
Dept. of Social Informatics
Kyoto University
Yoshida-Honmachi
Kyoto 606-8501, Japan

ishida@i.kyoto-u.ac.jp

Professor Nicholas R. Jennings
Intelligence, Agents Multimedia Group
School of Electronics & Computer Science
University of Southampton
Highfield, Southampton, SO17 1BJ, UK

nrj@ecs.soton.ac.uk

Professor Katia Sycara
The Robotics Institute
Carnegie Mellon University
5000 Forbes Ave., DH 3315
Pittsburgh, PA 15213, USA

katia@cs.cmu.edu

Library of Congress Control Number: 2005935330

ACM Computing Classification (1998): I.2.11, C.2.4, D.3.3

ISBN-10 3-540-27968-7 Springer Berlin Heidelberg New York
ISBN-13 978-3-540-27968-3 Springer Berlin Heidelberg New York

Springer is a part of Springer Science+Business Media

springeronline.com

© Springer-Verlag Berlin Heidelberg 2006
Printed in Germany

Typeset by the authors using a Springer TEX macro package
Production: LE-TEX Jelonek, Schmidt & Vöckler GbR, Leipzig
Cover design: KünkelLopka Werbeagentur, Heidelberg

Printed on acid-free paper   45/3142/YL - 5 4 3 2 1 0

To Elisabetta, Matteo, and my parents.
Marco

To Anna, Riccardo, and Veronica.
Franco

Preface

In the last few years, the search for radically new approaches to software engineering has witnessed a great momentum. These efforts are well justified by the troubling state of present day computer science.

Software engineering practices based on design-time architectural composition (the only assessed way of doing software engineering so far), lead to brittle and fragile systems, unable to gracefully cope with reconfiguration and faults. While such practices can be acceptable when dealing with software systems to be deployed in closed and static scenarios, they are definitely unsuitable for most emerging computing scenarios.

More and more, software systems involve autonomous and distributed software components that have to execute and interact in open and dynamic environments. This is the case of information economies, pervasive and mobile computing systems, wide-area Internet applications, and P2P computing. In all these scenarios, the dynamism, openness, and decentralization of the application's operational environments call for new approaches to software design and development, capable of supporting spontaneous configuration and networking, and capable of tolerating partial failures and adaptive reorganization of the software system.

Hints for the feasibility of such innovative approaches can come from a variety of natural systems. The process of morphogenesis in organisms demonstrates that well-defined shapes and functional structures can develop through the interaction of cells under the control of a genetic program, even though the precise arrangements and numbers of the individual cells are variable. The process of ant foraging demonstrates how the application goal of finding and carrying home food in hostile environments can be achieved by simple interactions among a multitude of individuals of limited intelligence.

By getting inspiration from natural systems, scientists and engineers are starting to understand that, to construct self-organizing and adaptive systems, it may be more appropriate focusing on the engineering of proper interaction mechanisms for the components of the system, rather than on the engineering of their overall system architecture.

In line with the above consideration, this book focuses on a physically inspired interaction model, i.e., field-based coordination. Field-based coordination relies on virtual computational fields, mimicking gravitational and electromagnetic fields, as the basic mechanisms with which to coordinate activities in open and dynamic ensembles of application components. This enables components to spontaneously interact with each other by the mediation of fields and – as in physical systems – to self-organize in an adaptive way their activity patterns. All of this with the additional advantage that – unlike in real-world physical systems – one can shape fields according to any needed virtual physical law, to achieve a variety of coordination patterns in support of a variety of application goals.

This book summarizes in a readable and accessible way some four years of work in the area of advanced field-based coordination models. The specific model presented in this book together with the middleware technologies that have been developed to support it, define a general-purpose approach for the engineering of self-organizing adaptive applications in a number of scenarios. The title of the book evokes the fact that the model was originally conceived for multiagent systems in pervasive computing scenarios. However, we invite readers to consider it as reflecting the fact that field-based coordination may be suitable for all systems made up of autonomous interacting components (agents *de facto*), from sensor networks to P2P computing systems, that will soon pervade our everyday environments.

Additional material for this book, including code of the simulations and of the TOTA middleware, can be found at the Web site of the Agents and Pervasive Computing Group, *http://www.agentgroup.unimore.it*.

Acknowledgments

A number of persons have directly or indirectly contributed to this book.

We thank all the members of the Agents and Pervasive Computing Group at the University of Modena and Reggio Emilia, for their continuous support and friendship during these years.

We thank Alfred Hofmann and Ralf Gerstner from Springer, for having supported this work and for having tolerated our delays.

A final special thanks is extended to all our students (now engineers) who have actively contributed to our researches with notable implementation and experimental work.

Reggio Emilia,
May 2005,
Marco Mamei and Franco Zambonelli

Contents

Part III Implementing Field-based Coordination

Part IV Advanced Applications

1

Introduction

Novel research findings in different areas are promoting radical changes in the upcoming Information and Communication Technology scenario. On the one hand, advances in pervasive and embedded computing systems (e.g., smart objects [44, 163], self-assembly [1, 102], sensor networks [33, 105], and distributed MEMS [11, 152]) will soon make our everyday environments populated by myriads of interacting computer-based systems. On the other hand, worldwide distributed computing (enabled by proposals for worldwide distributed service access [26, 98] and efficient approaches to adaptive distributed computing [3, 122, 45] and to location-based [119, 125, 22] and content-based data access [120, 129]) is eventually becoming a reality. Between these two extremes, various scenarios of use are arising, including personal-area networks (e.g., the ensemble of Bluetooth-enabled interacting computer-based components we could carry or find in our cars), MANETs (short for mobile ad hoc networks, e.g., dynamic networks of PDAs carried by members of a rescue team that have to directly interact and coordinate with each other in a disaster area), and networked furniture and appliances (e.g., Web-enabled fridges and ovens able to interact with each other and effectively support our culinary activities in a coordinated way).

1.1 The Challenge

Although the hardware technology for the above scenarios is rapidly maturing, the current state of software engineering models and practices – required to develop software applications in such huge and dynamic environments – seems not to be ready for such a revolution [77, 165]. In fact, software engineering practices have remained more or less the same since structured design and distributed programming methodologies were introduced: software is designed and developed in terms of components that are subject to a centralized flow of control and that are coupled at design time by fixed interaction patterns. Centralization of control and the static nature of interactions can make the design and development process simpler, but it typically leads to brittle and fragile software systems, unable to cope with dynamic reconfiguration and faults.

In recent years, researches on software agents and multiagent systems have fostered a programming paradigm based on autonomous components (i.e., components with independent threads of execution and control) that dynamically interact with each other toward the achievement of some application goals without being strictly coupled with each other at design time [10, 22, 112]. This paradigm shift is well motivated by the robustness, scalability, and flexibility of systems based on autonomous agents: if a component breaks down, the others can autonomously reorganize their interaction patterns to account for such a failure; if new components are added to the system, they can autonomously discover which other components are present and start to interact with them.

The key element leading to such robust, scalable, and flexible behaviors is, in addition to autonomy, the capability of self-organizing and adaptive coordination. Autonomous components must be able to spontaneously and dynamically coordinate their activity patterns to achieve goals exceeding their capabilities as single individuals, despite, and possibly taking advantage of, environment dynamism and unexpected situations [108, 132, 163]. Nature, for example, "adopts" these ideas at all scales, e.g., in colonies of social insects, in the cells of the immune systems, in the neurons of the brain [7, 8, 14]. The inherent dynamism of modern distributed computing scenarios invites one to get inspiration from these natural approaches to coordination, in order to promote the development and deployment of robust, self-organizing, and self-adaptive distributed applications.

Unfortunately, even though that nature can be a source of inspiration for the identification of novel coordination models, the general problem of programming and managing complex software systems that are deployed in dynamic scenarios is still open. The main conceptual difficulty is that while the developer can enforce direct control only on agents' local activities and local interactions, the application goal to be achieved is often expressed at the global scale [8, 14]. For example, the problem of routing in a MANET can be easily regarded as an adaptive coordination problem: autonomous nodes must cooperate, forwarding each other packets, to let the packets flow from sources to destinations. The reason routing in MANET is a difficult problem is that one can control only agents' local activities, specifying how an agent routes a packet to its immediate neighbors (the only ones reachable). However, the application goal is global: packets must flow from distant nodes across the whole network, which is typically dynamic and whose evolution cannot be controlled.

Bridging the gap between local and global activities is not easy, but it has been shown to be possible. By exploiting some nature-inspired interaction mechanisms with a proper application-specific tuning of parameters, it is possible to reproduce natural phenomena of adaptive self-organization (i.e., the emergence of globally coherent behaviors from local interactions) and put them to the service of specific application goals in specific scenarios. For example, the phenomenon of ant foraging has been proposed and successfully applied to routing in MANET [14].

The key problem is that the above success stories – dealing with specific solutions for specific application domains – do not provide lessons that can generalize to other scenarios. Indeed, what we really need are general-purpose approaches, supported by widely applicable methodologies, middleware, and tools, with which to promote the development of self-organizing adaptive applications in a variety of modern distributed computing scenarios [1, 132, 77, 165].

1.2 Contribution of the Book

The main contribution of this book is to present a novel coordination model that – together with its supporting middleware infrastructure – has the potential to form the basis for a general-purpose and widely applicable approach for the design and development of self-organizing and adaptive distributed applications.

The proposed coordination model takes its inspiration from the physical world, and in particular from the way masses and particles in our universe move and globally self-organize according to the contextual information represented by gravitational and electromagnetic fields. To acknowledge that inspiration, the model is called Field-based coordination. Field-based coordination aims at supporting agents' activities by providing, through the concept of "computational fields," a single abstraction to (i) promote uncoupled and adaptive interactions and (ii) provide agents with simple, yet expressive, contextual information.

These general ideas are embodied in our proposal called Co-Fields (short for "computational fields"). In Co-Fields, each agent in an environment (e.g., a mobile device carried by a human user as well as any embedded computing device) can generate and propagate, according to specific laws, component-specific fields conveying some application-specific information about the local environment and/or about itself. Other agents can then locally perceive these fields and can react according to the local configuration and shape of the perceived fields. Engineering a coordination policy within this model consists in specifying local interactions: how agents generate fields, how these fields are propagated, and how agents subscribe and react to the fields. The global coordination simply emerges in a self-organized and adaptive way from these local field-mediated interaction patterns.

The Co-Fields model can be used to develop and deploy application with the support of the Tuples On The Air (TOTA) middleware infrastructure, specifically conceived to support Co-Fields coordinated applications. In the

TOTA middleware, all interactions between agents take place in a fully un-coupled way by tuples' exchange. However, TOTA does not promote any sort of centralized shared tuple space. Rather, TOTA implements the abstraction of computational fields by tuples that can be "injected" into a networked system from any node and that can then propagate and diffuse in the system according to tuple-specific propagation patterns. The TOTA middleware takes care of tuple propagation by automatically readapting propagation patterns according to the dynamic changes that can occur in the network (as due to, e.g., mobile or ephemeral nodes). Agents can exploit a simple API to program and inject new tuples in the network and to locally sense both tuples and events associated with changes in the tuples' distributed structures (e.g., arrival and dismissing of tuples).

1.3 Structure of the Book

This book is divided into four main parts.

Part I presents an overview of the scenarios of interest and motivates the work by outlining the fundamental role of coordination in such scenarios. In particular, Chap. 2 describes our view of the future for Information and Communication Technologies, by showing that a vast range of scenarios, ranging from Internet-scale peer-to-peer (P2P) systems to networks of tiny microsensors, share very common issues and requirements with regard to application development and software engineering principles. Chapter 3 emphasizes the fundamental role of coordination in the context of such future scenarios and shows the inadequacy of current coordination models and middleware in supporting the development of self-organizing and adaptive applications.

Part II introduces field-based coordination models and details the Co-Fields model. Specifically, Chap. 4 describes field-based coordination as a powerful approach to support coordination in modern dynamic environments. A number of approaches in different areas exploiting some kinds of field-based coordination are presented and discussed. Chapter 5 presents in detail the Co-Fields model, emphasizing how Co-Fields abstractions overcome some problems at the heart of previous approaches. A formal description of the model, obtained by a dynamic system formalism, is presented along with several simulation results.

Part III focuses on the implementation and deployment of the field-based abstractions. Chapter 6 shows how the Co-Fields model can be implemented – with some limitations – by exploiting the services of "off the shelf" middleware. Chapter 7 describes TOTA, a middleware and a programming model specifically conceived to support field-based coordination at its best. The chapter shows how TOTA distributed tuples naturally match the Co-Fields abstractions. A prototype implementation of the middleware is discussed together with the implementation of an emulator enabling us to test the system in large-scale scenarios.

Part IV puts Co-Fields and TOTA at work, by presenting several advanced Co-Fields coordinated applications that have been developed (or simply designed) by making use of the TOTA middleware. Chapter 8 focuses on content-based approaches to distributed information access, and shows how Co-Fields and TOTA can flexibly implement it. Chapter 9 shows how Co-Fields and TOTA can be used to promote self-assembly and motion coordination in systems of mobile robots. Chapter 10 presents a visionary application, the cloak of invisibility, and shows how field-based coordination can be exploited within it.

Finally, Chap. 11 concludes the book and outlines open research issues.

Part I

The Scenario

2

Upcoming Information Technology Scenarios

Recent advances in electronics, telecommunications, and software technologies are making a variety of innovative distributed computing scenarios come to the fore. Robot swarms, sensor networks, pervasive computing systems, P2P networks, and Internet ecologies, promise to dramatically impact our future lives by supporting our social and professional activities in a ubiquitous and personalized way and by dramatically improving our interactions with both the physical and the cyberworlds.

This chapter details the key characteristics of several of the above scenarios and shows that all of them – although very diverse from each other in terms of both underlying hardware and application goals – share some common key characteristics. In fact, they all involve a large number of distributed and autonomous computational entities that interact with each other in decentralized networks with a highly dynamic structure.

The above common characteristics challenge traditional approaches to application design and development, calling for novel approaches supporting adaptive self-organization. However, the fact that there are common characteristics also lets us envision the possibility of identifying some general-purpose approaches that can apply with little or no modifications to scenarios as diverse as sensor networks and P2P networks.

2.1 From Robot Self-Assembly to Internet Ecologies

In order to present in a rational way a variety of diverse distributed systems scenarios, we can roughly classify them based on the type of computing devices involved and on the scale at which distribution occurs. The "micro scale" considers networks of low-end computing devices typically distributed over a geographically small area and interacting by short-range wireless connections (i.e., sensor networks and smart dust). The "medium scale" considers medium-end wearable, portable, and embedded devices interacting by short- and medium-range connections (i.e., pervasive computing environments). The "global scale" considers high-end computing devices participating in world-wide distributed applications (i.e., P2P and global service networks).

2.1.1 The Micro Scale

With the MEMS revolution in full swing, microsensors are now following manufacturing curves that are at least related to Moore's Law [114]. This trend, when combined with both the push for low power communication and computation devices and for the ubiquitous provisioning of data and services, paves the way for the "spray computers" revolution [161, 165]. It is not hard to envision a future in which networks of microcomputers will be literally sold as spray cans, to be sprayed in an environment or on specific artifacts to enrich them with functionalities that, as of today, may appear futuristic and visionary [1, 103, 163, 115]. The number of potential applications of the scenario is endless, ranging from smart and invisible clothes, intelligent interactive environments, self-assembly materials, and self-repairing artifacts.

As proved in the context of the Smart Dust project at Berkeley [11, 73], it is already possible to produce full-fledged computer-based systems smaller than a cubic centimeter, and even much smaller ones will be produced in the next few years [136]. Such computers, which can be enriched with communication capabilities (radio or optical), local sensing (e.g., optical, thermal, or inertial) and local effecting (e.g., optical and mechanical) capabilities, are the basic ingredients of our spray computer vision.

Spray computers, as we imagine them, are clouds of sub-millimeter-scale microcomputers, to be deployed in an environment or onto specific artifacts by a spraying or painting process. Once deployed, such components will spontaneously network with each other and will coordinate their actions (i.e., local sensing and effecting) to provide specific "smart" functionalities. We imagine it will be possible, say in 2020, to go to the local store and buy, for a few Euros, a "pipe repairing" spray, made up of a cloud of MEMS devices capable of navigating in a pipeline, recognizing the presence of holes, and self-assembling with each other so as to perfectly repair the pipe. Similarly, we could imagine a spray to transform our everyday desk into an active one, capable of recognizing the positions and characteristics of objects placed on it and letting them meaningfully interact [21].

Another peculiar application we envision is the "spray of invisibility" (described in Chap. 10 and in more detail in [163]): a spray of micro devices capable of receiving and retransmitting light emissions in a directional way, and capable of interacting with each other by short-range wireless communications. When an object is covered by a layer of such a spray, the emissions of the devices make external observers perceive exactly the same light configuration that they would have perceived if there was nothing in between. In fact, sensors on the rear side of the object can receive such a light configuration and, by distributed coordination, can communicate it to emitters on the observer's side to be retransmitted.

Other types of application one could envision include any type of self-assembly artifact [103], including things like the T1000 robot in the movie *Terminator 2*, the nanoswarms of Michael Chricton's novel *Prey* [24], and MEMS-based artificial immune systems and drugs [115].

Within the micro scale, and beside the spray computer vision, we can also classify recent efforts in the area of sensor networks [33]. Wireless networks of small computing devices enriched with various sensorial capabilities (e.g., thermal, inertial, or optical) have already been deployed in a variety of environments (e.g., buildings or landscapes) to monitor such environments in a cooperative way, by spontaneously networking with each other in order to coordinate their activities and to exchange sensorial information (see Fig. 2.1).

2.1.2 The Medium Scale

Besides micro devices to be literally sprayed, "spray computers" can also act as a power metaphor for the key characteristics of the emerging scenarios of ubiquitous and pervasive computing, as enabled by handheld, wearable, and embedded, networked computing systems. We already typically carry two or three computers (i.e., a cell phone, a laptop, and possibly a PDA). Also, our houses are already populated by a variety of microprocessor-based furniture (e.g., TVs, phones, etc.). However, at the moment, the networking capabilities of these computer-based systems are underexploited. Very soon, however, all these devices will start communicating and interacting with each other to provide new applications and value-added services (see Fig. 2.2). Our world will be densely populated by personal-area networks (e.g., the ensemble of Bluetooth-enabled interacting computer-based components we could carry or find in our cars), local ad hoc networks of handheld computers (e.g., networks of interacting PDAs carried by team members to interact and coordinate with each other in an open space), and furniture networks (e.g., Web-enabled fridges and ovens able to interact with each other and effectively support our culinary activities in a coordinated way).

Consider a scenario a few years hence in which a large city like Boston might have several wireless base stations in every building, i.e., a number of nodes in the order of 10^7. If most of the electrical devices in the buildings and those carried on by people are wirelessly networked too, then the total number of nodes could be as high as 10^{10}. If these nodes communicate peer-to-peer with nearby devices, then one could envision the entire city as connected into a huge mobile ad hoc network approximately 10^3 hops in diameter, comprised of extremely heterogeneous entities like workstations, computer-enabled furniture, cell phones, PDAs, and embedded sensors [9].

The possibilities of adopting these new technologies are endless and will be likely to impact every aspect of our lives: to support our cooperative activities [59], to monitor and control our environments [16], to improve our interactions with the physical world [87], in environmental sciences [139], in child and

Fig. 2.1. The micro scale: different micro scale devices. (a) A microsensor integrating processing unit, memory, wireless interface, and power supply; photo taken from [128]; (b) Sensor mote circuit [127]; (c) Sensor device deployed in a natural environment [143]; (d) Mobile wheeled micro device; photo from [127]; (e) Micro wireless robot; image from [100]; (f) T1000 terminator from the *Terminator 2* movie

health care [138], in entertainment [113], and in the military [130], to mention just a few examples.

Already today, for example, navigator-equipped cars can give us instructions on how to reach a specific address. However, in the near future, when computing and communication will be widespread, those navigators could provide much more added value: they could dynamically interact with traffic lights to negotiate on a specific green light timing policy, suggest alternative directions on the basis of the current traffic condition, notify other cars about a police car in ambush to hand off tickets, or – more ethically – automatically choke the engine to enforce speed limits.

As another application scenario, smart phones or palm computers could give us advice on restaurants and good pubs while visiting a new city, depending on our preferences and mood. Such an advice could be based on consulting online recommendation services, sharing of comments of past users or even dynamically exchanged on the fly between users (e.g., "hey, there is a good party going on at Griffin's Pub...," or in an Indian restaurant "this evening the Vindaloo chicken is not spicy enough...").

What we want here to emphasize is that the above kinds of applications involve dynamic networks of spontaneously interacting devices, thus resembling, at a different scale, the types of networks involved in the micro scale scenario described before. Consequently, they will also share with the micro scale the same issues as far as the development and management of distributed applications are concerned.

2.1.3 The Global Scale

In the case of macro-scale networks made up of high-end computer systems distributed at a worldwide scale, i.e., the Internet, the Web, and P2P networks, very similar issues arise.

The dramatic growth of these networks and of the information and traffic to be managed, together with the increasing request for ubiquitous connectivity, have recently raised researchers' attention to the need for radically novel approaches to distributed systems management [77]. Traditional approaches to management, requiring human configuration efforts and supervision, fall short when the number of nodes in the network (e.g., the number of inter-related services and links on the Web, or the number of peers in a P2P network) grows in a fully decentralized way, and when the presence of the nodes in a network is of an intrinsically ephemeral nature, as it is in the case of laptops on the Internet, of non-commercial services on the Web, and of peers in P2P networks (see Fig. 2.3).

The need for such novel approaches is even more fundamental and compelling when considering the endless range of applications lying ahead in the near future.

The Semantic Web [144], envisioned by the W3C, will provide a quantum leap to the functionalities (but also to the complexities) offered by the

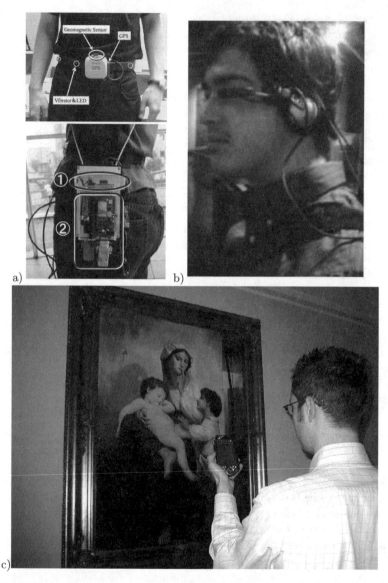

Fig. 2.2. The medium scale: wearable and handheld computing devices. (a) A belt wearable computing infrastructure; image taken from [149]; (b) Head-up wearable display; image taken from [134]; (c) A tourist accessing information on site by a PDA

Web. The Semantic Web is intended to complement humans in areas in which they do not perform well, such as processing large volumes of information quickly or analyzing large texts for certain pieces of information. While technologies for semantic data representation, like XML, RDF [158], and ontologies (DAML+OIL) [27], will provide the basic infrastructure, intelligent autonomous agents will process and distill such information on the fly to answer specific queries, avoiding information overload. The Semantic Web, and other developments such as multiagent systems economies – where intelligent agents will be fully delegated to being economic actors to buy, sell, and negotiate for good – and Grid computing [37] – where any one computer can tap the power of all computers – will possibly give rise to the concept of the "global brain" [146, 68]. According to this vision, the Web will act as a global superorganism, the "brain" of society. Intelligent agents, populating the Web, will scan and distill humanity's collective knowledge, identifying undiscovered relations between concepts and enabling communication of concepts even where there is no commonality of terms.

In all these cases, as visionary as the described applications can be, the development and management of distributed applications cannot of course rely on static architectural design and interaction patterns.

2.2 Distinguishing Characteristics

Embedded computing systems, sensor networks, pervasive computing environments, and worldwide computing systems, despite the apparent macro dissimilarity, share similar characteristics and introduce very similar issues with regard to programming and management, calling for context-aware interaction models capable of supporting adaptive self-organization of distributed activities.

- **Large Scale.** The various scenarios we have introduced in the previous subsection are all characterized by being composed of a possibly very high number of distributed components. The spray computer vision considers the possibility of deploying millions of micro devices; pervasive computing suggests that each and every object in an environment can become a computer-based device capable of networking with any number of nearby devices; current P2P networks already involve millions of users. Moreover, we must consider that all the above scenarios, now mostly studied as standalone systems, will be in the near future part of a huge network (with a flat, hierarchical, or somewhat clustered structure), including traditional Internet nodes, smart computer enriched objects and furniture, and networks of embedded and dispersed microsensors. For instance, the IPv6 addressing scheme will make it possible to assign an Internet address to every cubic millimeter of the earth surface [54], thus opening the possibility for each and every computer-based component to become part of a single worldwide network. Clearly, the large number of components involved makes

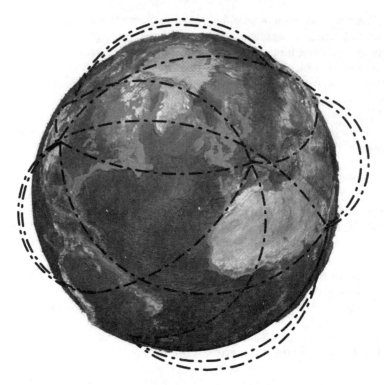

Fig. 2.3. The global scale: worldwide connectivity in distributed applications.

any traditional approach that implies the necessity of directly configuring each and every component of a system very hard to apply and, possibly, economically infeasible.

- **Decentralization.** One should also consider that the components of all these networks may not all be directly accessible for configuration and control, due to decentralization. Sensor networks may be deployed in hostile, uneasy to access landscapes. Pervasive computing environments may involve components developed in separate contexts and belonging to different stakeholders. P2P networks, by definition, involve a multiplicity of independent stakeholders which prevent direct access to individual components of the network. In addition, for spray computers, direct control over each component may be made impossible by the size of the components involved. This said, it is rather clear that those approaches considering the possibility of directly configuration and maintenance at the level of individual components may not only be difficult to enforce but simply impossible.
- **Network Dynamics.** Although the overall structures of, e.g., sensor networks, pervasive computing networks, and worldwide networks, may be

apparently very different from each other, they are all characterized by being intrinsically amorphous and dynamic. On the one hand, such networks tend to be amorphous either because they have been deployed without any determined configuration (think of a spray computer network or of a sensor network randomly deployed in a landscape) or because they grow and evolve without any central control (think of a pervasive computing network which continuously evolves as new smart objects are integrated in an environment, or at the way in which new users connect to a P2P community). On the other hand, such networks are characterized by an intrinsically dynamic structure, due to the presence of ephemeral nodes (e.g., sensors in a network can die or run out of power, the nodes in a worldwide P2P network can be shutdown or temporarily unreachable) and the presence of mobile nodes (e.g., mobile robots, laptops carried by humans). The above dynamics require the capability of a system to continue working in a proper way without being affected by the underlying changes in the network structure, i.e., to properly reconfigure its structure to reflect a changed situation. Clearly, these operations should by performed by the system in autonomy, without requiring any human intervention that, as previously outlined, is already hard to enforce at deployment time and can be impossible to enforce at runtime.

- **Need for Context-Awareness.** The dynamism of the network makes it impossible for application components to rely on strong a priori information about their execution context (e.g., the other application components with which to interact, their location in the network, the characteristics of the local environment in which they are executing). This forces applications to acquire at runtime all the contextual information required to dynamically adapt their behavior and proceed with their execution despite network dynamics [22, 125]. In other words, application components must become context-aware.

  The need for promoting context-awareness is also a consequence of the fact that most of modern scenarios are characterized by situated activities, i.e., are related with their being located in some sort of physical or virtual computational environment. On the one hand, situatedness can be at the very core of the application (e.g., in sensor networks and in pervasive computing systems the very goal is to exploit the physical location of nodes and their capabilities to collect environmental data to improve our interaction with the physical world). On the other hand, situatedness can relate to the fact that components can take advantage of some sort of computational environment to organize the access to distributed resources (as, e.g., on the Web and in P2P data sharing networks).

  In any case, any approach to design and development that does not properly account for context-awareness as a primary design development will simply be unsuitable for modern and future distributed computing scenarios.

All the above considerations suggest that the goal of identifying innovative software engineering approaches, uniformly accounting for the specific problems and issues arising at different scenarios, and proposing suitable solutions toward the development of self-organizing, adaptive, and context-aware applications, is a realistic goal, worth investigating.

2.3 Relevant Research Projects

Several projects around the world are starting to recognize the relevance of the above themes and are facing issues related, to different extents, to the identification of novel approaches for the engineering of what we can generally identify as "spray computing" systems and applications.

Without the ambition to be exhaustive, we present here a few relevant threads of activities and discuss what are, in our opinion, their shortcomings.

2.3.1 The Micro Scale

Very close to our spray computers vision, the Amorphous Computing project at MIT [1] focuses on the problem of identifying suitable models for programming applications over amorphous networks of "computing particles."

The goal of these applications is to enable locally interacting particles to self-organize coherent patterns of activity in the amorphous network [21, 103, 104]. So far, the Amorphous Computing project has defined a simple yet effective language for programming particles on the basis of an interaction model relying on the propagation of simple computational fields. On this basis, it has been shown how it is possible to exploit such a language and interaction model to let the particles self-organize a coordinate system and self-determine their position in it, and how it is possible to let a variety of global patterns get organized in a system from local interactions. What the project has still not addressed are the problems related to mobile and ephemeral particles: the network is considered static, and the relative position of particles is considered fixed. Also, the project so far has focused on very simple particles as finite-state machines with a limited number of states – not much different from cellular automata cells [154]. The effectiveness of their model and programming language in acting as a general-purpose programming approach for more complex particles in different scenarios is still to be verified . Besides amorphous computers, most of the researches in the area of micro-scale spray computers are performed in the context of the "sensor networks" research community [33, 85, 110].

The key issues being investigated in the area of sensor networks relate to the identification of effective algorithms and tools to perform distributed monitoring of activities by a cloud of distributed sensors in a physical environment. Representative goals pursued by these researches include tracing the position and movement of an object, determining the occurrence of specific environmental conditions, and reporting sensed data back to a base station in an efficient way. In general, these researches are indeed providing good insights on the theme of self-organized spontaneous interactions in amorphous ad hoc networks, and are leading to some very interesting results. Techniques for self-localization, self-synchronization of activities, and adaptive data distribution, all of which are of primary importance for any type of modern computing scenario, have been widely investigated.

Still, we feel these researches are somewhat limited by three main factors. Firstly, the accent on "sensing" tends to disregard the "actuating" factor – a potential source of a wide range of interesting applications. Secondly, most research work is being devoted to the definition of "power-aware" and "power-effective" algorithms for distributed sensing (where distributed sensors tend to self-organize their activities so as to minimize resource consumption). This is motivated by the current impossibility of providing such small computer systems with enough battery power to last for a long time. However, in our opinion, short life batteries and the consequent need for power-aware computing models are a current contingent problem, rather than a basic research issue likely to have long-term impact. Scavenging power from sunlight, vibration, thermal gradients, and background RF, the next generation of microcomputers will be fully autonomous in terms of power supply, and will be capable of long lasting, if not everlasting, activity. As Kris Pister (the inventor of the Smart Dust technology) envisions [114, 115], computer-based sensors and actuators, being entirely solid state and with no natural decay processes, may be everlasting and survive the human race. Thirdly, and possibly most importantly, these researches have little to say on the issue of identifying novel general-purpose approaches to application development, suitable for a wide range of applications and possibly suitable for scenarios beyond the specific area of sensor networks.

2.3.2 The Medium Scale

Coming to the medium scale, as far as we can see, most of the researches are focusing either on routing algorithms for mobile ad hoc networks of handheld computers [20] or on the definition of effective user-level ubiquitous environments [126, 49].

Researches on routing algorithms for MANETs [20] share several common issues with researches on algorithms for data distribution on sensor networks. In our opinion, these works are, again, too often focused on power and resources limitation problems and mostly disregard higher-level issues such as coordination of distributed behaviors and general-purpose programming approaches.

Researches on ubiquitous computing environments mostly focus on achieving dynamic interoperability between applications and pervasive computing devices. For instance, the Gaia system developed at PARC [126] and the

EventHeap [66] developed at Stanford, define an architecture based on "active" interaction spaces. These spaces are intended to act as a reification of a specific real-world environment (e.g., a meeting room), where pre-existing (and pre-programmed) devices and user-level software components can dynamically enter, acquire context-awareness, and leave and inter-operate dynamically with each other according to specific patterns specified as part of the active environment.

Although approaches based on active interaction spaces are very suitable to support context-aware user-level activities and interactions in a pervasive computing environment, neither Gaia or EventHeap nor most of the other proposals in this direction have something to say on the issue of designing, developing, and controlling self-organizing and adaptive distributed applications. Basically these systems limit themselves to enabling context-aware interactions, but disregard the problem of supporting an adaptive pattern of activities among components, which are instead statically specified in "old style" architectural terms.

The same thing is true also for a variety of related researches more focused on the specific issue of supporting context-aware computing in pervasive computing environments. The majority of proposals [125, 29, 31] presents methods to discover relevant sources of contextual information, merge them together, and provide meaningful, high-level descriptions of the data being gathered.

Although the proper and expressive provision of contextual information is indeed a relevant and fundamental topic, we think that the main shortcoming of these focused researches is the lack of concern on how the acquired contextual information is later exploited. Most of the researches simply assume humans and individual software components as the natural recipients of such information. This makes the above proposals inadequate in providing a context representation suitable to support adaptive self-organizing coordinated activities in distributed applications.

2.3.3 The Global Scale

As far as the global scale is involved, most researches on adaptive and unsupervised computing focus on the key idea of self-organizing overlay networks for peer-to-peer (P2P) computing.

The need to access data and services according to a variety of patterns and independently of the availability/location of specific servers calls for P2P approaches to distributed application development centered on the idea of overlay networks. This idea (promoted by first generation P2P systems such as Gnutella [122], and later improved by second generation P2P systems such as CAN [120], Chord [140], and Pastry [129]) is to have data and services organized into types of spontaneously organized virtual networks of acquaintances . In P2P networks, the allocation of software components that need to interact with each other (think, e.g., of file-sharing applications) can be intrinsically amorphous and dynamic, i.e., composed of an unpredictable number of possibly unknown peers placed almost anywhere in the physical network, as if it were a network of spray computers. However, such amorphous components can organize themselves into a virtual overlay network of acquaintances that enables easy and robust interactions. The constituted network, abstracting from the physical amorphous nature of the actual network, can survive events such as the arrival of new nodes or the dismissing of some nodes. The ideas and the results achieved in the area of overlay networks for P2P computing are outstanding. Still, in our opinion, they are focused on enabling communication only, and little is said about their potential support for coordinated distributed applications. Even when global communication is made possible and efficient by the overlay network, who should talk with whom? What shape of the overlay network is better suited to specific application needs? How can coordination of activities be supported by overlay networks? All these unanswered questions call for more than simply enabling communication in open and dynamic networks.

Research work in the area of multiagent systems [63] goes more in the direction of identifying novel approaches for the design and development of coordinated applications to be deployed in open, dynamic, and possibly worldwide scenarios. However, the focus of these researches is, in most of the cases, related to empowering agents with the intelligence to deal, as individuals, with the openness and dynamics of the operational environments and with the need to dynamically interact with other agents to achieve global application goals. Also, in several cases, the context-awareness dimension is underestimated, despite the fact that the canonical definition of agents explicitly consider them as situated entities [64]. A few proposals suggest using agents as a general paradigm for the development of context-aware, adaptive, and self-organizing applications [165, 162], but these are currently nothing more than declaration of intents or methodological guidelines, of little support in the actual development and deployment of large-scale dynamic applications.

A very peculiar – and, in our opinion, underestimated – approach actually supporting adaptive self-organization relates to the experiments conducted in [146, 68] and best described in [69]. Since all these examples are conceptually similar, here we will focus the description on the fascinating Slashdot.org story.

Slashdot.org is a discussion board Web site, where logged users can post information and comments at will. The problems of such discussion community Web sites are – rather intuitively – irrelevant posts and spammers. From the system architect point of view, the problem is how can the system filter between "good" and "bad" posts. The solution adopted by Slashdot is known as collaborative filtering. All the users can rate posted messages and all the rates are averaged out to create a number that represents how good a post is likely to be. Then, users can browse through Slashdot, with a quality filter on, effectively telling the software to hide those posts having a rating lower than a specified threshold. The power of this solution is its complete scalability in that the burden of rating is fairly partitioned between Slashdot users. It is rather easy to detect in this solution a mix of negative and positive feedbacks which universally form the basis of robust self-organization in complex adaptive systems [69]. It is worth noting that Amazon.com and eBay.com recommendation systems work on similar principles, and similar experiences have been applied in having a Web community semantically self-organize a set of common words [146] or perform other distributed problem solving tasks [68].

Although it is surely not easy to directly apply such experiences to distributed application development, they nevertheless suggest important ideas on the path to be followed and on the general methodologies to be pursued.

2.4 Final Considerations

The discussion in this chapter has outlined that a variety of emerging distributed computing scenarios, although apparently very diverse from each other, share some common key characteristics: (i) they all involve a large number of distributed computational and communication activities; (ii) they take place in decentralized networks that are (iii) characterized by an amorphous and highly dynamic structure; and (iv) they require components to dynamically acquire and properly exploit contextual information.

The above characteristics, far from being merely technological, introduce a number of conceptual and practical issues related to the design and development of distributed applications. In a word, they require novel software engineering approaches, promoting the development of self-organizing, adaptive, and context-aware software systems (or, adopting a recently highly hyped term, promoting the development of autonomic computing systems [77]). While a number of researches are proposing several specific solutions to promote adaptivity, self-organization, and context-awareness in specific scenarios, general-purpose approaches are still missing.

The need for novel general-purpose approaches – overcoming the limitations of traditional approaches – appears even compulsory when considering that most of the sketched scenarios will have a dramatic impact on every moment of our life. Thus, characteristics such as security, robustness, and ease of maintenance and testing, which only the presence of a suitable and sound software engineering methodology can ensure, will become even more necessary.

In a pervasive computing world, we should prevent companies from sending spyware in our computer-enriched furniture to spy on our habits, and we should avoid viruses that compromise the functionality of our car navigation system or of our sensor-based health-care network. In the emerging global information economy, we should prevent viruses and denial of service attacks that will possibly cause losses for billions and create unbalances in the world economy.

Whenever a system malfunctions, the classic solution, "shut down and restart the system", will not be an option. What if a traffic light control system needs to be repaired? Should we turn off all the traffic lights in a city? In some situation, the simple fact of finding and turning off everything may be impractical: what if the environment has been sprinkled with tiny microsensors?

Even worse, these systems are inherently difficult to test and debug. Emergent unexpected situations can arise only when the system is actually deployed and off-line simulations can lead to wrong forecasts. Moreover, in a dynamic system where components are mobile and wirelessly interacting, debugging is extremely difficult [32]: who is talking with whom? What happened in the past?

Considering the road ahead, any suitable approach for designing and developing systems exhibiting all the above characteristics will necessarily imply the capability of engineering prespecified, coherent, and useful behaviors from the cooperation of an immense number of unreliable parts interconnected in unknown, irregular, and time-varying ways and situated in dynamic operational environments.

The following chapter starts from these considerations and outlines the fundamental role that the adoption of a proper coordination model may have in this process.

3

The Role of Coordination and the Inadequacy of Current Approaches

In the previous chapter, we have identified the need for novel approaches to software engineering, promoting adaptive self-organization, and context-awareness. Now, we start to analyze the important role that will be played by the identification of proper coordination models in the process toward the definition of a suitable innovative software engineering approach.

In general terms, a *coordination model* identifies the mechanisms and the policies according to which an ensemble of "actors" can orchestrate the overall activities. Such an orchestration include mechanisms and policies for both exchange of information and synchronization of activities. The study of coordination models goes beyond computer science [86], in that also behavioral sciences, social sciences, business management, and logistics somewhat strictly deal with how various types of actors (e.g., animals, humans, trucks) can properly coordinate with each other.

In this book, we obviously focus on the coordination of computational actors, i.e., the components of distributed applications and systems. For the sake of simplicity, we will often adopt the generic term "agent" to indicate any component of a distributed network scenario hosting a computational activity that needs to coordinate with other components. These will this include actual software agents, processes in a distributed application, peers in a P2P network, as well as mobile devices and computer-based sensors (or, which is the same, the system-level processes running over them). Such a generalized adoption of the agent term, though, is not arbitrary [165]. In fact, it refers to entities with some degree of autonomy in execution, interacting with other entities, and situated in some context/environment. That is, entities matching the canonical definition of agents provided by the agent community [162].

3.1 The Fundamental Role of Coordination Models and Infrastructure

Whatever the scenario of interest, agents acting in the context of distributed applications and systems have the primary need to interact and coordinate with each other to achieve their goals. In all the scenarios described in the previous chapter, coordination between the agents constituting the system has a fundamental role.

- In the **micro scale**, where each single agent (i.e., micro device) has limited power and resources, coordination is mainly required to let the agents cooperate to accomplish tasks that exceed their capabilities as single individuals. In the "pipe repairing" application (described in Subsect. 2.1.1), for example, no single agent is large enough to repair a hole in the pipe; they must cooperate to aggregate into a suitable structure to fix the hole. As another example, in almost all sensor network applications, coordination between single sensors is enforced to exceed the sensing power of each single device or to implement power saving policies. Sensors, in fact, by coordinating with each other, can average their measures to wash out environmental noise, or can coordinate duty cycles to save battery energy.
- In the **medium scale**, agents are the applications running on handheld, wearable, and embedded devices. Coordinating their activities is at the core of a lot of pervasive computing applications, where humans can take advantage of a proper orchestration of distributed activities to improve their interactions with the surrounding environment. Consider, for example, the case of a housewife who "asks" the kitchen for suggestions about what she could prepare for dinner. The answer could be provided by having a computer-based fridge analyze what food is in it, by having computers embedded in the kitchen's shelves do the same, and by having them all exchange this information and cooperatively verify on an electronic recipe book what can be prepared on this basis. That is, answering to the housewife question implies a proper coordination of activities among the various pervasive computing devices in the kitchen.
- In the **global scale**, again, coordination is of primary importance. For example, in Internet-scale P2P applications, agents (i.e., peers) need to coordinate with each other in order to dynamically discover communication partners and to autonomously engage direct or third-party interaction patterns. For example, every kind of routing problem (whether on a real network [20] or on an overlay virtual network [120, 129]) can be easily regarded as a minimal coordination problem: autonomous nodes must cooperate, forwarding each other packets, to let the packets flow from sources to destinations.

The pervasiveness of coordination activities and their primary role in achieving global application goals in any distributed application and system, clearly make the identification of proper coordination models of fundamental importance. Not surprisingly, the research area of coordination models and middleware is particularly crowded and attracts researches from different communities like agents [56], software engineering [58], and distributed computing systems [57].

Coordination activities may vary from simple mutual exclusion policies to access shared resources to complex distributed artificial intelligence algorithms for collective problem solving. But, whatever the case, the design and development of complex distributed applications always call for the identification of a coordination model facilitating the overall design and development process. In the case of the emerging scenarios of interest to this book, such a coordination model should be able to facilitate adaptive self-organization of activities, and should be complemented by proper middleware to support the execution of distributed applications.

In particular, we think that any coordination model and the associated supporting middleware should provide

1. suitable mechanisms to enable coordination, i.e., interaction and synchronization mechanisms;
2. suitable means to promote context-awareness;

With regard to the first point, coordination requires by definition some form of communication between agents and some form of synchronization of activities. Besides sharp means to enforce communication and synchronization (e.g., messages, semaphores, etc.) one should also account for less obvious means, i.e., indirect interactions mediated by an environment (also known as "stigmergy") or behavioral interaction (i.e., indirect interactions induced by agents observing each other's actions).

With regard to the second point, a coordination model for dynamic and open scenarios also requires some forms of context-awareness. In fact, any agent has to be somehow aware of "what is around," i.e., its context, to meaningfully work in a specific operational environment, and to properly combine efforts with other agents. However, when agents are embedded in a possibly unknown, open, and dynamic environment (as in the case of the depicted emerging scenarios), they can hardly be provided with enough *a priori* up-to-date contextual knowledge, and should be supported in the process of dynamically acquiring it.

The above two points, interaction mechanisms and context-awareness, are indeed strictly intertwined, in that contextual information can be communicated only by the available interaction mechanisms. With this regard, it is worth anticipating that on the one hand, indirect interaction mechanisms appear much more suited for coordinating activities in open and dynamic scenarios, in which agents can appear and disappear at any time. In fact, these models uncouple the interacting entities and free them from the need for directly knowing each other to interact. This promotes spontaneous interaction, which is the basic ingredient to support self-organization. On the other hand, for spontaneous indirect interactions to take place in an adaptive way, agents must somehow affect the surrounding environment by their actions in a way that can be somewhat perceived by other agents. That is, indirect interactions require the capability of affecting the context and of perceiving the context.

As a simple example, in cooperative distributed robotics, a lot of implementations rely on robots interacting by merely observing each other's actions. Robots can acquire a picture of the surroundings with their cameras and, using such a picture, decide what to do without any explicit communication being involved [67].

In addition, the characteristics of modern distributed scenarios analyzed in the previous section also alert us that any coordination model, for being effective, should also promote locality both in interactions and in the acquisition of contextual information. In fact, for systems which can be characterized by a large number of decentralized agents, any approach requiring global-scale interactions is doomed to fail. Scalability and ease of management can be properly supported only by a model in which most interactions occur at a local and localized scale. In the simple case of cooperative robotics, for instance, one cannot rely on the fact that each robot sees and understands the actions of all other robots: that could work only for small environments with full line of sight, and in any case the presence of a large number of robots would challenge the limited capabilities of robots.

3.2 An Exemplary Case Study Application

To exemplify and fix ideas on what has been discussed so far, it may be useful to introduce a case study application. The chosen application involves a pervasive computing scenario, and in particular a computer-enriched museum in which tourists, while visiting it, can exploit PDAs or smart phones to get a better and more immersive experience. A number of devices embedded in the museum can provide tourists with a sort of interactive guide, but they can also be exploited by museum guards for the sake of monitoring and control.

In particular, for tourists, the pervasive services provided by the museum infrastructure may be of help to retrieve information about art pieces, effectively orient themselves in the museum, and meet with each other (in the case of organized groups). For museum guards, the pervasive services can be used to improve their monitoring capabilities over art pieces and tourist actions, and to coordinate each other's actions and movements. In the following, we will concentrate on two specific representative problems: (i) how tourists can gather and exploit information related to an art piece they want to see; and (ii) how they can be supported in planning and coordinating their movements with other, possibly unknown, tourists (e.g., to avoid crowd or queues, or to meet together at a suitable location).

To this end, we assume that (i) tourists are provided with a software agent running on some wireless handheld device, like a PDA or a cell phone, giving them information on art pieces and suggestions on how and where to move; (ii) the museum is provided with an adequate embedded computer network. In particular, embedded in the museum walls (associated either with each art item or each museum room), there are a number of computers capable of communicating with each other (by wired or wireless links) and with the mobile devices located in their proximity (e.g., by the use of short-range wireless links); and (iii) both the devices and the infrastructure hosts are provided with a localization mechanism to find out where they are actually located in the museum; this could be implemented by some kind of cheap mechanism relying on well-known algorithms based on radio or acoustic signal triangulation [50].

Despite this coarse description we think that this kind of case study captures in a powerful way features and constraints of next-generation application scenarios:

- It can be of very large size. In fact, in huge museums there can be thousands of embedded electronic devices and hundreds of tourists with mobile devices. There can be multiple systems concurrently running within the museum computer infrastructure (e.g., light and heating control systems) and other systems connected to these other services. In addition, since a huge museum can have multiple sections managed by different organizations, some degree of decentralization may also be present.
- It represents a very open and dynamic scenario. In fact, a variable number of unknown tourists may enter and leave the museum at any time, each following unpredictable schedules and visiting plans. In addition, the museum too can exhibit high dynamics, in that huge museums very often restructure their topology to host temporary special exhibitions, and very often art pieces are moved from room to room and new art pieces are added.
- The need for context-awareness is intrinsic in the goals to be pursued by tourists and museum guards when exploiting the infrastructure, in that they all somewhat relate in understanding what is happening in the museum and act accordingly.

The above characteristics carry on a number of implications. Despite the high dynamics of the scenario, the system should be robust and flexible. When embedded hosts break down, wireless networks have glitches, or other unexpected malfunctioning occurs, the system should exhibit a limited and gradual decay of performance. When special exhibitions take place or new art pieces are introduced, the system should immediately reflect the new configuration in the way it provides its services, and without any temporary unavailability. Whenever a tourist enters the museum, he must be immediately allowed to take advantage of the museum services.

From the viewpoint of the museum infrastructure, one cannot rely on manual configuration and reconfiguration for the above requirements to be fulfilled. In fact, the human efforts required to do that would be nearly continuous and dramatically expensive. Also, for very large museums, the time required for such reconfigurations would lead either to temporary unavailability or to services providing obsolete information. The only feasible solution is to have the system be able to autonomously configure its operational parameters in response to changed conditions, in an adaptive and context-aware fashion, without requiring human intervention and without exhibiting perceivable service malfunctioning.

From the viewpoint of tourists, they must be properly enabled to access all the available information in an up-to-date way, and they must be given the possibility of understanding how to move in the museum. Clearly, this should be done on the fly for each tourist, by having his mobile device spontaneously connect with the embedded infrastructure, and by having the whole system dynamically provide personalized services (e.g., "Since you are interested in both Egyptian art and Greek sculpture, here the best path for you to follow based on current crowd conditions"). Also, tourists and museum guards should be enabled to dynamically coordinate with each other (e.g., "All students of my class please report to me!"). For this to occur, tourists and museum guards must be able to start interacting possibly without knowing each other a priori (e.g., "Anyone here interested in discussing Egyptian art?") and in a context-aware way (e.g., "Alice, this is Bob, let's walk toward each other to meet in between"). Again, since we cannot assume any possibility of centralized control, all these types of context-aware interactions must be promoted by the system in an adaptive way without requiring any manual configuration.

As an additional note, it is worth noting that even testing and debugging a system of that kind is extremely difficult. That would imply accounting for an uncountable number of possible situations (e.g., what is the typical group behavior of a class of children visiting the museum? What happens when someone shouts "fire!" in a packed room?). For this reason, testing should also follow a different approach. Rather than trying to account for all possible situations to verify that the system is flawless, one should structure the system so as to make it able to dynamically adapt itself to face any unexpected situation.

To be successful, any approach to designing and developing a system capable of exhibiting the above characteristics should rely on the choice of a proper coordination model and by a corresponding supporting middleware infrastructure. The model should promote spontaneous interactions among agents that possibly do not know each other a priori (e.g., a new art piece that connects to the museum infrastructure, or two tourists with common interests that want to meet to discuss with each other) and should enforce context-aware interactions in an expressive way, to ensure that any dynamic adaptation of the system and any coordination activity (e.g., a group of museum guards that wants to monitor in a coordinated way different areas of the museum) properly reflect the current conditions of the system and of the other agents in it.

In the rest of this chapter, we will refer to the above case study to evaluate the inadequacy of current coordination models and middleware to face the complexities of modern scenarios. Moreover, from time to time in the book, we will again revert to this case study to ground the discussion.

Although the case study focuses on pervasive computing (which also unveils our specific specific area of interest) it introduces issues which are of a very general nature. In fact, it is analogous to a number of different scenarios, e.g., traffic management and forklift activity in a warehouse, where navigator-equipped vehicles can guide their pilots on what to do; mobile robots and unmanned vehicles exploring an environment; spray computers having to organize their relative positions and activity patterns; software agents exploring the Web, where mobile software agents coordinate distributed researches on various Web sites. Therefore, all our considerations will be of a more general validity.

3.3 Inadequacy of Current Approaches in Supporting Coordination

Most coordination models and middleware used so far in the development of distributed applications appear, in our opinion, inadequate in supporting coordination activities in dynamic network scenarios, such as those described in the previous chapter and in the above case study. In the following paragraphs, we are going to survey various coordination models and middleware to illustrate their inadequacies from a software engineering perspective. The analysis will be mainly focused on evaluating how those models and middleware provide agents with contextual information and whether the information provided is suitable for supporting effective coordination activities.

We identified three main general classes of coordination models encompassing almost all the proposals. These include (i) direct coordination models, i.e., message passing and client-server ones; (ii) shared data space models, i.e., tuple space ones; and (iii) event-based models. The implementation of middleware infrastructures to support a specific model within a class can be very different from each other (e.g., centralized vs. distributed, or using proprietary vs. open protocols). Still, they are mostly equivalent from the software engineering viewpoint, in that the overall design of an application developed adopting a specific middleware would not be substantially affected by being ported on a different middleware relying on a coordination model of the same class.

3.3.1 Direct Coordination Models

Models based on direct coordination promote designing a distributed application by means of a group of agents that can coordinate by directly communicating with each other in a direct and explicit way, by message passing or in a client-server way (i.e., adopting some kind of remote procedure call mechanism). Client-server middleware systems like Jini [65], and message-oriented middleware like UPnP [150] and JADE [10], are examples of middleware infrastructures rooted on a direct coordination model.

The model

Since, from a software engineering point of view, all the implementations of direct coordination models are rather similar, here, for simplicity, we will focus the description according to the terminology adopted by the Jini middleware (see Fig. 3.1). At the end of this section we will briefly review the main differences between client-server and message passing implementations.

The main service offered by direct communication models, like Jini, is lookup and discovery. The main idea at the bottom line of this service is to provide agents with a shared middleware in which they can store their identities and capabilities, and in which they can look for other identities and declared capabilities to find suitable interaction partners. In particular, this service can be implemented by means of either white or yellow pages.

- A *white page* server basically provides a database where agents can store their name together with the network address and port they are listening to. Agents connect to the server either to publish themselves on the network by storing their own identities, or to look for the address of agents with which they want to interact. After obtaining such information agents can communicate directly (i.e., through sockets) with each other. Although this service decouples the agent symbolic names from the host in which they are running, it actually requires an a priori (i.e., compile time) acquaintanceship between the agents.
- A *yellow page* complements white pages, by allowing an agent to associate a machine readable description of their capabilities with their network address. This allows a better decoupling of agent interaction, in that an agent can look for the specific service it needs, disregarding the identity of the agent providing that service.

In Jini, for example, a specific lookup and discovery server provides the above functionalities. To give agents access to the server it is possible to install it at a well-known network address, or the agents can start a local network broadcast search.

Once an agent connects to a newly discovered one, a communication problem arises: *the agents need to talk the same language.* Earlier proposals, like Jini, adopt a client-server approach: agents export an interface (in the object-oriented sense) and other agents can invoke methods on that interface disregarding the methods' actual implementation. More recent proposals like JADE [10] do not encode the agents' interaction by means of method invocation, but by means of formatted text messages. Agents receiving such messages must be able to understand the message syntactic and semantic content to decide which action to undertake. Such understanding is typically promoted by the adoption of shared ontologies between agents [10].

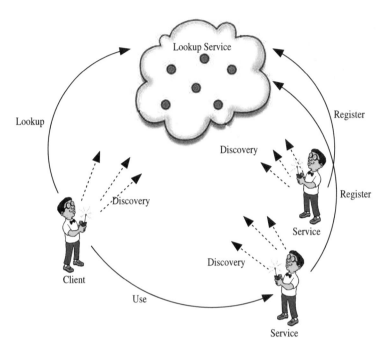

Fig. 3.1. Direct coordination: Jini main operations

Inadequacy

One problem of direct coordination approaches, as promoted by the adoption of the Jini middleware or of an alike middleware, is that agents have to interact directly with each other and can hardly sustain the openness and dynamics of near future computing scenarios. Firstly, explicit and expensive discovery of communication partners – as supported by directory services – has to be enforced for enabling agents that do not previously know each other to interact. Secondly, agents are typically placed in a "void" space: the model, per se, does not provide any contextual information: agents can only perceive and interact with (or request services from) other agents, without any higher-level contextual abstraction.

In the case study scenario, tourists have to explicitly discover locations of art pieces and of other tourists. Also, to orchestrate their movements, tourist must explicitly keep in touch with each other and agree on their respective movements by direct negotiation. These activities require notable computational and communications efforts and typically end up with ad hoc solutions – brittle, inflexible, and nonadaptive – for a contingent coordination problem.

To better clarify these ideas, let us focus the attention on the meeting problem in the museum case study. Specifically, let us consider the case in which a group of agents wants to meet in the best room according to the current locations of the agents (i.e., at the center of gravity of their current positions). The pseudo-code in Fig. 3.2 implements an agent performing the meeting application by exploiting the services of a Jini-like middleware.

```
01: // register myself to the discovery middleware
02: middleware.register(this)
03: // get a reference to the other agents in the meeting group
04: for every name in the meeting group
05:  agent[i] = middleware.get(name)
06: end for
07: // get the museum map
08: museum = middleware.get(MuseumMap)
09: //proceed with the meeting
10: while not meet
11:  // find where the other agents are
12:  for every agent in agent[]
13:   location[i] = agent[i].getLocation()
14:  end for
15:  // compute the best room for the meting on the basis
16:  // of the agent current locations and museum map
17:  room = computeBestRoom(museum, location[])
18:  // move toward the meting room
19:  goTo(museum, room)
20: end while
```

Fig. 3.2. Pseudo code of the meeting application with a direct coordination middleware

Looking at the pseudo-code, the problems inherent in direct coordination models are immediately evident. First of all, the system relies on global middleware services that can be difficult to implement and can represent a bottleneck or a single point of failure. Secondly, the system does not cope gracefully with situations in which agents can dynamically join or leave the meeting group (in rows 4-6 and 12-14, the members of the meeting group are supposed to be fixed). Thirdly, a notable decision burden is left to the agents. Agents have to exchange information about their current positions and evaluate by themselves the best room for the meeting, by merging information about the museum map and other agent current locations (row 17). Moreover, they have to implement some navigation (i.e., routing) algorithm to move to the destination room within the museum map (row 19). Whenever some contingency occurs or some new information is available (i.e., a room in the path of an agent is discovered to be so crowded that it should be best avoided), the agents have to explicitly renegotiate a new meeting point.

For all these reasons, direct coordination models are not suited to effectively support agent coordination activities in dynamic scenarios.

3.3.2 Shared Data Space Models

Coordination models based on shared data spaces support agent interactions with the mediation of localized shared data structures, which agents can read and write, and which could also be used for representing contextual information. These data structures can be hosted in some data space such as a tuple space, as in EventHeap [66], JavaSpaces [39], and TSpace [83], or they can be carried by agents themselves and dynamically merged with each other to enable interactions, as in Lime [112] or XMiddle [96].

The model

Let us refer to the tuple space model, the most general and widely used model based on shared data spaces.

A tuple space is a shared, associatively addressed, memory space, organized as a multiset, i.e., as a bag of tuples. The tuplespace concept was originally proposed in the context of the Linda coordination language [43], and has recently received renewed attention because of several innovative proposals, like Sun's JavaSpaces [39].

The basic element of a tuple space system is the tuple, which is simply a vector of typed values, or fields. Templates are used to associatively address tuples by pattern matching. A template (often called anti-tuple) is also tuple, but with some (zero or more) fields in the vector replaced by typed placeholders (with no value) called formal fields. A formal field in a template is said to match an actual tuple field if they have the same type, whatever the value in the actual field of the tuple. If the field of the template is not formal, both fields must also have the same value to match. Thus, a template matches a tuple if they have an equal number of fields, with types respectively corresponding, and each field of the template matches the corresponding tuple field.

A tuple is created by an agent and placed in a tuple space by a *write* primitive (called *in* in the original version of Linda). Tuples are read or extracted by a tuple space with *read* and *take* primitives respectively (the latter called *out* in the original version of Linda), which take a template and return the first matching tuple. Since a tuple space is an unstructured multiset, the choice among multiple matching tuples is arbitrary and implementation-dependent. Most tuple space implementations provide both blocking and non-blocking versions of the tuple retrieval primitives. A blocking read, for example, waits until a matching tuple is found in the tuple space, whereas a non-blocking version will return a "tuple not found" value if no matching tuple is immediately available.

Tuple spaces provide a simple, yet powerful mechanism for agent coordination. Tuple space-based programs are easier to write and maintain, because tuple-based interactions uncouple interacting agents. Destination uncoupling is enforced because the creator of a tuple requires no knowledge about the future use of that tuple, i.e., about which other agent will read that tuple. Time uncoupling is enforced because tuples have their own life span, independent of the life cycle of the processes that generate them, or of the processes that may read them in the future. These two types of uncoupling enable time-disjoint processes and processes that do not know each other to coordinate seamlessly.

In addition, tuple-based coordination models provide for notable flexibility, which is an important requirement for open and dynamic software systems. Lacking a schema or a predefined organization, a tuple space does not restrict the format of the tuples it stores or the types of data it can contain, thus making it suitable for unexpected types of interactions. In addition, the scalability of a tuple space system is provided by the complete anonymity of tuple operations. No one has to keep track of connected processes to a specific tuple space. Thus, it is possible to conceive systems based on a multiplicity of independent localized tuple spaces [112], to enforce locality in interactions (see Fig. 3.3).

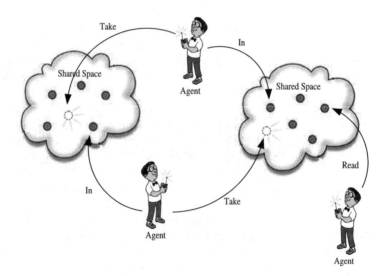

Fig. 3.3. Shared data space model: main operations on a tuple space, as provided in Javaspaces

Inadequacy

When adopting a tuple-based coordination model (i.e., when developing applications exploiting a middleware relying on tuple-based services), agents are no longer strictly coupled in their interactions, because shared tuple spaces mediate interactions promoting uncoupling. Also, a shared localized tuple space can be effectively used as a repository of local, contextual information. Still, such contextual information can only represent a strictly local description of the context that can hardly support the achievement of global coordination tasks.

In the case study, one can assume that the museum provides a set of tuple spaces, storing information such as a list of nearby art pieces as well as message tuples left by the other agents. Tourists can easily discover what art pieces are near them, but to locate a distant art piece they should query either a centralized shared tuple space or a multiplicity of localized tuple spaces, and agents have to internally synthesize all the information to compute the best route to the target. To meet with each other, tourists can build an internal representation of the other people's positioning by accessing several distributed data spaces, by reading tuples reporting about their presence, and then by locally computing a path in the museum. However, the availability of such information does not free them from the need for negotiating with each other to orchestrate movements.

The pseudo-code in Fig. 3.4 implements an agent performing the meeting application by accessing a shared (Javaspaces-like) tuple space middleware. Here, we have assumed the presence of a global space (whether provided by a specific server or obtained by merging agents' private spaces) on which all the agents can post and retrieve information in the form of tuples. It is rather easy to see that this kind of middleware is much more suited to manage open meeting groups than direct coordination middleware. In fact, the space uncouples the interaction between the agents in the meeting group (on rows 7-9, the agent retrieves tuples independently for who actually wrote them), and somehow provides a suitable means by which to access contextual information (i.e., the location of other tourists). However, in our opinion, a key problem is that agents are left alone in discovering relevant contextual information, in evaluating and possibly negotiating a meeting room, and in navigating across the museum (rows 12-14). This can lead to noticeable computational and communication burden.

It is fair to say that models like MARS [22] and TuCSoN [121], by relying on *programmable* tuple spaces, are better suited for dealing with coordination. In fact, agents can program the middleware so that it can perform low-level coordination tasks on the agents' behalf. In the case study, for example, an agent could program the middleware to properly aggregate relevant information about other agent locations. In this way the agent would have access to the already aggregated information without the burden of doing it on its own.

```
01: // get the museum map
02: Tuple mapT = new Tuple("MUSEUM MAP")
03: museum = middleware.read(mapT)
04: // proceed with the meting
05: while not meet
06:   // find where the other agents are
07:   Tuple readT = new Tuple("MEETING", *, *)
08:   Tuple[] locT = middleware.read(readT)
09:   location[] = parse(locT[])
10:   //compute the best room for the meting on the basis
11:   // of the agents current location and museum map
12:   room = computeBestRoom(museum, location[])
13:   // move toward the meting room
14:   goTo(museum, room)
15:   // update my location
16:   Tuple writeT = new Tuple("MEETING", this,this.getLocation())
17:   middleware.write(writeT)
18: end while
```

Fig. 3.4. Pseudo-code of the meeting application with a shared data space middleware

3.3.3 Event-Based Models

Event-based models relying on *publish/subscribe* mechanisms make agents interact with each other by generating events and by reacting to events of interest, without having them to interact explicitly with each other. Typical infrastructures rooted on this model are Jedi [26] and Siena [23]. In [35] is presented a complete survey on this kind of model.

The model

A software event is a piece of data generated to indicate that something has occurred in a system, e.g., a user moved the mouse, or a datagram has arrived from the network, or a sensor has detected that someone is knocking at the door. All of these occurrences can be modeled as events, and information about what happened can be included as attributes in the events themselves.

Event-based programming, i.e., writing software systems in terms of event processing, is a commonly accepted practice: programming becomes a process of specifying "when this happens, do that." This is particularly evident in graphics programming: if the mouse moved, move the cursor with it; if the user clicks this button, execute that procedure.

The simplicity of event-based programming is a key to its success: identify the events of interest; identify who (which processes/objects/agents) are interested in handling those events; and identify what procedures event handlers have to execute upon the occurrence of specific events. Events and event handlers are coupled by exploiting a publish-subscribe schema: agents interact by publishing events and by subscribing to the classes of events they are interested in (subscriptions are associated with event handlers). An operating system component, called event dispatcher, is in charge of collecting subscriptions and events, and of triggering the proper reactions in event handlers (see Fig. 3.5).

In distributed systems, event-based programming can be supported by means of middleware services acting as event dispatchers, in charge of collecting subscriptions from agents interested in specific classes of events, and in charge of distributing events (i.e., in triggering reactions) to subscribers whenever appropriate. A variety of schemas can be conceived for subscriptions [26] (e.g., subscribing to specific classes of events, or to events whose attributes match a specific template, or to events occurring at specific sites and/or at specific times). A variety of solutions can also be conceived for how to implement event dispatchers (e.g., centralized vs. distributed) and for how to distribute events to subscribers (e.g., broadcasting vs. direct forwarding).

Whatever the solution adopted, event-based coordination models clearly provide for full uncoupling among interacting entities (the same as tuple space models), and also provide for an effective way to achieve contextual information at runtime (indeed, an event represents something that has happened in a context).

Inadequacy

The fact that event-based models promote both uncoupling (all interactions occur by asynchronous and typically anonymous events) and context-awareness (agents can be considered as embedded in an active environment capable of notifying them about what is happening) represent important features for large-scale, open, and dynamic systems.

In the case study example, a possible use of an event-based approach would be to have each tourist notify his movements across the building to the rest of the group. Notified agents can then easily obtain an updated picture of the current group distribution in a simpler and less expensive way than required by adopting shared data spaces. However, such information still relies on agents for the negotiating of coordinated movements and does not alleviate their computational tasks (i.e., in the case study, tourists still have to explicitly negotiate their movements, as from the pseudo-code in Fig. 3.6).

It is rather easy to see that here agents are indeed provided with an active middleware that notifies them about other agents' movements (the react method in row 9 is invoked by the middleware upon the detection of an agent movement). However, agents need to process these events on their own and, in this case, the *computeBestRoom* and *goTo* methods can be source of complexity, brittleness and inflexibility.

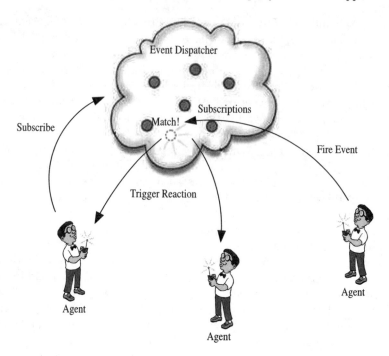

Fig. 3.5. Event based model: publish-subscribe operations

3.4 Requirements for Next-Generation Coordination Models and Systems

In this chapter, we have outlined the fundamental role of coordination for the engineering of adaptive self-organizing applications. At the same time, we have shown how current coordination models and infrastructures appear inadequate to the needs of emerging computing scenarios.

To summarize, the key characteristics that a proper coordination model should exhibit include

- the uncoupling of application agents, to properly facilitate spontaneous interactions and coordination activities in an open world;
- the integration of expressive means to acquire context-awareness, in order to facilitate agents in actually exploiting such information for their application purposes;
- the promotion of locality in interactions, to support scalability in large-scale and decentralized systems.

In the following chapter, we introduce field-based coordination as a potential candidate meeting the above requirements.

```
01: main() {
02:   // get the museum map
03:   museum = middleware.read(map)
04:   // subscribe to other agents movements
05:   Event newLocation = new Event("MEETING",*,*)
06:   middleware.subscribe(newLocation)
07: }
08:
09: react(Event newLocation) {
10:   // update my internal representation of the agents distribution
11:   location[].add(newLocation.source, newLocation.location)
12:   //compute the best room for the meting on the basis
13:   // of the agents current distribution and museum map
14:   room = computeBestRoom(museum, location[])
15:   // move toward the meting room
16:   goTo(museum, room)
17:   // notify other agents about my movement
18:   Event move = new Event("MEETING", this,this.getLocation())
19:   middleware.fireEvent(move)
20: }
```

Fig. 3.6. Pseudo-code of the meeting application with an event-based middleware

Part II

Modeling Field-based Coordination

4

Field-Based Coordination

The general problem of the coordination models described in the previous chapter is that they either couple interacting agents (direct coordination models) or provide contextual information that is not expressive enough (shared data spaces and event-based coordination models). These models, for the achievement of complex distributed coordination tasks and for the acquisition of relevant contextual information, typically force agents to perform global searches and execute complex algorithms to elaborate the acquired information, to interpret it, and to decide what to do.

The meeting problem in the case study application (in which a set of agents in the museum have to meet each other at a convenient place), for example, requires agents' notable efforts in acquiring information about the museum floor plan and about the position of other agents in the meeting group. Moreover, even when such information is a *complete* representation of the operational environment, agents still have to execute possibly complex algorithms to decide and/or negotiate where to meet and how to get there.

In our opinion, a proper coordination model for modern distributed computing scenarios should promote mediated interactions by exploiting some sort of distributed information that can be used as a means to enforce indirect (uncoupled) interactions among agents and that can also be expressive enough to represent contextual information in a form locally accessible and immediately usable by agents. By simply accessing such local information, expressing even non-local properties of the context or information communicated by remote agents, an agent should be able to immediately recognize what is happening and what it has to do. In the meeting application, if agents would be able to locally perceive in their environment something like a "red carpet" leading to a suitable meeting room, it would be trivial for them to exploit the information: just walk on the red carpet! The key point, though, is how can one create such a "red carpet," i.e., how can one effectively represent context for the sake of specific coordination problems?

4.1 Key Concepts in Field-Based Approaches

An intriguing possibility toward the definition of a coordination model suitable for modern open and dynamic scenarios is to take inspiration from the physical world, and in particular from the way masses and particles in our universe move and globally self-organize their movements according to the local contextual information that is represented by gravitational and electromagnetic fields.

In the physical word, particles interact in an uncoupled way, by the mediation of fields, and without having to know each other. Gravitational (or electro-magnetic) fields represent information about other particles/masses in the system in a sort of summarized contextual information. Contextual information is distributed in fields, and fields – although expressing some global information – are locally perceived by particles/masses. The local perception of a field by a particle/mass is a sort of "red carpet": a particle/mass can know what to do, i.e., how to globally coordinate its movement with other particles/masses, simply by following the local field's gradient.

The above properties summarize the key concept of field-based coordination models: computational fields, propagated in a distributed environment and locally sensed by agents, can provide suitable contextual information to support agent coordination. Moreover one can also immediately recognize that field-based coordination can meet the requirements identified at the end of the previous chapter: uncoupled and local (i.e., scalable) interactions, and expressive contextual information.

Finally, field-based coordination naturally promotes self-organization and self-adaptation: agents, in fact, can be considered as entities that do not act as individuals, but as entities that are part of a system in which fields naturally force agents to globally coordinate their activities. This also implies that the agents' activities are automatically adapted to the environmental dynamics, which is reflected in a changing field-based representation, without forcing agents to re-adapt themselves. In the above "red carpet" metaphor, dynamics of the environment are reflected in a "red carpet" that gets timely rearranged as environmental conditions change. Agents do not worry about such changes; they just keep on walking on the "red carpet."

Operatively, the key points of field-based coordination models can be summarized as follows:

1. Agents' interactions are enabled and mediated by virtual "computational fields," propagated in the system by the agents themselves or by the environment in which agents operate (typically with the support of a proper middleware infrastructure). These fields are types of distributed data structures conveying information about other agents and about the context in general, and can provide agents with strong coordination task tailored context-awareness.

2. The local value of propagated fields can be locally accessed by agents. This can be used to acquire contextual information and also to have agents

coordinate in a very simple way with other agents, i.e., by having agents act and move following the "waveform" of these fields.

3. Openness and environmental dynamics are adaptively taken into account in that any change in the system (e.g., a new agent entering the system or a change in the network topology) may induce changes in the fields' waveform that, consequently, tend to influence agents' behaviors (point 2).

4. The above feedback cycle lets the system self-organize so that a global coordination pattern is eventually achieved.

A field-based coordination model could clearly assume that, in a given environment/system, several different types of fields can exist and be propagated for the sake of providing to agents different types of contextual information and for supporting a variety of different coordination patterns.

With reference to the case study, one can consider that each museum guide spread in the museum network a computational field identifying him, and including a data value monotonically increasing as the field gets farther from him (see Fig. 4.1). Any agent (i.e., tourist) perceiving the field of a guide could thus locally sense how distant the guide is and where (in which direction) he is. That is, this field – as simple as it can be – represents indeed a very expressive contextual information.

Again with reference to the case study, let us consider another example of agent coordination supported by fields. In particular, let us assume that a group of tourists have to meet together at a convenient room in the museum, and that each tourist propagates a field similar to the monotonically increasing one of the museum guide just described. In this case, simply by having tourists start following downhill the fields of the other tourists in the group, as if they were gravitationally attracted by them, the result is that all tourists will eventually meet at their center of gravity.

Dynamic changes in the environment and agents' actions induce changes in the fields' surface, producing a feedback cycle that consequently influences agents' actions. Again, in application examples, should the museum guide be moving around in the museum, the corresponding computational field would be automatically updated and would, consequently, have any agent looking for a guide readapt its movement accordingly. Should there be multiple guides in the museum, they could decide to sense each other's fields so as to stay as far as possible from each other to improve their reachability by tourists, and possibly dynamically reshape their formation when a guide, for contingent problems, has to move or go away.

Further examples follow later in this book. Here, we emphasize that coordinated actions in a field-based system – following its physical inspiration – can be considered as expressions of a simple dynamic system: agents are seen as balls rolling upon a surface, and complex coordinated actions or movements are achieved not because of the agents' will, but because of dynamic reshaping of this surface.

Of course, the physical inspiration of field-based coordination approaches
and the strictly local perspective in which agents act promote a strictly greedy
approach in their coordinated actions. In fact, agents act on the basis of their
local viewpoint only, disregarding that a small sacrifice now can possibly lead
to greater advantages in the future. Let us consider again the case study,
and the problem of having a tourist follow a guide to ask him information.
In a circular track, for example, a tourist looking for a guide who is moving
clockwise could, instead of greedily following the guide field downhill, decide
to move uphill to meet the guide counterclockwise. However, this is a general
drawback of distributed problem solving, where efficiency reasons often rule
out the possibility of globally informed decisions by distributed agents, rather
than a specific drawback of field-based coordination.

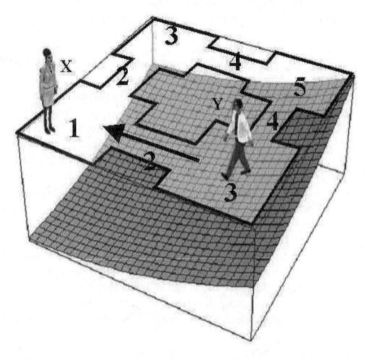

Fig. 4.1. The tourist Y follows downhill the field generated by the tourist guide X
(increasing with the distance from the source, as the numeric values in each room
indicate)

4.2 A Survey of Field-Based Approaches

Several recent proposals in different areas are adopting approaches to enforce context-awareness and distributed coordination that can be – to different extents – assimilated to field-based coordination approaches. Without the ambition of being exhaustive, in this section we survey a few representative proposals in that direction.

4.2.1 Amorphous Computing

Domain Scenario

The amorphous computing project has been already introduced in Chap. 2 [1, 21]. In general terms, the project focuses on a visionary scenario in which a massive numbers of identically programmed and locally interacting computational particles are randomly dispersed on a surface or mixed throughout a volume, and are possibly capable of sensing and affecting the environment.

Particles are assumed to have limited resources and local information, and to be subject to faults. All particles are programmed identically, although each of them has an autonomous thread of execution, is capable of generating autonomously random numbers, and has an internal local state that can depend on past actions (i.e., a particle is a minimal agent). Particles can communicate with each other by short-distance radio connections, or through the substrate itself [21], or (in an even more visionary perspective) by emission of chemicals [153]. One can generally assume that there is a communication radius r, large compared with the size of individual particles and small compared with the area in which they are distributed, and that two particles can communicate if they are within distance r.

The key characteristic of amorphous computing, although it somewhat resembles cellular automata [154], is that particles have no a priori knowledge about the topology of the resulting communication network. No centralized source of information is available, and there are no global clocks, and no global beacons for triangulating positions. Thus, particles must engage in processes of self-organization for all their activities.

Field-Based Approach

The research activity in amorphous computing is heavily inspired by biological systems. Most biological systems, in fact, achieve coherent, reliable, and complex behaviors from the cooperation of large numbers of identical organic elements. One of the most fascinating examples is embryogenesis. Cells, all with the same genetic code, reliably cooperate to form complex structures by reproduction from a single cell [156]. There is a plethora of examples of regulation in different organisms that can compensate for large variations in cell size, cell numbers, cell division rates, and development time [30]. Even after development, many organisms preserve incredible abilities for self-repair and regeneration.

A key mechanism adopted in embryogenesis is the use of gradients of proteins to determine positional information and polarity. In the embryos of many species (e.g., in the *Drosophila*), cells at one extreme of the embryo emit a protein (called morphogen) that diffuses along the length of the embryo. The concentration of this morphogen (morphogen gradient) is then used by other cells to determine whether they lie in the head, thorax, or abdominal regions [82], and these cells react by differentiating their behavior accordingly. Different morphogens are used for determining the dorsal-ventral axis, wing and limb development, and even leg bristle polarity. Gradients of morphogens are believed to play an important role in providing position and polarity information in many different organisms, and even in regeneration [156].

The concept of morphogen gradients can be clearly assimilated to that of fields in field-based coordination. In fact, a morphogen gradient resembles a distributed data structure that propagates through a network, by changing its values as it propagates. Accordingly, it can be reproduced in an amorphous network of computational particles and it can be used for a variety of purposes related to self-organization of activities.

The key mechanism can work as follow. In a network of undifferentiated particles, an initial "source" particle, chosen by a cue from the environment or by generating a random value, creates a gradient by sending a message to its local neighborhood with the morphogen name and a value of zero. The neighboring particles forward the message to their neighbors with the value increased by one, and so on, until the morphogen has propagated through the entire population. Each particle stores and forwards only the minimum value it has received for a particular morphogen name; thus the morphogen value represents the shortest path from the source. The value provides an estimate of distance from the source: a point reached in n steps will be roughly distance nr away. The quality of this estimate depends on the density of the particles and can be reasonably predicted for random distributions [105].

This very simple program can be used in powerful ways. By limiting the maximum value of a morphogen, one can create regions of controlled size. The morphogen can also be used to provide a sense of local orientation; a particle can compare values in its local neighborhood to determine the direction toward or away from the source. More than one particle could be the source for the same morphogen, in which case the morphogen value reflects the shortest distance to *any* of the sources. Thus, if a single particle emits a morphogen then the value increases as one moves radially away from the particle, but if a line of particles emits a morphogen then the value increases as one moves perpendicularly away from the line. In this way, complex spatial patterning can be created by positioning without any change to the particle program (see Fig. 4.2). The particles can also be programmed so that they can selectively choose which morphogens to propagate. Thus, particles in a particular state can act as barriers to specific morphogens, or as obstacles around

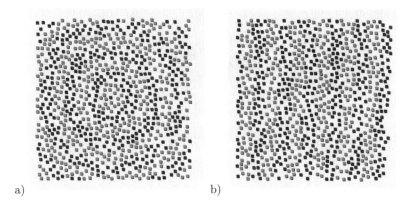

a)   b)

Fig. 4.2. Morphogen Gradient: (a) Radially propagating from a source node; (b) Propagating from a line of nodes thus creating vertical stripes equidistant from the source line

which the morphogen must travel; or, similarly, morphogens can be limited to propagate only within certain spatial regions. As an additional example, the source particle can constantly produce a morphogen message, and have the morphogen value stored by any agent lose significance if not constantly reinforced. The result is that the morphogen values adapt as source particles appear and disappear.

These are just a few of the ways in which morphogen gradients can be used. The key point is that the described basic mechanism, which is also the basic mechanism for field-based propagation in any network, can act as the basis for many distributed self-organizing algorithms, e.g., self-establishment of coordinate systems, distributed storage, and ad hoc routing [104, 105].

In general, morphogen gradients (and thus fields) are well matched to amorphous and dynamic network settings, because the phenomenon of diffusion at its basis is insensitive to the precise arrangement of the individual particles, so long as the distribution is reasonably dense. In addition, if individual particles do not function, or stop broadcasting, the result will not change very much, so long as there are sufficiently many left.

One of the most fascinating applications of morphogen gradients, already developed by the amorphous computer group, is about obtaining three-dimensional shapes by letting a sheet composed of amorphous computer particles fold autonomously following origami techniques [102]. The idea is to let particles spread several morphogen gradients across the sheet. The local configuration of such morphogen gradients identifies where the sheet should bend (see Fig. 4.3). Particles actually bend the sheet collectively, each trying to locally deform the sheet (i.e., the particles' local distribution).

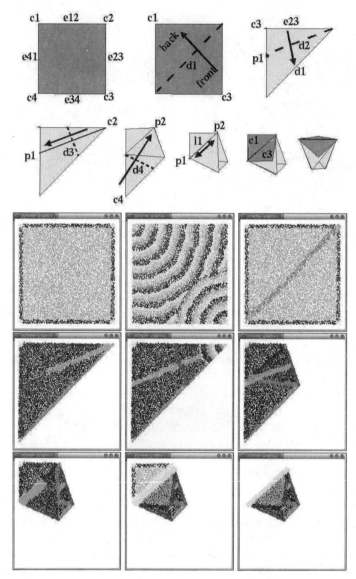

Fig. 4.3. (top) Origami program for folding a cup. (bottom) Simulation snapshots of the actual folding. These pictures have been taken from [104]

4.2.2 Modular Robots

Domain Scenario

A modular (or self-reconfigurable) robot is a flexible robot made up of a collection of (typically simple) autonomous elements (actuators) connected with each other and with some degree of freedom in their relative movements.

The key idea underlying modular robots is to have their components execute distributed control algorithms so as to coordinate their movements and let a robot assume specific shapes or move according to some motion pattern (i.e., gait).

The flexibility of modular robots is highly desirable for tasks to be performed in hostile environments, such as fire fighting, search and rescue after an earthquake, and battlefield reconnaissance. In these cases, robots can encounter unexpected situations and obstacles, hard to overcome for fixed-shape monolithic robots. A modular robot, instead, could shape itself depending on needs. For example, to pass through a hole, the robot can transform itself into a sort of snake; to move through a difficult terrain, it can assume a circular shape and move in a way similar to that of a tank; to enter a room through a closed door, a modular robot may disassemble itself into a set of smaller units, crawl under the door, and then reassemble itself in the room (see Fig. 4.4).

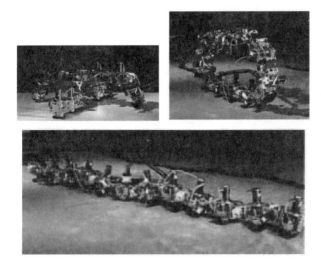

Fig. 4.4. Examples of different shapes a modular robot can assume. Images taken from [159]

CONRO modular robots are one of the most interesting examples [133]. CONRO modular robots are made of a set of connectable modules, each computer-based, and each containing batteries, two motors, four pairs of IR transmitters/receivers for communication and proximity sensing, and four docking connectors to allow connections with other modules. Each module has two degrees of freedom for pitch (up and down) and for yaw (left and right). The state of a module is determined based on how it is connected to other modules. Each module can self-determine its state locally by checking to which links of the neighboring modules it is connected. This information can be communicated among neighbors to establish a local topology in the network.

Field-Based Approach

Several approaches to control shapes and movements of modular robots rely on predetermined centralized control tables [160]. Although this is a comprehensive and simple mechanism, it can hardly deal with the intrinsically dynamic nature of robot reconfiguration in dynamic and a priori unknown environments. Control tables must be set up in advance, and every time the configuration is changed, no matter how slight the modification, the control table must be rewritten.

To increase the flexibility of controlling modular robots, the interesting possibility adapted by CONRO robots is to exploit a biologically inspired concept, very similar to that morphogen gradients (and, thus, representing a field-based approach), i.e., the concept of "hormones" [133].

A hormone is a message that propagates in a system and that tends to trigger different actions in the different subsystems in which it propagates, leaving the execution and coordination of these triggered actions to the local autonomous subsystems. For example, when a human experiences sudden fear, a hormone released by the brain and propagated in the body causes different actions, e.g., the mouth opens and the legs jerk. In particular, a hormone is a message that has three important properties: (i) it has no specific destination but floats in a distributed system, as a field; (ii) it has a life span (and thus tends to vanish if not reinforced, which makes it different from the morphogen gradients of the amorphous computing approach); and (iii) it can trigger different actions at different receiving sites.

The actions caused by a hormone may include modification and relay of other hormones, execution of certain local actions like bending an actuator, or just ignoring the received hormone. It is worth noting that hormones as used in modular robots are very different from simple broadcast messages or content-based messages. Hormones are propagated signals that may be modified, be delayed, or disappear while propagating from the source to the rest of the system, and thus they are de facto fields. Given this, hormones can be used, the same way as morphogen gradients and fields, to accomplish self-organizing tasks that are beyond the abilities of conventional messaging systems.

To give an example, the so-called caterpillar gait is a motion pattern that lets a snake-like modular robot advance as a "wave" of activity moves from the head of the robot to its tail (see Fig. 4.5). This gait is achieved by having a hormone propagate from the head to the tail of the robot at regular intervals (or synchronized by other mechanisms). Such a hormone lets the pitch joints of the robots assume the wave configuration that brings the robot forward.

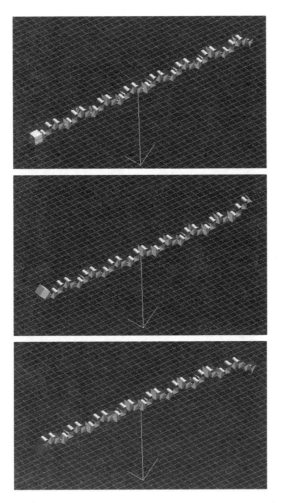

Fig. 4.5. Caterpillar gait, in a chain-type modular robot composed of six actuators

4.2.3 Routing in Mobile Ad Hoc and Sensor Networks

Domain Scenario

Wireless ad hoc networks and wireless sensor networks are very representative examples of those classes of large-scale dynamic network scenarios discussed in Chap. 2. Such networks have recently received growing attention because of their promise of providing pervasive communication infrastructures that are cheap and trivial to deploy. However, they challenge current approaches to routing and network control, typically requiring manual configuration and suited for fixed or slowly changing network topologies.

On the one hand, lacking any centralized point of control, nodes in ad hoc networks must cooperatively self-organize routing and medium access functions. On the other hand, nodes in ad hoc networks may be mobile (consider, e.g., a network of PDAs carried by humans) or ephemeral (consider, e.g., the limited lifetime of battery-powered sensors), inducing continual changes in the network topology.

For these reasons, new routing algorithms inspired by new principles must be conceived.

Field-Based Approach

In the last decade, a number of ad hoc network routing protocols have been proposed, which usually dynamically build – by flooding the network – a sort of routing overlay structure, and which then exploit this overlaid structure for routing. Among the others, (i) "Gradient Routing (GRAd)" [116] and (ii) "Directed Diffusion" [55] make a field-based metaphor in building the overlay particularly explicit.

Gradient Routing is a routing algorithm specifically conceived for mobile ad hoc networks. In very general terms, when a node "A" wants to send a message to a node "B," it actually floods the network with a field-like data structure that holds, the source id, i.e., "A," the message, and the number of hops from the source of the message to the current node. Such structure not only trivially hands off the message to "B" (since the message reaches all nodes), but also creates a sort of overlay field leading back to "A," to be exploited for further uses. If node "B" wants to reply, it can just send a message that follows the "A" field downhill toward node "A." In this case no flooding is involved. The field-like distributed data structures created in this process can be used further also by other peers to communicate (see Fig. 4.6). However, such a field-based data structure has a limited life, in that changes in the network topology due to mobility may invalidate it. The next message sent by "A" will eventually help in rebuilding it.

Directed Diffusion is a routing algorithm proposed in the sensor network domain. Here the problem is how to collect sensed information from a vast network of sensors dispersed in an environment. The idea is that a workstation at the edge of the network can inject a field-like data structure expressing an interest for a particular set of events ("query" field). Sensors are able to route relevant sensed information back to the workstation, exploiting the field data structure as a guide with a mechanism similar to the one described above for the Gradient Routing. Moreover, in this algorithm, the workstation can reinforce some part of the fields, applying a sort of reinforcement learning algorithm. This enables those sensors that have acquired "good" information to report back to the workstation, while allowing other sensors to forget about the "query" field (and thus save battery energy) if they are not able to provide relevant information.

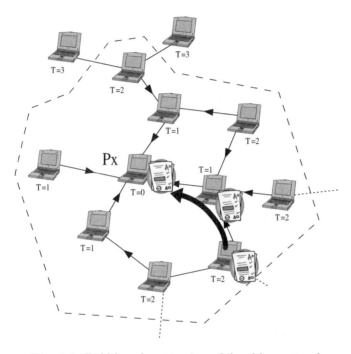

Fig. 4.6. Field-based routing in mobile ad hoc network

4.2.4 Navigation in Sensor Networks

Domain Scenario

Sensor networks [33], besides being ad hoc networks with specific routing problems, have a wide range of potential applications. In particular, a network of sensors distributed in a landscape can also be used as a distributed information repository allowing users (people, robots, unmanned vehicles, etc.) to exploit this information to traverse the sensor-enriched landscape, as described in [84].

A moving object can be guided, by distributed sensors across the landscape along a safe path, away from the type of danger that can be detected by the sensors. The dangerous areas of the sensor network are represented as obstacles. Danger may include fire, holes, distrusted people, etc. It is assumed that each sensor can sense the presence or absence of such types of danger. A danger configuration protocol running across all nodes of the network creates a danger map. It is not likely that the network will create an accurate geometric map, distributed across the nodes. Instead, it is important for the nodes in the network to provide some information about how far from danger each node is. If the sensors are uniformly distributed, the smallest number of communication hops to a sensor that triggers "yes" to danger is a reasonable measure of the distance to danger.

The overall goal of this "danger avoiding" navigation is to find a safe path to lead a user to a specific destination. This path can be either computed offline by a planning algorithm, or it can be dynamically evaluated by a user accessing online (e.g., by a wireless PDA) the closest nodes of the sensor network.

Field-Based Approach

In [84], the "avoid danger" navigation has been implemented over a grid of Mica Motes sensors [114] (see Fig. 4.7). In particular, a sort of field-based approach (called potential fields) has been conveniently used. In such a potential fields approach, users move under the actuation of artificial forces. The goal (i.e., the intended destination) generates an attractive potential field pulling the user to it. The recognized obstacles generate a repulsive potential which pushes the user away from them. The (negated) gradient of the total potential is the artificial force acting on the user. The direction of this force at a point in the landscape is the current best direction of motion from that point.

The potential fields in this approach are computed as follows. Each node whose sensor triggers a danger diffuses the information about the danger to its neighbors. The message includes the source node id, the potential value, and the number of hops from the source of the message to the current node. The propagation occurs with the basic mechanism of fields and morphogen gradients: when a node receives multiple messages from the same source node, it keeps only the message with the smallest number of hops; the current node computes the new potential value from this source node; the node then broadcasts a message with its potential value and number of hops to its neighbors. After this bootstrap procedure, nodes may have several potentials from multiple sources. To compute its current danger level information, each node adds all the potentials.

The potential field protocol, can be used to build a plan offline of movements across a landscape. Moreover, if the potential field information is con-

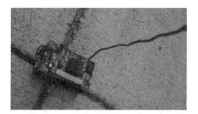

Fig. 4.7. A Grid of motes suitable to be employed in a navigation application. Image taken from [4]

tinuously adapted in response to sensor failures, to addition of new nodes into the network, and to dynamic danger sources moving across the network, then it is a precious source of contextual information. This information can be used to guide a PDA-equipped user who connects online to the network to get awareness of the current situation and dynamically plan his movements. A user of the sensor network can rely on the information to choose the best possibility from the returned values, i.e., to move to the direction corresponding to the minimum value of potential danger. Such a path inevitably leads the user to the goal (see Fig. 4.8).

4.2.5 Situated Multiagent Ecologies

Domain Scenario

Multiagent systems executing in the context of large-scale Internet applications are typically characterized by involving agents that do not know each other and that have to interact and execute in a dynamic computational environment. While most approaches still rely on direct communications between agents (supported by heavyweight middleware) and on a minimal (sometimes inadequate) modeling of the environment [162], some recent proposals are recognizing the importance of approaches based on appropriate environmental abstractions for both interactions and situatedness. An interesting proposal in that direction is the Multilayered Multi Agent Situated System (MMASS) [6, 106], defining a formal and computational framework relying on a layered environmental abstraction.

MMASS explicitly promotes the environment and the agents as first-class entities. On the one hand, the basic MMASS environment is described by a

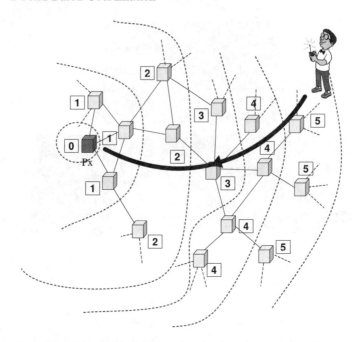

Fig. 4.8. Field-based navigation in a sensor network

network structure, made up of sites that may contain an agent. The main role of this network is to provide agents with a suitable network of acquaintance on which to ground interactions. On the other hand, agents are defined in terms of their capabilities of perceiving the environmental properties and behaving accordingly.

The key idea underlying the MMASS model is that, through a suitable definition of physical and conceptual spatial structures, it is possible to effectively obtain context-aware behavior for modeled agents. In fact, different spatial representations layered one over the other may be defined to model different aspects of the agent environment. Concepts such as agent preferences, membership to groups or organizations, and assignment to tasks may determine some kind of neighborhood or distance in an abstract space according to specific aspects of their activities or preferences. This kind of modeling naturally supports agent activities. Once such spaces have been defined, an agent can interact with all the other neighbor agents in some specific space (e.g., send a query for the file "Hey-Jude.mp3" to all the neighbors in the "music" space).

To better clarify, let us focus our attention on an Internet file sharing application (see Fig. 4.9). At the base level, agents are embedded in the physical network space. Neighbor relationships are based upon the IP connectivity (i.e., two nodes are neighbors if they know each other's IP addresses – they can open sockets to each other). Moreover, agents can build upon such physical space several different logical spaces according to some criteria. Specifically, agents can store in a specific table the IP addresses of the nodes that are neighbors in a specific space. Provided with that information, agents can trivially exploit it: if they want to send messages to neighbor nodes in some space (e.g., the "music" space) they have just to access the corresponding table and open the sockets.

In any case, it is worth reporting that the application scenarios originally considered in MMASS were related to the simulation of artificial societies and social phenomena, for which the physical layers of the environment were also virtual spatial abstractions. Only recently did MMASS start considering Internet-based application scenarios, where the physical layer is realized by the available IP network and logical spaces are built in the way described above [106].

Field-Based Approach

In MMASS, agents are provided with two interaction modalities. First, agents that are adjacent in space can agree to perform a simultaneous change in their internal states (in a way similar to that of cellular automata [154]). Second, asynchronous interaction between agents, as well as access to contextual information, can occur by the mediation of fields diffused in the environment.

Fields in MMASS are conceived as signals that can be emitted by agents and are spread over the environment according to a diffusion function related to the specific field type. Field intensity is thus modulated throughout their path from source to destination sites.

Agents are characterized by two methods with which to interact by means of fields: *emit*, which allows an agent to add a field of a certain type in its site and to let it diffuse according to the spatial structure of the environment and of the field's diffusion function; *trigger*, which allows the definition of a change in the state of an agent that takes place when a specific field is perceived.

The general idea in MMASS is to exploit fields to define the different environments where agents' actions take place. Since fields can easily create routing data structures (as depicted in a number of scenarios before), they can easily create networks of acquaintance between agents, i.e., *space* in the MMASS terminology.

In particular, following such an approach, different layers of acquaintances can be established in a multiagent system. For example, in a file-sharing application, each agent interested in, say, "mp3 files" could propagate a field storing the keyword "mp3" and its own IP address. Upon the receipt of fields marked with the keyword "mp3" other interested agents could store their corresponding IP address, thus creating a topology for a, let us call it, "mp3" logical space. This could be represented in the first logical layer of Fig. 4.9. Adopting a similar approach other fields could be propagated on such a novel established network creating, say, the "dance music mp3" network (i.e., second logical layer). Changes in an agent's preferences or internal state could lead to the update of the networks.

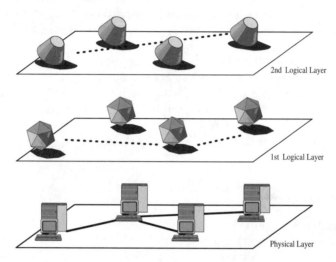

Fig. 4.9. The MMASS layered environment

4.2.6 Coordination of Robot Teams

Domain Scenario

The systems surveyed so far exploit field-based coordination as an actual mechanism to enforce coordination and context-awareness. That is, in the above systems, some field-based data structure is actually propagated in a distributed system (e.g., in the nodes of a network) either by agents or by some sort of supporting middleware, to be sensed by distributed agents.

However, proposals exist that exploit field-based coordination as a pure conceptual mechanism, without having fields propagated and without requiring a supporting infrastructure, but simply as a way to better model and engineer situated and coordinated behaviors.

Consider the case of a group of robots distributed in an environment, having to orient themselves and to coordinate their movements. To interact meaningfully, they have to exploit their sensing capabilities (e.g., cameras) to acquire contextual information. In addition, if they do not have direct means to communicate with each other's (e.g., they do not have wireless network interfaces) they necessarily have to coordinate with each other by detecting each other movements and adapt their behavior accordingly (in a sort of mediated, behavior-driven interaction).

In these cases, robots could take advantage from interpreting the environment and the other robots' behavior in terms of a field-based representation and acting on the basis of fields. As a simple example, an agent seeing an obstacle through its camera could represent it as a repelling field, whose strength increases as the perceived dimensions of the obstacle increase. As another example, it could perceive an object it has to carry as an attracting field. The main advantage of this approach is that it promotes a clean separation of concerns between the phase of processing sensorial stimuli (e.g., understanding that an object is an obstacle) and the phase of acting on the basis of such stimuli.

Fig. 4.10. Robocup competition. Images taken from [12, 74]

Field-Based Approach

The idea of fields driving robots' movements is not new [79]. One of the most recent reissues of this idea, the Electric Field Approach (EFA) [67], has been exploited in the control of a team of Sony Aibo legged robots in the context of RoboCup competitions (see Fig. 4.10). In this approach, each Aibo robot builds a field-based representation of the environment from the images captured by its two head-mounted cameras (which also provides for stereo vision), and then decides its actions and movements by examining the gradients of the so-built environmental representation.

Compared to previous approaches of robot coordination based on internal field representations, EFA is more general in that it is not restricted only to inter-robot coordination, but can be used for various other contextual actions as well. In fact, the EFA field-based representation takes into account the playfield itself (to force the robot to stay within the playfield), the ball (to move and kick it), as well as the other robots (to interfere with opponent actions).

In EFA, the inspiration from electromagnetic fields (also reflected in the name of the approach) is due to the fact that each robot represents all the perceived entities, except the ball, as positively or negatively charged entities, emitting the corresponding electric fields. Opponent robots and the playfield border will be represented by negatively charged entities. The robot itself, its mates, and the opponents' goal will be represented by positively charged objects. Given this representation, each robot computes the electric field distribution across the playfield, by combining the effects of all the electric charges being modeled. The basic rationale at the bottom line of this representation is that, following this approach, the robot represents "good" areas of the playfield by means of a positive electric field, while it represents "bad" areas by means of negative electric field.

The robot measures the electric field where the ball is located. For this reason in [67] the ball is referenced as the *probe*. The robot aims at performing some action to move the ball into areas where the field is more positively charged. Since the opponents' goal is the most positively charged object, this approach should lead the robots to score.

There are two main actions a robot can undertake to move the ball toward positively charged areas: if the ball is within reach the robot can kick the ball toward the opponents' goal or toward a mate robot; alternatively, the robot can move so as to change the background field representation, and thus bring the ball to more positively charged areas indirectly.

Following this approach EFA robots operate within this activity loop:

1. The robot updates its electric field representation on the basis of the entities perceived.
2. The robot measures the field at the ball's location.
3. The robot simulates internally the set of actions it can undertake (e.g., try to kick the ball, move toward the ball, move toward the closest opponent robot, etc.).
4. For each action, it computes the expected value of the electric field at the expected final location of the ball. For example, if the robot simulates – i.e., thinks – that kicking the ball will move the ball to the opponents' goal, then that action will be associated with a very high electric field value.
5. The action that obtained the greatest electric field value, i.e., the one that is expected to bring the ball to the most positively charged place in reach, is executed.

Adopting this field-based approach, the EFA robots are capable of nontrivial actions such as passing the ball to each other (i.e., moving the ball to a positively charged area closer to the opponents' goal) and obstructing opponents' actions by moving between the opponents and their own goal (i.e., opposing a positive charge to the opponents' field).

4.2.7 Artificial Worlds

Domain Scenario

Another confirmation of the fact that field-based coordination is, other than simply a coordination model, a reasonable abstraction to model coordinated and situated contextual activities, comes from its adoption in the simulation of artificial worlds, e.g., in videogames.

The sharper example comes from the specific solution to coordinate activities of virtual characters in the Sims [145] videogame. In the Sims, the main goal for the player is to run a simulated life by creating and owning a virtual person, shaping his family, building his home, and run his life (see Fig. 4.11). To drive a character to act in the simulated city where he lives, the player interact with the virtual world as is usual in videogames. For example, clicking on an object of the virtual world (e.g., a television) makes a bunch of options appear expressing actions that the character can do with that object (e.g., switching on the television, changing the channel). In addition, specific needs of the simulated character that the player has to satisfy (e.g., the need to sleep) appear as bars on the bottom of the screen. Keeping the owned virtual character happy and having him run a successful life is the goal of the player.

Field-Based Approach

While the activities of the owned character are directly driven by the player, a number of additional computer-driven non-player characters exists in the Sims virtual world. For the activities of these non-player characters, the Sims adopts a peculiar approach based on computational fields, called "happiness landscapes," spread in the virtual city in which characters live, and driving their movements [70].

In particular, non-player characters autonomously move in the virtual Sims city with the goal of increasing their degree of satisfaction by climbing the gradients of specific computational fields. If a character is hungry, she perceives and follows a happiness landscape whose peaks correspond to places where food can be found, e.g., a fridge or a restaurant. After having eaten, a new landscape will be followed by the character depending on her needs. Different kinds of fields can have different extents. The slope of the bed extends all the way across the house, while the pinball machine extends only a few feet. A fatigued character will start climbing the slope toward the bed no matter where she is; if she needs some entertainment, she will migrate to the pinball machine but only if it is nearby. This provides quite realistic behaviors for non-player characters, and also make their movements very easy to model and enforce.

In addition to the Sims example, our research group has also successfully experimented with a field-based approach applied to the Quake III Arena videogame [92]. Quake III Arena (Q3A) [117] belongs to the kind of first person

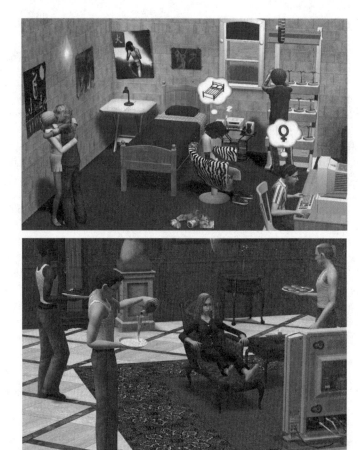

Fig. 4.11. Two snapshots of the videogame "The Sims" [145]

shooter (FPS) computer games. The player controls a character (bot) fighting against other artificial bots (i.e., software agents) in a dungeon. The whole point in the game is staying alive and killing opponents. The game provides a first-person perspective on the current situation 4.12. What we have done with this regard is modifying the algorithms adopted by evil bots (typically self-interested and unable to cooperate with each other toward the capturing of the player character) to have groups of evil bots coordinate their movements according to a field-based approach. In particular, we have enforced the virtual propagation in the environment (by both evil bots and the player character) of computational fields that (as with the fields of tourists and museum guides in the case study application discussed in Chap. 3) have a value that increases as the field propagates farther from the source. Then, by having evil bots move in the virtual environment by following the gradients of these fields, we have been able to enforce a variety of coordinated movements for bots, overall increasing their capability of capturing the player character. For instance (see Fig. 4.12) the evil bots in our modified version of the game are able to orchestrate their movements and surround the player in order to leave him no escape.

In both Sims and Quake III Arena, the field-based approach is not exploited to actually coordinate activities of distributed agents (the execution of these games and of all their characters is indeed centralized on a single computer). Rather, it is used to effectively model the properties of a virtual environment and to effectively promote context-aware virtual movements of agents in it. This confirms the effectiveness of field-based coordination not only as an interaction mechanism, but also as a modeling approach to facilitate engineering in a complex software system.

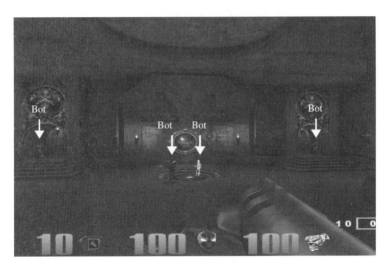

Fig. 4.12. A snapshot of Quake III Arena. By means of field-based coordination, the evil characters (bots) are able to effectively surround the player, blocking all the exit doors

4.3 Swarm Intelligence as a Form of Field-based Coordination

Researchers are paying an increasing attention to engineering approaches getting inspiration from the behavior of social animals, e.g., ants and termites. The interesting fact is that social animals – although not very intelligent as individuals – are able to collectively solve a wide variety of different hard problems (e.g., finding food, using shortest paths to reach the nest, adaptively organizing task division) in a very robust and flexible way.

Robustness arises in social animals because a large group can achieve goals even when some individuals die or simply fail to behave as expected. Flexibility arises from the fact that the patterns of interactions between the individuals are not fixed once and for all. Rather, they dynamically reshape to adapt to changing environments. These kinds of smart behaviors are often referred to as behaviors of *swarm intelligence* [14], to stress the fact that they do not emerge from the capabilities of individuals, but rather from the interactions between individuals.

Swarm intelligence attracts computer scientists and software engineers [108] because several problems solved by groups of animals have direct counterparts in engineering and computer science: finding food strategies can be exploited in an information retrieval context; the strategies used to find the shortest path connecting two locations can be exploited in routing algorithms for telecommunication and computer networks; mechanisms for ants' division of labor can be exploited in manufacturing or workflow management scenarios. Therefore, it is no surprise that several works [3, 14, 15, 69, 76, 107] describe specific applications of swarm intelligence in a variety of areas.

While the opportunity to exploit these new concepts has already been spotted, the next challenge is to leverage their exploitation in a systematic and engineered way. This is not a simple task and the research community is still far from proposing a solution. A prerequisite to develop such a methodology is to identify a common and general framework in which all the swarm intelligent systems could fit.

From our viewpoint, field-based coordination can work as a unifying abstraction (and thus a general framework) for a large class of swarm intelligent systems. In the rest of this section, we survey some widely known swarm intelligence behaviors (more deeply analyzed in [14, 107]) and show how can they be modeled in terms of field-based coordination.

4.3.1 Wolves Surrounding a Prey

To capture a prey (e.g., a moose), a group of wolves tends to act in a coordinated way, being able to surround the prey and leaving it no escape. The wolves' coordinated behavior can be explained in terms of swarm intelligence without assuming long-range communication mechanisms or complex intelligent decision making by wolves [107]. Wolves simply hunt for the moose trying to maintain a suitable distance from other wolves. Simulations of this simple strategy, with a moose that simply tries to escape by moving farthest away from the nearest wolf, reproduce the actual behavior of a group of wolves in nature.

In any case, it is also possible to model the same behavior in terms of a field-based approach, by assuming that the moose and the wolves generate fields like the ones depicted in Fig. 4.13, updated in real time depending on their movements and actual positions.

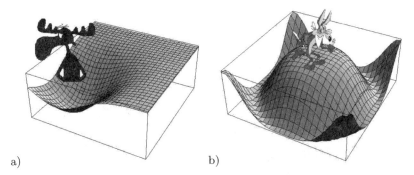

a)   b)

Fig. 4.13. (a) Moose field. (b) Wolf field

Now, the moose behavior can be modeled by considering that the moose tries to follow downhill all the wolves' fields, to escape from them. More specifically, it is possible to imagine that the moose adds the wolves' fields together and follows downhill the result. Similarly, each wolf tries to follow downhill the fields of the other wolves and of the moose. In this way, a wolf is directed toward the moose, but is also repelled from other wolves. This simple description is perfectly analogous to the description based on distances and, by a proper tuning of the fields' coefficients, can lead to the same results.

4.3.2 Birds Flocking

Flocks of birds stay together, coordinate turns, and avoid colliding into each other, by following a very simple swarm algorithm [107]. Since similar coordination problems may happen in air-traffic control, robot swarms, and unmanned vehicles, flocking behavior in birds could be a source of inspiration to these areas, and could be possibly addressed by using a similar algorithm.

The behavior of bird flocks can be explained by assuming that each bird tries to maintain a specified separation from the nearest birds and to match the nearby birds' velocity. The flock is a self-constraining structure in which each entity's individual action simultaneously responds to and changes the overall structure of the flock. Although each bird senses only the movements of its nearest peers, its responses to these movements transitively propagate to others, so that the system overall exhibits global coordination.

To model this strategy under a field-based modeling framework, it is possible to imagine that each bird generates a field like the one shown in Fig. 4.14a, and that this field is updated in real time to match the bird's movements.

Now, saying that birds have to stay a specified distance from each other is equivalent to saying that birds have to follow the decrease of other birds' generated fields (see Fig. 4.14b). In fact the shape of the field constrains birds to stay close each other in an almost regular grid; the movement of a bird and the consequent change in the field it generates will force other birds to move as well.

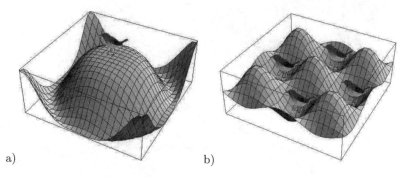

a)   b)

Fig. 4.14. (a) The flocking field of an individual bird. (b) The birds moving in a regular grid formation

4.3.3 Ant Foraging

Ant colonies are able to find food in any environment, and to carry this food back to the nest. To do this, ants do not directly communicate with each other. Rather, they indirectly communicate in a stigmergic way, by cooperatively constructing a network of pheromone (scent markers that many insects generate) paths that connects their nest with available food sources [14]. The global structure of paths emerges from the simple actions of the individual ants that do not even know they are involved in this distributed building process. Several authors spotted the possibility to exploit the technique used by ants in this process in a routing or in an information retrieval context.

The swarm intelligent behavior of ant foraging works basically as follows. Each ant that forages for food is able to produce two kinds of pheromones. A home pheromone is produced after leaving the anthill wandering looking for food. A food pheromone is produced when the ant goes back to the anthill after some food has been found. Ants wander randomly following the food pheromone when looking for food, and following the home pheromone when bringing food back to the anthill. The overall system behavior is based on the fact that pheromone tracks deployed by an ant can be exploited by the same ant or by other ants in the future. The natural tendency of the pheromones to evaporate if not reinforced allows the pheromone network to remain up-to-date: when a food source is extinguished the corresponding pheromone trial disappears, because it is no longer used and reinforced.

To describe the ants' foraging strategy under a field-based coordination model, one should conceive pheromones in terms of deformation to distributed fields. In fact, one can imagine that the environment in which ants move can be considered as perceived by ants in terms of two initially flat fields. These two fields, which can be named the home and the food fields, are generated and spread by the environment itself. The environment reacts to ants' movements by wrinkling the fields' surface, while ants' movements are affected by the "waveform" of the field. This feedback cycle constitutes the key to let the system auto-organize. The algorithm followed by ants can in fact be restated by supposing that each ant wanders, avoiding obstacles, following (probabilistically) the decrease of the food field when it is looking for food and following (probabilistically) the decrease of the home field when it is bringing food back to the anthill. Then, to close successfully the feedback cycle, it is simply possible to imagine that the environment reacts to the ants' presence, by locally wrinkling the home field surface in correspondence with the points in which ants looking for food are located and it wrinkles the food field surface at the points at which ants carrying food are located. The form of the wrinkle is depicted in Fig. 4.15a. Moreover, suppose that the environment is able to control the deepness of the wrinkle, so that each new (or renewed) wrinkle is deeper that all the wrinkles in its neighborhood.

Following these principles, ants' movements create a network of channels in the fields' surfaces. In the food field surface these channels descend from the anthill to the food sources, in the home field surface these channels descend from the food sources to the anthill. In Fig. 4.15b a channel created by an ant movement is shown. Of course this is a pure abstraction and a natural environment cannot provide the described capabilities. However this does not matter for our purposes, the aim is to demonstrate that the field model can abstract these phenomena, and then use this model to build software systems in an artificial environment, where these functionalities can easily be gathered.

Finally, to account for pheromone evaporation, it is possible to imagine that each of the fields' surfaces has some form of memory and it gradually reshapes to its original flat form if untouched.

It is worth noting that this kind of field-based representation of ant foraging is the very one adopted in some routing mechanisms in MANET like "Rumor Routing" [19] and in other swarm-inspired approaches and middleware like "Anthill" [3] and "Swarm Linda" [98].

4.3.4 Ant Labor Division and Task Succession

In social insects, different activities are often performed simultaneously by specialized individuals; this phenomenon is called division of labor. A key feature of division of labor is plasticity: the ratios of workers performing different tasks can vary in response to internal perturbations or external challenges. A simple model, which relies on response threshold, can explain how ants achieve

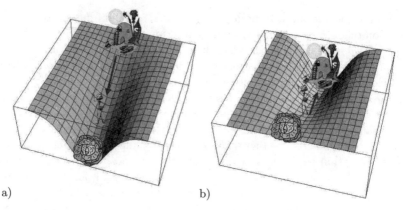

Fig. 4.15. (a) A wrinkle induced on a field's surface by the presence of an ant. (b) The channel in the field surface created by the ant's movement

flexibility and specialization in labor division [14]. Each individual has a response threshold for every task; it engages in task performance when the level of the task-associated stimuli exceeds its threshold; it drops a task when the task associated stimuli falls under another threshold. In this way each ant adjusts its duties according to the colony's needs. Moreover, by performing a certain task, individuals' task-associated thresholds decrease. This simple strategy is the key for specialization: the more an individual performed a task in the past, the more likely the same individual will perform the task in the future.

This example is particularly interesting and challenging for modeling with field-based concepts, because it involves fields propagated in a space which is not the physical space in which ants are embedded.

To model the above-described coordination task within the field-based approach, it is possible to imagine that there exists a logical virtual space, separated by the physical one, in which ants are embedded. This is a multi-dimensional space containing one dimension for each of the possible tasks in which an ant may be involved. If an ant can be involved just in three tasks, let us say, Task A, Task B, and Task C, then this space will be the one depicted in Fig. 4.16a. An ant is placed within the space depending on its duties: suppose that each axis measures the fraction of the time, an ant performs that particular task. So that the ant in Fig. 4.16a performs Task A for 33% of its time, Task B for 33% of its time and Task C for 33% of its time. Of course, in general, every ant is constrained to the subspace. An ant can move in this space, but its movement does not correspond to an actual movement in its physical space, but in a change in the ant's duties. So, for example, the movement depicted in Fig. 4.16b, represents an agent that gradually stops doing Task C and starts doing Task B. Of course, fields can be spread and sensed by ants also in this space. In particular the environment generates fields encoding the stimuli that encourage ants in performing a task. Basically the shape of these fields is almost like a steep flat surface, decreasing in the direction of the associated axis. The more urgent the task achievement, the more the environment increases the steepness of the field surface. In Fig. 4.17, three different Task A's associated fields are shown. The more steep the surface gets, the more urgent Task A's achievement becomes.

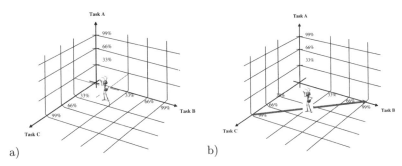

Fig. 4.16. (a) Representation of the task space. (b) Movement in the task space

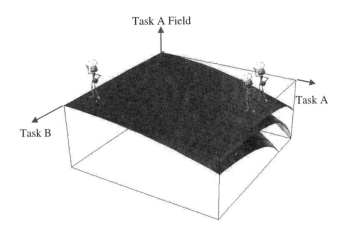

Fig. 4.17. Task A stimuli-associated fields. The more urgent Task A's achievement becomes, the more steep the overall surface gets

The ants' algorithm for division of labor can thus be restated by means of the following actions: each ant evaluates a combination of the sensed fields, by considering only those fields whose steepness where the ant is located exceeds a certain threshold. Then the ant follows downhill the field obtained. As the ants move along the task space the field's surface tends to get flattened, because the associated tasks are achieved. The ants' duties get stabilized in a suitable configuration, until new stimuli and thus fields' surfaces' deformations appear.

As depicted in Fig. 4.17, a task-associated field's surface is not actually a steep flat surface, but its steepness increases both in the direction of the associated axis and in the proximity of the associated axis itself. The reason for this nonlinear shape is to enforce specialization. In fact, on the one hand, by increasing the steepness in the direction of the associated axis, the more an ant is placed in that direction (i.e., the more it is performing that task), the more easy it will be for that ant to perform the task in the future because the field's steepness is particularly high there. On the other hand, the increase of the steepness toward the axis itself (i.e., toward the zero) renders it easier for "unemployed" ants, rather than already fully committed ants, to engage the task.

4.4 Summing Up

In this chapter we have analyzed the key concepts of field-based coordination, and have discussed how it exhibits those key characteristics that are necessary for supporting adaptive self-organization in modern distributed computing scenarios. This suitability is somewhat confirmed by the fact that, on the one hand, a variety of recent proposals successfully adopt solutions that conform to field-based ones, and on the other hand, several swarm intelligence behaviors can be easily modeled in terms of field-based coordination.

The question of whether it is possible to generalize from the variety of examples reported in this chapter and identify a single unifying model for field-based coordination, integrating the necessary characteristics for supporting the design and development of field-based coordinated applications in a variety of scenarios, and suitable to model a variety of coordination patterns, is still open.

The Co-Fields model, discussed in the next chapter, may represent a preliminary answer to this question.

5

Co-Fields and Motion Coordination

After having introduced, in the previous chapter, the key concepts of field-based coordination and its potential in supporting context-aware coordination activities in a variety of scenarios, we are now ready to go into details about a specific approach to field-based coordination, developed within our research group, i.e., *Co-Fields*.

Co-Fields (short for "Computational Fields") is a model to promote field-based coordination in pervasive computing scenarios [95]. In particular, Co-Fields has been conceived to support, by a single general-purpose field-based mechanism, context-aware execution and coordination in ensembles of distributed agents executing on mobile and embedded devices.

In this chapter, we show how Co-Fields promotes an easy modeling of field-based coordinated applications by dynamic system formalism, and present several examples of field-based coordinated applications in a pervasive computing scenario. A specific emphasis is given to motion coordination, i.e., the problem of orchestrating – in a robust and adaptive way – the movements of agents distributed in the environment. Depending on the specific context, such agents may represent humans, the mobile devices they carry, the software running on the mobile devices, and mobile robots and sensors.

Despite its intrinsic orientation to pervasive computing, Co-Fields is indeed a very general model of field-based coordination, and most of what we discuss in this chapter naturally applies also when Co-Fields is ported in other scenarios, such as mobile ad hoc and sensor networks, modular robots, or global multiagent systems.

5.1 The Co-Fields Approach

5.1.1 Structure of Fields

In Co-Fields, fields are considered simple data structures spread across an environment according to a field-specific propagation rule. A multiplicity of independent fields can coexist and be propagated in a network environment.

Each field is characterized by an unique identifier (e.g., a number or a string), by a location-dependent numeric value (expressing the strength of a field at a specific location, and taking values that depend on the propagation rule), plus any needed number of additional data (to encode and propagate in fields any information that can be of use to application agents).

Fields are propagated in a network environment according to the simple mechanism already sketched in Chap. 4. A field is generated by a source agent at a specific location in the network, with an initial numerical value of strength. The field is then sent to all neighbor nodes in the network, which update the strength according to the propagation rule and locally store the field. Then, if this is the case (i.e., if the field requires to be further propagated), these nodes send the field to their neighbors in turn, and so on recursively until the field has been fully propagated. Each node stores and forwards a field only if it has not already done so, to ensure that a specific field is propagated only once.

The propagation rules for fields can be various and application-dependent. Basically, a field can rely on any computable rule for how its strength value will have to vary as it gets propagated. The strength can simply increase from hop to hop in the network, either linearly or according to other monotonic functions. The strength can increase up to a specific distance from the source and can start decreasing. Or it could even vary according to some periodic function of the distance from the source.

Fields can be static or dynamic. A field is static if once propagated its strength does not change over time. A field is dynamic if its strength varies either due to some time-dependent propagation rule or due to dynamics in the network environment. For example, if the source of a field moves in the network, the field it has generated should update its propagated structure accordingly.

Co-Fields assumes that fields can be propagated in a network environment by application agents to enforce some application-specific coordination task, or by system-level agents to support specific system-level tasks and to provide application agents with any needed system-level and contextual information. In addition, Co-Fields assumes that agents have the capability of only locally sensing fields and their strength gradients (i.e., they can sense the value and gradients of fields only as they result from their current location).

5.1.2 The Coordination Field

Individual fields propagated in a network environment can give agents some clue about some specific aspects of the context in which the agents execute. For instance, coming back to the museum case study, a tourist looking for a guide can simply perceive the field propagated by that guide to understand if he is within the museum, how far he is, and in which direction he could be found. In other words, individual fields encode in a distributed way some kind of location-dependent contextual information, which enables agents to act in both context-aware and location-aware fashion.

However, the achievement of application-specific coordination tasks, involving more complex activities than simply finding something in an environment, is rarely relying on the evaluation, per se, of an existing individual computational field. Rather, in most cases, an application-specific task relies on the evaluation of an application-specific combination of locally perceived fields. We call this the *coordination field*. The coordination field can be considered a new field in itself that, although not existing as an actually propagated structure, is internally built by agents with the goal of reaching a proper more comprehensive view of the context, tailored to the achievement of some application-specific tasks. Once a proper coordination field is computed, agents can achieve their coordination task in a strict reactive way, depending on the local configuration of the coordination field. For example, to understand where the closest guide is, a tourist in the museum can compute a coordination field resulting from the minimum of all locally perceived fields of guides, and evaluate the gradient of such a coordination field. The evaluation of a coordination field is particularly relevant when a group of agents has to orchestrate its activities in a distributed way. In these cases, all the agents involved in a specific coordinated task will spread their own fields in the environment, and will act on the basis of some combination of all the fields spread by the agents of the group (and possibly of additional fields spread by other agents of the system).

With regard to distributed motion coordination, this translates to having agents simply follow (deterministically or with some probabilistic rule) the shape of their coordination field uphill, downhill, or along its equipotential lines (depending on the specific problem) as if they were walking upon the coordination field associated surface. For example, turning the attention to the case study, museum guides can simply coordinate so as to stay as far as possible from each other simply by (i) having each of them inject into the museum the usual field having a value that increases with the distance from the source, and (ii) following uphill a coordination field resulting from the sum of all the fields of each guide.

In the following we will always refer to the coordination field as the only field driving the agent actions and movements. In any case, we emphasize that although agents act on the basis of the coordination field, they are nevertheless preserved with the capability of perceiving the individual fields. Thus, whenever necessary, they can discriminate their actions also based on the analysis of the individual components of a coordination field.

5.1.3 Practical Issues

Specific Co-Fields implementation issues related to, e.g., how fields can be propagated in a specific environment, how can one ensure that a field is propagated only once, and how can agents actually be made accessing and propagating fields, will be discussed in the following chapters. Nevertheless, we anticipate here the discussion of some key infrastructure-related issues.

In general, to support field propagation, a proper infrastructure or middleware is required. In pervasive computing scenarios, such an infrastructure could be defined by an ad hoc network of devices – embedded sensors and PDAs carried by humans – through which fields propagate. However, it could also be defined by a multitude of networked computers embedded in the environment and providing wireless connectivity to agents (e.g., to PDAs). The shape of a field surface (i.e., its propagated distributed data structure) is determined both by the field's propagation rule and by the underlying infrastructure topology.

With reference to the museum case study, we can assume that (i) each tourist and museum guide is provided with a software agent running on some wireless PDA device in charge of giving him suggestions on how to act; and (ii) the museum is provided with an adequate embedded computer network to which agents connect to create and access field data structures. The number of the embedded hosts and the topology of the network may depend on the museum, but the basic requirement is that the embedded network topology mimics the topology of the museum plan (i.e., no network links between physical barriers, like walls). In this way, the propagation of fields through the infrastructure follows patterns that reflect the physical topology of the museum. For example, an agent from anywhere can reach the source of a field whose strength increases as it gets farther from the source, by simply following the field gradient downhill. The absence of network links between physical barriers is required to avoid agents stumbling into walls.

The above fundamental hypothesis is easy to achieve. In fact, one can suppose that each node of the network infrastructure is provided with only the IP addresses of the nodes that are spatial neighbors in the target museum topology, and the communication between nodes is restricted to the provided virtual neighbors. Or one can suppose that nodes spontaneously connect to each other, but devices are able to detect and drop the network links crossing physical barriers (e.g., by relying on signal strength attenuation or some other sensor installed on devices).

5.2 Modeling Co-Fields Coordination

The physical inspiration of Co-Fields encourages modeling field-based coordinated systems in terms of a dynamic system formalism. In fact, the gradient of fields can be considered simply as kinds of forces, that locally act on agents and influence their activities.

If, as in the museum case study (and more in general in pervasive computing scenarios), the propagation of fields across a network reflects some propagation in physical space, it is possible to define a field in analytical terms, by writing the equations defining its values in space. Accordingly, by combining different fields into some coordination field function, it is possible to model the virtual forces that act on agents at any location in the system.

This kind of modeling is particularly suited for motion coordination, in that the virtual forces deriving from the coordination field and acting on agents produce, as in real physical systems, a movement of the agents. In particular, for each agent in the system, one can write the differential equations governing the motion of the agent, which will be driven by the gradient of a specific coordination field. Once the analytical shape of a field is defined, writing and solving numerically the differential equations of the system is rather simple (e.g., by proper software tools). This provides a very effective way to analyze the system, and it can be regarded as an easy and powerful tool to support the design of field-based coordinated applications, e.g., to quickly verify that a coordination field correctly enables the achievement of a specific coordination task, to experience its effectiveness in doing that, and to tune coefficients.

5.2.1 Analytical Modeling

In more detail, it is rather easy to see that if we consider the agent i, denote its coordinates in a particular space as $(x_1^i(t), x_2^i(t), ..., x_n^i(t))$ and its coordination field as $CF_i(x_1, x_2, ..., x_n, t)$, the differential equations governing i motion are in the form

$$\frac{dx_j^i}{dt} = v \frac{\partial CF_i(x_1, x_2, ..., x_n, t)}{\partial x_j}(x_1, x_2, ..., x_n, t) \qquad j = 1, 2..., n$$

if i follows uphill the increase of the coordination field, and

$$\frac{dx_j^i}{dt} = -v \frac{\partial CF_i(x_1, x_2, ..., x_n, t)}{\partial x_j}(x_1, x_2, ..., x_n, t) \qquad j = 1, 2..., n$$

if i follows downhill the decrease of the coordination field.

This is because the direction of the gradient of the agent's coordination field, evaluated toward the spatial coordinates, points to the direction in which the coordination field increases. So the agent i will follow this gradient or will go in the opposite direction depending on whether it wants to follow the increase or the decrease of its coordination field. We indicate with v a term that can model an agent's constant speed.

The case in which the agent follows an equipotential line of the coordination field is slightly more complicated, because if the space dimension is greater than two, we cannot talk about an equipotential line, but in general we have to talk about an equipotential hypersurface. This hypersurface will be the one orthogonal to the gradient of the coordination field evaluated only toward the spatial coordinates, which will be thus a function of time:

$$\nabla CF_i(x_1, x_2, ..., x_n)(t).$$

So, the only differential equation it is possible to write in this case is the one that specifies that the agent's movements belong to this hypersurface:

$$(\frac{dx_1^i}{dt}, \frac{dx_2^i}{dt}, ..., \frac{dx_n^i}{dt}) \cdot \nabla CF_i(x_1^i, x_2^i, ..., x_n^i)(t) = 0,$$

where the dot stands for the classical scalar product.

In the rest of this chapter we apply the Co-Field approach and the dynamic system formalism to a number of motion coordination problems, contextualized in the case study scenario. In such a scenario, the possibility of enforcing motion coordination has a variety of applications: letting tourists effectively move in the museum in a reasonable way, have group of tourists meet somewhere [22], have museum guides distribute themselves according to specific spatial patterns [1, 101], or simply move without interfering with each other [53]. However, motion coordination (and, thus, the described modeling approach) finds a variety of applications in a variety of other scenarios, from self-assembly to routing in complex networks (see also the survey in Chap. 4).

Before proceeding, it is worth noting that, in realistic scenarios, the agents' movements are likely to be constrained by environmental conditions (e.g., museum walls). Such constraints should be in our dynamic system model. This could involve either some artificial force fields that constrain agents to stay within the museum plan (without crossing walls) or a spatial domain not based on simple $\Re^n$, but on a more general and complex differentiable manifold. We have successfully experienced the former approach, by defining walls and other constraints in terms of fields with infinity values. However, due to the complexities involved in the description of such equations, this chapter considers and discusses the Co-Field modeling only in open, unconstrained spaces, an approach which is anyway valuable to evaluate the potentials of a specific motion coordination solution.

5.2.2 Simulating Co-Fields

To overcome the limitations of the dynamic system formalism, it can be useful to complement the analytical description with some kind of simulation tools, enabling one to easily verify the effectiveness of a Co-Fields coordinated solution even in complex environments.

To this end, we have developed a multiagent simulation framework for Co-Fields by exploiting the Swarm simulation toolkit [147]. Such frameworks enables us to model any required spatial environment (e.g., any specific museum map), the presence in such environment of any needed number of fields with any conceivable propagation rule, and the presence of any needed number of system-level and application-level agents each with its own goals (e.g., any number of tourists each with a specific plan of visit to the museum). Each of the next subsections will present, together with the analytical modeling of various motion coordination tasks, some snapshots of the Swarm simulation of these motion coordination tasks in various simulated museum maps.

5.3 Motion Coordination in Co-Fields

Let us now put Co-Fields at work in the museum case study, to show how it can support a variety of motion coordination patterns in a robust, adaptive, and self-organizing way.

5.3.1 Room Field: Plain Navigation

The aim of this application is simply to guide individual tourists across the museum. Specifically, we assume that each tourist selects a personal schedule with the rooms he wants to visit. Agents on the PDAs of tourists will give them suggestions about where to go at a given time to visit all selected rooms in the most effective way, without requiring the tourists to know anything a priori about the museum map.

For the sake of this application, we need to introduce a specific field. The *room field* is generated by every building's room and has a value that increases with the distance from the source room. The analytical description of this field is the following: if we consider the room i to be located at the coordinates (X_R^i, Y_R^i) – the center of the room is taken as a reference – then we can describe its room field by the equation

$$ROOM_i(x, y, t) = (x - X_R^i)^2 + (y - Y_R^i)^2.$$

From an implementation point view (i.e., in the Swarm simulation), we can assume that each $ROOM$ field is just a data structure reflecting the hop count from the source room (i.e., once propagated across the infrastructure, it increases its strength value by one at every hop; see Fig. 5.1).

It is worth noting that the mathematical description of the fields does not coincide precisely with the implemented one. This is because, dealing with differential equations, we preferred to avoid discontinuities and to work with simple functions. However, from a conceptual point of view, the two descriptions are perfectly coherent despite these slight mismatches.

Given the above fields spread in the museum and given the list of rooms a tourist wants to visit, realizing this application is straightforward. Users' agents evaluate their coordination field CF as a minimum combination (fields are combined by taking at each point the minimum one) of the room fields $ROOM_i$ in which their users are interested:

$$CF(x, y, t) = min(ROOM_i(x, y, t) : i = 1, 2, ..., n).$$

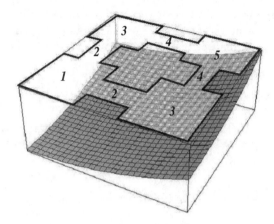

Fig. 5.1. The ROOM field generated from the bottom left room and spread across the museum

The coordination field produced models a surface having minimum points in correspondence with the rooms the user wants to visit. The user follows greedily the decrease of the coordination field, thus visiting the associated rooms. In order not to get trapped in a minimum, when the user completes the visit of a room, the corresponding field is removed from the combination and so it does not represent a minimum any more.

Starting from these simple equations, one can write, for each of the agents involved, the differential equations ruling the dynamic behavior of the system, i.e., expressing the fact that agents follow downhill their coordination fields. In the following we will restrict them to two dimensions for concreteness and notation simplicity. They have the form

$$
\begin{cases}
\frac{dx_i}{dt} = -v\frac{\partial CF_i(x,y,t)}{\partial x}(x_i, y_i) & i = 1, 2..., n, \\
\frac{dy_i}{dt} = -v\frac{\partial CF_i(x,y,t)}{\partial y}(x_i, y_i) & i = 1, 2..., n;
\end{cases}
$$

$$
\begin{cases}
\frac{dx_i}{dt} = -v\frac{\partial min(ROOM_i(x,y,t):i=1,2,...,n)}{\partial x}(x_i, y_i) & i = 1, 2..., n, \\
\frac{dy_i}{dt} = -v\frac{\partial min(ROOM_i(x,y,t):i=1,2,...,n)}{\partial y}(x_i, y_i) & i = 1, 2..., n.
\end{cases}
$$

Such equations can be numerically integrated by making use of any suitable mathematical software. In our studies, we used the Mathematica package [97]. Fig. 5.2 shows the results obtained by integrating the above equations for a system composed of just one agent. In particular, the Fig. shows an xy-plane with the trajectory of the agent (i.e., the solution of $(x_i(t), y_i(t))$ evaluated for a certain time interval) while moving in an open space.

In addition, such a motion coordination approach can be easily simulated with the simulation toolkit by modeling a specific museum map. Figure 5.3

shows some snapshots of the simulation in a simple museum with one agent (the white dot) moving in it.

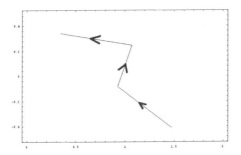

Fig. 5.2. Solution of the navigation differential equations. Note that, due to the mathematical difficulties involved in removing a field from the combination when a specific room is eventually reached, the picture has been obtained by pasting together the solutions of different equations, evaluated with "sequential" initial conditions

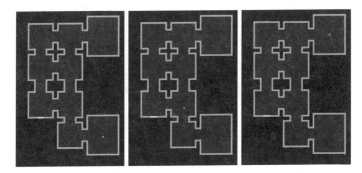

Fig. 5.3. Plain navigation: from left to right, different stages in the simulated movement of an agent through the museum building.

5.3.2 Flock Field: Moving Maintaining a Formation

Let us consider the problem of having agents distribute in space (i.e., in the museum) according to specific geometrical patterns ("flocks"), and to let them preserve such patterns while moving. More specifically, agents can represent security guards (or security robots) in charge of cooperatively monitoring the building by spreading in it so as to stay at specified distances from each other [53]. To this end, we can take inspiration from the work done in swarm intelligence research [14] and described in the previous chapter. Flocks of birds stay together, coordinate turns, and avoid each other, by following a very simple swarm algorithm. Their coordinated behavior can be explained by assuming that each bird tries to maintain a specified separation from the nearest birds and to match nearby birds' velocity.

To implement such a self-organized coordinated behavior with Co-Fields and apply it in our case study, we can have each agent generate a flock field (FLOCK) whose strength assumes the minimal value at a specific distance from the source, the distance expressing the intended spatial separation between security guards. The final shape of this field approaches the function depicted in Fig. 5.4(top). Fields are always updated to reflect peers' movements. To coordinate movements, peers have simply to (i) locally perceive the generated fields, (ii) combine sensed fields in a coordination field CF by taking the field having minimum value, and (iii) follow downhill the gradient of the resulting coordination field CF. The result is a globally self-organized movement in which peers maintain an almost regular grid formation (see Fig. 5.4(bottom)).

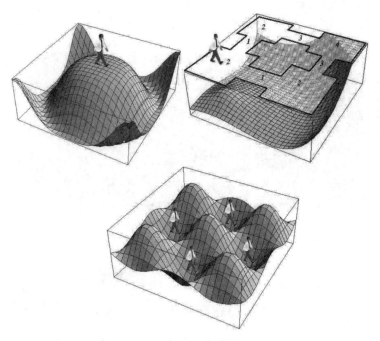

Fig. 5.4. (top) Ideal shape of the $FLOCK$ field. (bottom) When all the agents follow other agents' fields they collapse in a regular grid formation

Analytically, the $FLOCK_i$ field generated by an agent i located at (X_P^i, Y_P^i) can be simply described as follows:

$$d = \sqrt{(x - X_P^i)^2 + (y - Y_P^i)^2}$$

$$FLOCK_i(x, y, t) = d^4 - 2a^2 d^2,$$

where a is the distance at which agents must stay away from each other. Starting from these simple equations, one can write, for each of the agents in the set, the differential equations ruling the dynamic behavior of the system, i.e., expressing that agents follow downhill the minimum of the $FLOCK$ fields. They have the form

$$
\begin{cases}
\frac{dx_i}{dt} = -v \frac{\partial CF_i(x,y,t)}{\partial x}(x_i, y_i) & i = 1, 2..., n, \\
\frac{dy_i}{dt} = -v \frac{\partial CF_i(x,y,t)}{\partial y}(x_i, y_i) & i = 1, 2..., n;
\end{cases}
$$

$$
\begin{cases}
\frac{dx_i}{dt} = -v \frac{\partial min(FLOCK_1, FLOCK_2,..., FLOCK_n)}{\partial x}(x_i, y_i) & i = 1, 2..., n, \\
\frac{dy_i}{dt} = -v \frac{\partial min(FLOCK_1, FLOCK_2,..., FLOCK_n)}{\partial y}(x_i, y_i) & i = 1, 2..., n.
\end{cases}
$$

The results of the numerical integration of these equations for different initial conditions and for a system composed of four agents are displayed in Fig. 5.5, which shows a common xy-plane with the trajectories of the elements of the system (i.e., the solutions of $(x_i(t), y_i(t))$ evaluated for a certain time interval). It is rather easy to see that the four agents maintain a formation, keeping themselves at specified distances from each other.

Figure 5.6 shows the result of the motion coordination in the simulated environment. Specifically, a simple museum map has been drawn, with three agents (the white dots) moving in it. The formation consists in having the agents remain in adjacent rooms from each other.

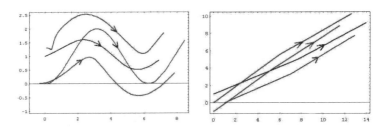

Fig. 5.5. Solutions of the flock fields' differential equations, for different initial conditions

5.3.3 Person Presence Field: Surrounding a Prey

The aim of this coordination task is to allow a group of agents ("predators") moving in the building to surround and eventually capture another agent

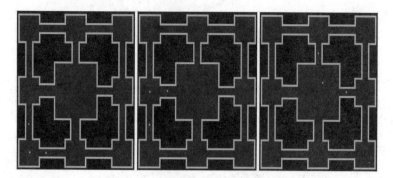

Fig. 5.6. Flocking: from left to right, different stages in the movement of a group of agents through the building, coordinating with each other so as to stay always in neighboring rooms

("prey"). As an example, one may think of a group of security guards in charge of searching for and catching a child who got lost in a large museum and who is frightened by big military men.

The task of surrounding a prey relies on a field that must be generated by every agent in the building. We will refer to this field as the *person presence field*(*PRES*), to stress the fact it represents the presence of a person in the building. The *PRES* field simply has a strength value that increases monotonically as the distance from the source person increases. Specifically, as already discussed, such a field can be realized as a distributed data structure that propagates while keeping the hop count from the source.

The analytical description of this field is straightforward and can be represented as the fields depicted in Fig. 5.7. If the agent i is at the coordinates (X_P^i, Y_P^i), then it generates a $PRES_i$ field whose equation can be written as

$$PRES_i(x, y, t) = (x - X_P^i)^2 + (y - Y_P^i)^2.$$

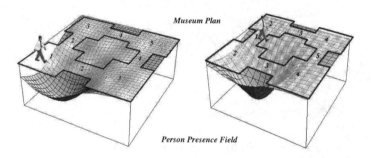

Fig. 5.7. Person presence fields (*PRES*) in a building

Now, if we consider the prey's coordination field CF^{prey}, it can consists of a (negative) linear combination of all the predators' fields. The prey runs away from the predators, by following the decrease of the resulting coordination field:

$$CF^{prey}(x,y,t) = \sum_{i=1}^{n} -PRES_i^{pred}(x,y,t),$$

where $PRES_i^{pred}$ is the person presence field of the predator agent i.

Similarly, if we consider each predator's coordination fields CF^{pred} consisting of the linear combination between the prey's field and all the other predators' fields (negative), then a predator is attracted toward the prey, but avoids other predators:

$$CF_i^{pred}(x,y,t) = PRES^{prey}(x,y,t) + \sum_{j=1,j\neq i}^{n} -PRES_i^{pred}(x,y,t),$$

where $PRES^{prey}$ is the person presence field of the prey agent.

Obtaining the differential equations governing the system is now just a matter of substituting the fields' analytical description together with the coordination field's description in the differential equations describing the field-based model:

$$\begin{cases} \frac{dx^{prey}}{dt} = -v^{prey}\frac{\partial CF^{prey}(x,y,t)}{\partial x}\left(x^{prey},y^{prey}\right), \\\\ \frac{dy^{prey}}{dt} = -v^{prey}\frac{\partial CF^{prey}(x,y,t)}{\partial y}\left(x^{prey},y^{prey}\right), \\\\ \frac{dx_i^{pred}}{dt} = -v^{pred}\frac{\partial CF_i^{pred}(x,y,t)}{\partial x}\left(x_i^{pred},y_i^{pred}\right) \quad i=1,2...,n, \\\\ \frac{dy_i^{pred}}{dt} = -v^{pred}\frac{\partial CF_i^{pred}(x,y,t)}{\partial y}\left(x_i^{pred},y_i^{pred}\right) \quad i=1,2...,n. \end{cases}$$

The results of the numerical integration of these equations, in the case of three predators and one prey, are displayed in Fig. 5.8, which shows a common xy-plane with the trajectories of the elements of the system (i.e., the solutions of $(x_i(t), y_i(t))$ evaluated for a certain time interval). Here we can see (Fig. 5.8(left)) that if the predators do not repel one another they are not able to surround the prey and all reach the prey from the same direction. In contrast (Fig. 5.8(right)), if they repel each other, they reach the prey from different directions, surrounding it.

Figure 5.9 shows the result of the motion coordination in the simulated environment. Predator agents surround the prey without leaving any escape path, by simply maintaining a certain distance from each other.

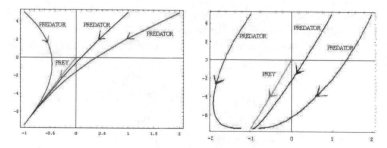

Fig. 5.8. Surrounding a prey: predators that simply follow the prey without enacting any coordination strategy are not able to surround the prey (left); predators being repulsed by other predators' fields are able to surround the prey (right)

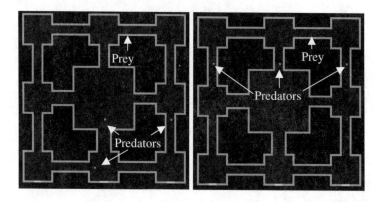

Fig. 5.9. Surrounding a prey: from left to right, different stages in the movements of a group of three predator agents, coordinating with each other so as to surround a prey agent

5.3.4 Crowd Field: Load-Balancing

The aim of this coordination task is to allow the users to avoid queues while visiting the museum. For this reason their agents will drive them to visit the rooms in their schedule by trying to avoid crowded areas. At the global scale, this realizes a load-balancing policy between users and the museum's rooms.

To this end, we need to introduce the *crowd fields*(*CROWD*), measuring the amount of crowd in a room. Such a field is assumed to be evaluated by system-level agents in the infrastructure, by manipulating the already introduced person presence fields (*PRES*) spread by all the people in the building. The analytical description of the *CROWD* fields is a bit more complicated than the previous ones, because we are trying to abstract as a continuous field an entity that is strictly coupled with the discrete nature of the space considered.

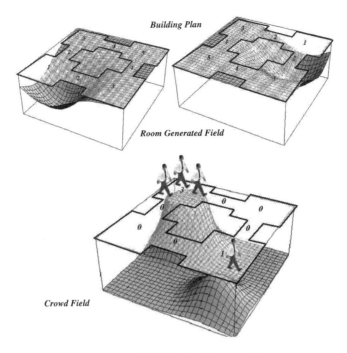

Fig. 5.10. CROWD field in a building

The crowd field $CROWD_i$ for a room i, in fact, should in principle have a constant strength value in the area of a room and drop to zero (or to another value) outside that area. However, in order to avoid discontinuities, we model the $CROWD_i$ field generated by the room i at the coordinates (X_R^i, Y_R^i), by means of the following function (see Fig. 5.10).

$$CROWD_i(x, y, t) = k_c^i e^{-h_c((x-X_R^i)^2 + (y-Y_R^i)^2)}$$

where h_c is chosen so that the strength of the field outside the room is almost 0, while $k_c^i > 0$ is a coefficient that represents how much crowded the room is. It is important to understand that, because of its role, k_c^i cannot be a fixed coefficient, but it must vary over time to reflect the different crowd conditions, so in general $k_c^i = k_c^i(t)$. For our purposes $k_c^i(t)$ is simply given by the number of people present in room i at time t (whose coordinates are within the room's perimeter) normalized to the dimension of the room. It is clear that the $k_c^i(t)$ defined in this way is an effective measure of how crowded a room is.

Eventually, the global crowd field $CROWD_g$ can be defined by means of the sum of all the individual rooms' crowd fields:

$$CROWD_g(x, y, t) = \sum_{i \in rooms} CROWD_i(x, y, t).$$

Clearly, if all agents always follow the $CROWD_g$ field downhill, the overall result is (as in a diffusion process) a global convergence toward a balance of the crowding conditions in the museum rooms.

To realize an effective service to tourists, we need to combine this process of escaping from crowds to the plain navigation application described above. So, if an agent wants, at the same time, to visit the room in its schedule and to avoid crowd conditions, it can use the following coordination field:

$$CF(x, y, t) = (1 - w) \cdot min(ROOM_i(x, y, t) : i = 1, 2, ..., n) +$$
$$w \cdot CROWD_g(x, y, t)$$

The first term of the coordination field tends to attract the agent toward the rooms in its visit schedule, while the second tends to repel it from crowded areas. The weight w can be used to specify the relevance of the crowd field, and we assume it can be specified by a tourist by the help of some user interface. For $w = 0$, the load-balancing mechanism is turned off and agents proceed toward their closest destinations in the "greed" path, disregarding crowded areas. If w is low, the agents will proceed toward their destination rooms following a "greed" path most of the time, and being diverted to alternative paths only in the case of very crowded conditions. As w gets higher, alternative (possibly longer) paths are suggested more often, whenever the "greed" path will be a bit crowded. For $w = 1$, agents ignore their visit schedule and simply move to balance the load in a diffusion process.

The result of the numerical integration of the differential equations is depicted in Fig. 5.11. Here an agent is willing to proceed from $(0, 0)$ to $(10, 0)$. If it does not consider crowd (Fig. 5.11(left)) it follows a straight line from source to destination (eventually queuing in the middle). Otherwise, it is able to avoid the crowded area in the middle, by walking around it (Fig. 5.11(right)).

Figure 5.12 shows the result of the motion coordination in two different simulated environments. On the left, the crowd is not considered in the agents'coordination field and thus crowds and queues arise. On the right, the crowd term is considered and thus crowds are avoided.

The Co-Fields enforcement of load-balancing sharply proves the already claimed advantages of field-based coordination in general and of Co-Fields in particular. First, it is an expressive means to achieve context-awareness. By means of a very limited number of fields, and with only local perception, agents can nevertheless acquire a lot of information about the environment (e.g., who is around and where, how many persons are around in the museum, where are the less crowded zones). Second, fields (when properly combined into a coordination field) represent a sort of red carpet for agents, which simply have to follow the gradients of the coordination field to achieve their coordinated goals (e.g., visiting specific rooms while avoiding crowds). Third, it supports adaptive self-organization. Once agents know which coordination field to evaluate, they can start evaluating and following it without knowing anything a priori about the environment (e.g., the same coordination field can be effectively exploited independently of the specific characteristics of the environment, as shown in Fig. 5.12), without worrying if the environmental situation changes continuously (in fact fields, as in the load-balancing example, are dynamically updated to reflect the current situation), and yet end up with some sort of globally coordinated self-organized behavior.

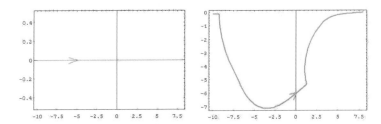

Fig. 5.11. Load-balancing: (top) Trajectory followed by an agent when no crowd is encountered. (bottom) Following downhill the coordination field the agent avoids a crowd between itself and its target

5.3.5 Room Field and Crowd Field: Meetings

Let us turn our attention to a "meeting" service whose aim is to help a group of users (e.g., tourists of museum guides) to dynamically find each other and move to meet in a suitable room.

The definition of this coordination policy can rely on the already introduced fields simply by changing the coordination field perceived by agents, which proves the effectiveness of the Co-Fields choice of preserving the separation between individual and combined fields. Also, this coordination policy can be fully integrated with the already described load-balancing policy based on $CROWD$ fields, so as to retain the capability of avoiding crowds when agents are moving to meet with each other.

Several different policies can be thought related to how a group of agents should meet.

1. The group of users wants to meet in a particular room x. This is the simplest case and each of the user has to compute the following coordination field:

$$CF(x, y, t) = ROOM_x(x, y, t) + \mu CROWD_g(x, y, t).$$

In this way every agent is directed to the minimum of the coordination field that inevitably leads to the meeting room (i.e., x). The $CROWD_g$ field term can enforce (with any desired weight μ) the load-balancing policy in this case also.

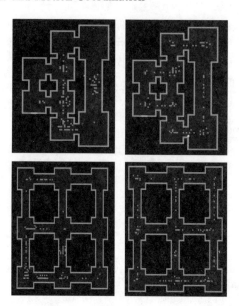

Fig. 5.12. Load-balancing in two different simulated museums. (left) When agents do not exploit Co-Fields, crowded zones appear. (right) These crowded zones are mostly avoided when agents follow the proper coordination field. The same load-balancing policy can be applied by agents with the same effectiveness independently of the specific museum topology, without having to change a bit in their code

2. The group of users wants to meet in the room where person x is located. This is very simple as well: each of the users has to compute the following coordination field:

$$CF(x, y, t) = PRES_x(x, y, t) + \mu CROWD_g(x, y, t)$$

where $PRES_x$ is the field generated by person x. In this way, every agent is directed to the minimum of $PRES_x$ that leads to the meeting room (where person x is located). It is interesting to notice that this approach works even if person x moves after the meeting has been scheduled. The meeting will be automatically rescheduled in the new minimum of $PRES_x$.

3. The group of users wants to meet in the room that is between them (at their barycenter, i.e., center of gravity). For this purpose each user i can compose its coordination field by combining the fields of all the other users:

$$CF(x, y, t) = \sum_{i \neq x} PRES_x(x, y, t) + \mu CROWD_g(x, y, t).$$

In this way all the users collapse toward each other, and they eventually meet in the room that is the center of gravity of their starting positions.

It is interesting to note that this "middle room" is evaluated dynamically, and the evaluation process can take into consideration the crowd that users may encounter at the meeting point or during the meeting process. If a room is overcrowded, it will not be chosen as the meeting point even if it represents the center of gravity. Similarly, if some users are slowed down by crowds in their paths to the meeting room, the meeting room is automatically changed to one closer to these unfortunate users. The strength of this approach is that it is fully integrated with the field concept, and that the overall coordination pattern enforced is the result of an adaptive self-organized process, accounting for the current (possibly dynamically changing) situation of the context.

By considering the third of the above three possibilities, the dynamic system description for this problem is straightforward and the integration of the differential equations is depicted in Fig. 5.13, showing how agents effectively converge to each other at the center of gravity in an open space. Specifically, it depicts the xy-plane where agents live, with the trajectories of the agents of the system (i.e., the solutions of $(x_i(t), y_i(t))$ evaluated for a certain time interval).

Figure 5.14 shows the various stages in the meeting process in two different simulated environments. Again, the meeting policy applies to any museum map, without requiring any a priori knowledge.

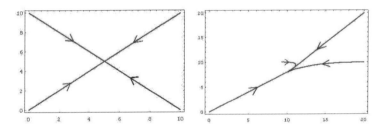

Fig. 5.13. Meeting: solutions of the system's differential equations, for different initial conditions

5.3.6 The Hint for a Methodology

It is interesting to notice that the equations governing the motion of a Co-Field agent can be also interpreted as partial differential equations prescribing what coordination field an agent has to sense in order to move according to a specified pattern.

In theory this is very useful since, from a methodology point of view, it enables answering the question: *What kind of coordination field is required to*

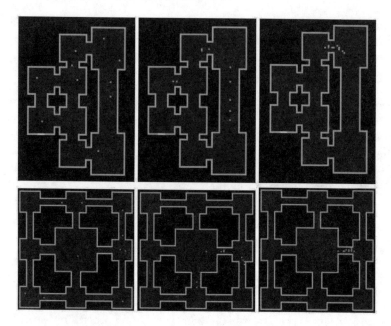

Fig. 5.14. Meeting: from left to right different stages in the meeting process showing, for two different museum maps, how agents converge toward each other

move following a specific trajectory? This is a fundamental question, since one of the main problems of field-based approaches is the lack of a methodology to help identify, given a specific motion pattern to be enforced, which fields have to be defined, how they should be propagated, and how they should be combined in a coordination field.

For example, if the coordination problem at hand requires an agent to move along a sinusoidal path:

$$\begin{cases} x(t) = t, \\ y(t) = sin(t). \end{cases}$$

Then, one has basically to find a coordination field that solves the following partial differential equations, and let it guide the agent:

$$\begin{cases} v\frac{\partial CF_i(x,y,t)}{\partial x}(x,y,t) = 1, \\ v\frac{\partial CF_i(x,y,t)}{\partial y}(x,y,t) = cos(t). \end{cases}$$

In principle, solving (numerically) the above equations provides a complete representation of the required coordination field. It is worth noting that although a closed-form smooth solution may not exist, close enough solutions with possible discontinuities may do the work (see [163]).

Although the above equations can provide useful hints, they do not solve the methodology problem completely. In fact, one has to consider that the coordination field is not something actually spread in the environment by an abstract being. It is computed by an agent by combining the fields spread by other agents and/or by some infrastructure. In turn, these fields may change due to the agents' movements. This feedback cycle, which is also the one at the basis of the field-based approach, makes it rather difficult to devise which fields are spread by the agents and how they should be composed to obtain the coordination field satisfying the above equations.

Despite these difficulties, solving the above equations may provide useful hints on which kinds of fields to employ to achieve a desired motion pattern.

Complementarily to the above approach, the immediate applicability of Co-Fields is guaranteed by the possibility of getting inspiration from (and of reverse engineering) a wide variety of motion patterns found in nature. We have already outlined in Chap. 4 how phenomena such as, birds' flocking, ants' foraging, etc. [14], can all be easily modeled with field-based coordination and, this, with Co-Fields (i.e., in terms of agents climbing/descending a coordination field as the composition of some computational fields), and all have practical application in pervasive and mobile computing scenarios.

Finally, it is also important to remark that the field-based approach is not limited to a single coordination field to be followed from the beginning to the end of the application. On the contrary, complex coordination actions can be divided into simpler sub-applications and agents can shift between different field configurations, incrementally realizing complex tasks [103, 141]. This, for example, can be useful to realize more complex, non-greedy behaviors [109].

5.4 Important Remarks and Corrections to the Model

Let us now provide some insights and important remarks about the Co-Fields model. Some corrections to what was previously stated are in fact required to overcome some subtle, but critical issues. More specifically, we will provide some guidelines dealing with (i) how different fields should be actually combined to create an effective coordination field and (ii) how agents can cope with false minima that are likely to arise in their coordination fields.

5.4.1 Propagate and Combine Fields

In the Co-Fields applications presented above we often adopted nonlinear approaches to combine different fields in a coordination field (e.g., the minimum combination).

At first, when we started developing the Co-Fields model and the concept of coordination fields, we ventured limiting ourselves to a natural, easy to understand, and analytically tractable linear combination of fields. However, although we had been able to actually model most coordination tasks with a linear combination of fields, we discovered that this basic approach can lead, in several cases, to poor performances and even deadlocks. For this reason, we decided to switch to nonlinear combinations. In this section we are going to examine what problems arise with the linear combination and how they are addressed in the actual implementation.

Before we proceed in the discussion, it is important to remark the fact that many fields, like the *ROOM* ones, other than be possibly linearly combined, are also linearly propagated. That is to say, they are fields whose strengths increase, with a constant slope, as the fields get farther from the source (e.g., +1 per hop).

In the rest of this section we will focus on the plain navigation problem to ground the discussion.

Problems with linear propagation and linear combination

There are mainly two problems arising when linearly propagated fields are also linearly combined to obtain a coordination field. The first is that linear propagation and linear combination tend to generate a coordination field with a constant value in wide areas. This fact badly affects system performance because when an agent is in a flat area it cannot be guided by the system (there is no gradient decrease to follow). The second problem is that, even disregarding the coefficients in the linear combination (e.g., all equal to one), this approach generates a field surface whose minima have different values and, worse of all, the minima can be deleted in the combination process.

To better explain these problems, let us consider the simple building map depicted in Fig. 5.15. This map can be represented in just one dimension by considering a line segment with wrapped edges. Such a representation is used as the abscissa axis in Fig. 5.16 and Fig. 5.17. In the segment, the different rooms from "A" to "R" will be reported, implicitly assuming that the edges are also connected to form a ring.

Such a representation is particularly suitable to depict fields on the map. For example, in Fig. 5.16, the black diamond line, represents the *ROOM* field generated by room H and spread across the building.

Adopting this representation it is clear how the problems related to the coordination fields arise. The problem of constant value in wide areas is depicted in Fig. 5.16, the problem of minima deletion is depicted in Fig. 5.17.

Alternatives to linear propagation and linear combination

In order to overcome the above limitations there are mainly two options: (i) it is possible to change the fields propagation rule or (ii) it is possible to change the way in which fields are combined in the coordination field.

However, as we are going to prove, only the second possibility can lead to good results. To justify this assertion, we have to consider that, both from a

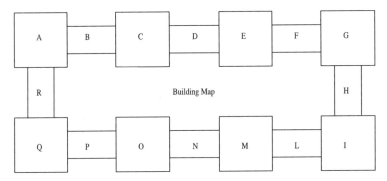

Fig. 5.15. A simple museum map that can mapped as a wrapped line of rooms

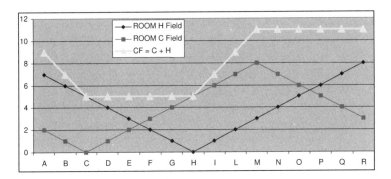

Fig. 5.16. In this example, two fields are spread in the museum: *ROOM C* and *ROOM H* fields (square and diamond lines, respectively). The coordination field (triangle line) presents constant values in all the rooms from C to H and from M to R. An agent in one of those rooms could not be directed by the coordination field

conceptual point of view and in order to avoid the minimum-deletion problem, the coordination field should appear as having equally deep minimum points in correspondence with the minima of the fields being pursued (i.e., selected rooms in the navigation example). A coordination field whose values are higher or lower depending on the building topology is not only conceptually unjustified, but is also the basis for the minimum deletion problem.

So our question is, is there a field propagation rule that generates equally deep minimum points, once fields are linearly combined? The answer is no, as demonstrated in the next few paragraphs. To perform this demonstration we need to consider a building map slightly more complicated than the one presented in Fig. 5.15. Specifically, let us consider the building plan in Fig. 5.18).

Now, consider the value the coordination field assumes in rooms A, B, and C, under the hypothesis that the agent is interested in visiting all the

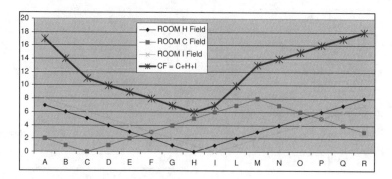

Fig. 5.17. In this example, three fields are spread in the museum: *ROOM C, ROOM H* and *ROOM I* fields (square, diamond, and cross lines, respectively). The coordination field (star line) has only one minimum point corresponding to room H. Minima associated with rooms C and I have been deleted in the combination process

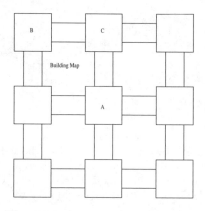

Fig. 5.18. An example building plan

big rooms, but not the corridors (i.e., smaller rooms). If we indicate with $p(x)$ the value assumed by a room field on the xth hop then we have that the coordination field in A, B, and C, which will be called CoordA, CoordB, and CoordC, is

$$\begin{cases} CoordA = 4p(1) + 4p(2), \\ CoordB = 2p(1) + 3p(2) + 2p(3) + 1p(4), \\ CoordC = 3p(1) + 3p(3) + 2p(3). \end{cases}$$

The previous requirements mean solving the following sets of equations:

$$\begin{cases} CoordA = CoordB, \\ CoordA = CoordC, \\ p(1) \le p(2) \le p(3) \le p(4); \end{cases}$$

$$\begin{cases} 2p(1) + 3p(2) + 2p(3) + 1p(4) = 4p(1) + 4p(2), \\ 4p(1) + 4p(2) = 23p(1) + 3p(3) + 2p(3), \\ p(1) \leq p(2) \leq p(3) \leq p(4), \end{cases}$$

where the second is required to lead to a meaningful guide. Unfortunately, the only solution for this set of equations is $p(1) = 0, p(2) = 0, p(3) = 0, p(4) = 0$, which does not make sense in our context. This proves that even with very simple building maps the solution based on changing the propagation function is not viable.

In contrast, by changing the way in which agents evaluate their coordination fields it is very easy to solve the above problems.

For the sake of visualization simplicity, let us turn the attention back to the simple museum plan of Fig. 5.15. Instead of adding the different fields' values, their minimum is taken as the coordination field (see Fig. 5.19). This approach guarantees that all the minimum points are preserved and have the same value.

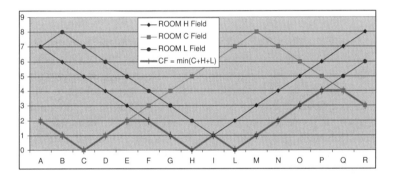

Fig. 5.19. In this example, three fields are spread in the museum: *ROOM C*, *ROOM H*, and *ROOM L* fields (square, diamond, and circle lines, respectively). The coordination field (cut line) is obtained by considering, at each point, the minimum of the propagated fields. This minimum combination maintains all the minima

5.4.2 Escaping from an Attraction Basin or Following an Alternative Path

A potential problem that may affect the load-balancing and the meeting strategy (if the latter is modified to take crowd into account) relates to the emergence of spurious local minima in the coordination fields. These spurious minima can trap an agent in unwanted locations.

In general, whenever two fields expressing an attracting part (e.g., the *ROOM* fields) and a repelling one (e.g., the *CROWD* field) are combined by agents in a coordination field, spurious local minima in the coordination fields

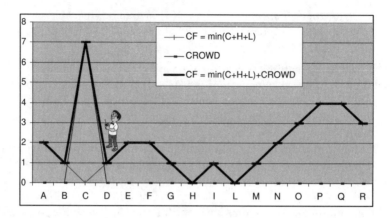

Fig. 5.20. The coordination field creates a false minimum in room D. This room was not inserted in the original agent schedule; however, the agent is directed there by the application

may arise (see Fig. 5.20). This is of course a big problem, because the user is directed from the application toward a room not inserted in his schedule.

To overcome this problem, the model has to be refined so as to require more intelligence from the agent's viewpoint. When an agent arrives at a minimum of its perceived field, it has to discover whether it is at a real minimum (a room inserted in its schedule) or a false minimum (a minimum created by the combination with the crowd field). To this end, an agent can exploit the fact that, besides typically acting on the basis of the coordination field, it is still preserving the capability of perceiving individual fields. Accordingly, to recognize a false minimum, an agent can remove the crowd field from the combination and reevaluate the coordination field. If it is again at a minimum then the minimum is a real one, otherwise it is a false one. Of course problems arise if it is a false one.

Basically, an agent at a false minimum has to decide whether to queue, to visit something else on its schedule, or, if there are alternative paths leading to its target, to follow an alternative path toward its original destination. The decision to queue or to try something different is simply a matter of preference of the user, who can simply look at the crowd and decide what to do. The details of this decision process are not analyzed. Instead, we enter into details about the specific algorithms that an agent can follow to escape to the false minimum attraction basin or to determine alternative paths to reach the original destination, since these are more strictly related to the field approach.

Before doing that, we want emphasize that the capability of agents to somewhat understand what determines the shape of a coordination field, and to take alternative actions to blindly following the attracting force of a coordination field, clearly distinguish Co-Fields from other (even field-based) approaches to adaptive self-organization. In general, most approaches to self-organization assume that agents are very simple components devoted to reacting to specific environmental stimuli (e.g., fields or pheromones), without requiring any cognitive ability [107]. In Co-Fields, agents can indeed rely on such simple reactive behaviors to self-organize their activities. However, an agent can also try to understand what and why it is being invited to react in some ways, and it can exploit its cognitive abilities to autonomously decide how to act. In other words, Co-Fields leverage reactive self-organization toward more sophisticated forms of cognitive or *semantic self-organization*, which in our opinion will play an important role in the future.

Escape from an attraction basin

The situation of an agent trapped at a false minimum can be visualized from Fig. 5.20. A first strategy the agent could adopt to escape from this false minimum is to remove temporarily from its combination those fields that attract it toward the crowded direction (left, in Fig. 5.20). This would allow the agent to visit the room in a different order: visiting first the rooms not crowded (see Fig. 5.21). This is accomplished by finding all the fields in the agent's original combination that push it toward the blocked direction, and removing them iteratively (starting from the closest) and checking every time if the agent is still at a false minimum.

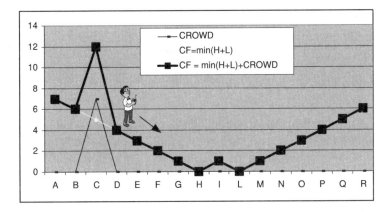

Fig. 5.21. The agent can escape a false minimum, by temporarily removing from its combination those fields that push it toward the blocked direction (i.e., remove *ROOM C* that brings it to the left)

Following an alternative path

When it is not possible to escape from the false minimum using the previous approach because all the rooms in the schedule are past the blocked direction, it may be possible to follow an alternative path toward the agent's original destination. The most interesting part of this process is how to determine if there are alternative paths, exploiting only local information. In the Co-Fields approach it is easy to prove the following alternative path theorem.

Let us consider the map in Fig. 5.22. Starting from the top-left room of the map and proceeding clockwise, we will name the rooms A, B, C, D, E, F, G and H.

If an agent is in a room C and it wants to go toward a room A in direction i, and if there is a field $ROOMG$ ($ROOMG \neq ROOMA$) so that $ROOMG$ decreases toward i and decreases also toward another direction j ($j \neq i$), then there exists a path toward A alternative to the one indicated only by the $ROOMA$ field.

To follow this alternative path the agent can change its coordination field to follow $ROOMG$; once the minimum of $ROOMG$ has been reached, the agent can switch back to $ROOMA$ to go toward its original destination (see Fig. 5.22).

This can be also visualized by reverting the representation to just one dimension, as already done in the previous section. In such a representation, the agent trapped in room C is shown in Fig. 5.23(top). The agent proceeding to the alternative path is depicted in Fig. 5.23(bottom).

Alternative Path Theorem

In order to state the alternative path theorem and to prove its correctness, it is useful to introduce a formalism to abstract a building plan into an undirected graph, and to formalize the fields concept as abstract functions on this graph.

Definition. A **building** can be defined as an undirected graph **M=** **(R,C)**, where **R** (Rooms) is the set of the graph's nodes and **C** (Connections) is the set of arcs between the building's rooms. By definition, $C \subset R \times R$. $\forall c \in C$ we can indicate $c = (r_1, r_2)$, with $r_1, r_2 \in R$, to say that c connects room r_1 with room r_2. Because the graph is undirected the connection (r_1, r_2) is equal to (r_2, r_1) and one implies the existence of the other.

Definition. A **path** through the building $M = (R, C)$ can be defined as an **ordered list of connections**: $path = (c_1, c_2, ..., c_n)$ where $\forall i = 1, 2, ..., n$, $c_i \in C$ and if $c_i = (a_i, b_i)$ and $c_{i+1} = (a_{i+1}, b_{i+1})$ then $b_i = a_{i+1}$. In particular given $c_1 = (a_1, b_1)$, a_1 will be the path starting point, while given $c_n = (a_n, b_n)$, b_n will be the path destination.

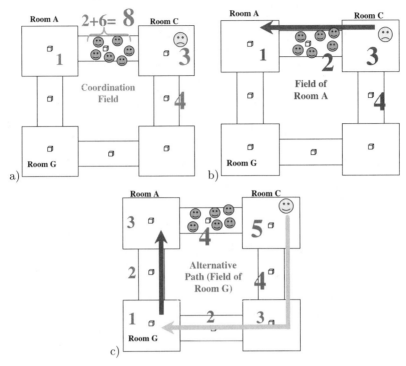

Fig. 5.22. (a) An agent willing to visit room A, gets trapped in room C due to a local minimum of the coordination field; (b) the agent can analyze the components of its coordination field, discover the presence of the local minimum, and decide to proceed, ignoring the *CROWD* field, toward A; (c) Alternatively, the agent can evaluate the existence of alternative paths by looking for *ROOM* fields decreasing both toward A and in another direction (e.g., the field of *ROOM G*). If such a field exists, the agent can follow the field of G and, once the minimum of *ROOM G* has been reached, it can switch back to the original coordination field

Definition. Given a building $M = (R, C)$, and two rooms $r_i, r_j \in R$, we will indicate with $path(r_i, r_j)$ the set of all the paths having r_i as starting point and r_j as destination. A building will be **totally connected** if $\forall r_i, r_j \in R$, $path(r_i, r_j) \neq \emptyset$

Definition. The **hop distance** between two rooms in $M = (R, C)$ is defined by the following function

$$d_{hop} : R \times R \rightarrow N$$

$$d_{hop}(r_i, r_j) = \begin{cases} +\infty & if \quad path(r_i, r_j) = \emptyset \\ min\{card(p_i) : p(i) \in path(r_i, r_j)\} & if \quad path(r_i, r_j) \neq \emptyset \end{cases}$$

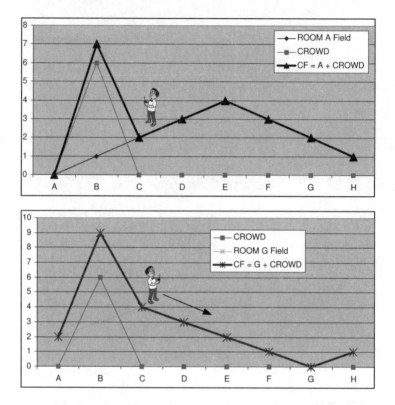

Fig. 5.23. (top) An agent trapped in a false minima. (bottom) The agent applies the alternative path theorem

Definition. Given a building $M = (R, C)$, a field is defined as a function $f : R \to N$, with $f(r_i)$ the field value in room r_i

Definition. Given a building $M = (R, C)$, a **room field** $f_{\bar{r}}, \bar{r} \in R$ is defined as a field so that $\forall r_i, r_j \in R, d_{hop}(\bar{r}, r_i) < d_{hop}(\bar{r}, r_j) \Leftrightarrow f_{\bar{r}}(r_i) < f_{\bar{r}}(r_j)$. That is to say that $f_{\bar{r}}$ is a monotonic increasing field, with respect to hop distance, and has its minimum in $\bar{r}$.

Alternative Path Theorem

Hypothesis.
Given a totally connected building $M = (R, C)$. Suppose that every room in the building generates its corresponding room field: $\forall \bar{r} \in R, \exists f_{\bar{r}} room\ field$. Let $\hat{r}$ a room with more than one connection, i.e., $\exists c_x, c_y \in C : c_x =$

$(\hat{r}, x), c_y = (\hat{r}, y); x, y \in R, x \neq y$. Let $\tilde{r}$ be a room so that: $f_{\tilde{r}}(x) < f_{\tilde{r}}(\hat{r})$ and $f_{\tilde{r}}(y) < f_{\tilde{r}}(\hat{r})$. That is to say that the room field $\tilde{r}$, in $\hat{r}$, decreases toward both x and y (see Fig. 5.24(left)).

Thesis.
There exist at least two distinct paths connecting $\hat{r}$ and $\tilde{r}$. That is to say $\exists p_1, p_2 \in path(\hat{r}, \tilde{r}) : p_1 \neq p2$.

Proof.
Let us consider $c_x = (\hat{r}, x)$, and $c_y = (\hat{r}, y)$, $c_x, c_y \in C, c_x \neq c_y$ because $x \neq y$.

Now it is easy to prove that $\exists p_x \in path(x, \tilde{r})$ so that $\hat{r} \notin path(x, \tilde{r})$ and $\forall(a_i, b_i) \in path(x, \tilde{r}), f_{\tilde{r}}(b_i) < f_{\tilde{r}}(a_i)$.

In fact because M is totally connected there exists a path between x and $\tilde{r}$. Let us indicate this path with $(c_1, c_2, ..., c_k)$ (see Fig. 5.24(right)).

Of course we can assume that this path does not contain closed loops, otherwise we could cut the path short by bypassing the loops.

Now $(c_k, ..., c_2, c_1)$ is a path that goes from $\tilde{r}$ to x. By definition of d_{hop} we have: $\forall c_i, c_{i+1} \in (c_k, ..., c_1), c_i = (a_i, b_i), c_{i+1} = (a_{i+1}, b_{i+1}) f_{\tilde{r}}(b_i) = f_{\tilde{r}}(a_{i+1}) < f_{\tilde{r}}(a_i)$, because $card(c_k, ..., c_{i+1}) = card(c_k, ..., c_i) + 1$.

So $\forall(a_i, b_i) \in (c_1, c_2, ..., c_k) f_{\tilde{r}}(b_i) < f_{\tilde{r}}(a_i)$. Moreover because $f_{\tilde{r}}(x) < f_{\tilde{r}}(\hat{r})$, $\hat{r} \notin (c_1, c_2, ..., c_k)$.

So $p_x = (c_1, c_2, ..., c_k)$.

Now for the same reasons $\exists p_y \in path(y, \tilde{r})$ so that $\hat{r} \notin path(y, \tilde{r})$ and that $\forall(a_i, b_i) \in path(y, \tilde{r}) f_{\tilde{r}}(b_i) < f_{\tilde{r}}(a_i)$.

Finally $c_x \cup p_x$ and $c_y \cup p_y$ are two paths that satisfy the thesis.
q.e.d.

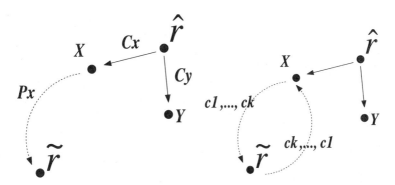

Fig. 5.24. The alternative path theorem

5.5 Scalability Issues

An important issue to be analyzed in field-based coordination and, thus, in Co-Fields, relates to scalability. By disregarding scalability issues related to storage management (after all, fields are simple data structures that occupy very little memory), an infrastructure supporting Co-Fields must be able to timely propagate the fields spread by the agents and to promptly update their values according to the agents' movements and network dynamics. In this regard, some key questions arise: how much bandwidth is required to handle field propagation? How much time does it takes to update the fields' landscape in response to dynamic changes? How much does this cost in terms of communication bandwidth and computational resources?

In the following chapters we will analyze the above issues with regard to specific implementations of the Co-Fields approach. Here, we can only sketch some general analysis (on the lines of [84]), hinting at the feasibility of the Co-Fields approach.

To ground the discussion, let us focus on the person presence fields of the case study. These fields are the worst ones to be considered, since they have to be updated according to people's movements. Let n be the average number of neighbors of a network node (because the network topology must resemble the building one, we assume $n \sim 4$ corridors for a room). Let p be the number of people roaming the building. Let t be the transmission rate for each node measured in field messages per second. Because the MAC protocol of most network links avoids collisions between packets, by avoiding neighboring nodes to talk simultaneously, each node has an actual transmission rate of t/n or equivalently, it takes a node n/t seconds to propagate a field. Now, a person moving at speed v, provided with a localization mechanism with a resolution of d, will repropagate its person presence field v/d times per second. Thus, to assure that all the field messages are timely managed the following equation must hold in the network: $t/n > p(v/d)$. This means that, assuming that a field message is four bytes (three for the person id, and one for the hop value), each network node will sustain an average traffic of $4np(v/d)$. Under foreseeable circumstances ($n = 4, p = 100, v = 1, d = 1$), this translates to a bandwidth requirement of 12.8 Kbit/s. So under these conditions, scalability and communication bandwidth do not appear to be of any concern.

Analogously, it is rather easy to see that pn/t is the time needed for a node to let the fields forward by one hop. So, for a building with a network diameter of m, the time to have the fields updated is mpn/t. Under foreseeable circumstances (t=1 Mbit/s, p=100, n=4, m=50, message=4 bytes), this results in 0.64 s. Of course, this is not a problem, especially considering the average speed at which people can proceed in a building! These simple calculations, surely overlook lots of important aspects (e.g., latency), but still the results represent good hints about the feasibility of the model.

More on this topic will be in any case discussed in the next chapters.

Part III

Implementing Field-based Coordination

6

Commercial Off-The-Shelf Implementations

Co-Fields coordination can potentially be implemented, by means of specific overlay services, on any middleware infrastructure providing basic support for data storage, communication, and localization. In fact, what is required from the middleware infrastructure to implement Co-Fields is a simple storage mechanism (to store field values), a basic communication mechanism (to propagate fields and to make agents aware of the value of fields and of the changes in field values), and some kind of network localization mechanism (to properly support the propagation of fields on a network, and to provide agents with the correct fields' magnitude at their current location). In addition, some kind of mobile code service may be required to dynamically configure field propagation algorithms and coordination field composition rules [40].

The aim of this short chapter is to present an overview of how Co-Fields – and field-based coordination in general – can be realized on top of Commercial Off-The-Shelf (COTS) middleware infrastructures. In particular, we will present how to realize Co-Fields by means of (i) infrastructures based on direct coordination models, (ii) on shared data space models, and (iii) on event-based models.

From a very basic perspective, implementing Co-Fields as an overlay service over existing middleware infrastructures amounts to creating a software substrate providing agents with the following two methods: *inject(Field f)* and *read(Field template)*. The former allows an agent to inject and spread a field across the environment (of course, some linguistic mechanisms must also be available to define fields and their propagation rules). The latter allows an agent to read the values of a field in a neighborhood so as to be able to compute the coordination field, its gradient, and to decide about further actions (see Fig. 6.1).

In the following, by exploiting again the museum case study to ground the discussion, we analyze how the existing models and infrastructures can be made supporting the above *inject* and *read* methods.

Before going on, it is important to remark that although we intend to show that infrastructures based on existing models can somehow support

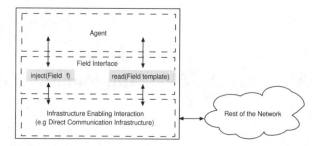

Fig. 6.1. The structure of an abstract Co-Fields implementation

field-based coordination, this does not contradict the claims about the inadequacy of these models made in Chap. 3. All these models (direct coordination, shared data spaces, and event-based ones), being general-purpose, provide basic mechanisms that can be exploited to enforce any type of coordination in a distributed system. In fact, they can be employed to build any overlay coordination models above them. But this is not the point. The point is that the provided mechanisms per se are inadequate in easily supporting uncoupled context-aware coordination activities. Thus, the need for adaptive context-aware mechanisms can hardly be easily satisfied by these models – calling for notable design and implementation efforts. For this reason, the provisioning of overlay field-based coordination services does not overcome the problem but simply shifts it to a different level.

By building additional "overlay" field-based coordination services on top of existing middleware, the application level can take effective advantage of the simplicity and suitability of the model for dynamic context-aware applications. However, the mismatch between the underlying basic model and the field-based abstractions offered at the application level leads to complex and tricky solutions for implementing field-based services. This problem, analyzed in the following, motivates the implementation of a special-purpose middleware, explicitly conceived to handle field-based coordination, that will be described in the next chapter.

6.1 Co-Fields with Direct Coordination

The main difficulty in realizing Co-Fields on top of an infrastructure supporting a direct coordination model is about the fact that Co-Fields promote a completely uncoupled approach, while direct coordination models, by definition, tend to enforce strict coupling between interacting components.

To bridge this gap, we can envision two possible solutions:

- We can think that agents communicate directly eventually relying on a proper discovery facility to exchange information about fields' values.

- We can envision the presence of *middle agents* [111, 157] located within the building and providing a field-based service. Middle agents can uncouple agents' interaction by storing fields, contributing in propagating them, and later providing fields' values to application agents.

Although the role of middle agents has been well recognized within direct coordination models, we focus on the former solution for two main reasons: on the one hand, the former approach best embodies the principles underlying direct coordination models and infrastructures. On the other hand, when middle agents are introduced, direct coordination models become very similar to shared data space and event-based models, in that the role of the middle agent can be assimilated to that of a data space that is also capable of handling events (see the rest of this chapter).

Focusing on the case study, the "direct coordination" implementation can be rooted on few key assumptions.

1. Users carry wireless mobile devices, running an agent that is able to access and spread fields (see below) by properly accessing the middleware services.
2. The museum provides also a "direct coordination" middleware infrastructure that enables unconstrained (i.e., long range) communications between all the agents within the building. Moreover, a globally accessible naming and discovery service is available to resolve names and find suitable interaction partners.
3. The museum provides a globally accessible location service that is able to localize agents within the building and has access to the building map. In particular, this service should easily provide a measure expressing the distance (in terms of either length of walking path or room distance) between the inquiring and the inquired agents.
4. Sorts of system level "Room Agents" are associated with each museum room. These agents are of limited activity, being mainly devoted to injecting the corresponding room fields (see below).

To actually propagate and read fields, agents have to implement the *inject* and *read* methods sketched above. In particular a possible (among many others) implementation of these methods is reported below.

1. When an agent X injects a field it basically registers a new entry in the globally accessible naming and discovery service of the museum. A field identifier, or better a general description of the field F, is associated with the field together with the reference (e.g., the network address) of the agent that has injected it X (see Fig. 6.2a).
2. When an agent Y tries to read a field, it basically looks up its description F in the naming and discovery service, to retrieve a reference to the agent X that injected it. Then, it can communicate directly with that agent X. Specifically agent Y asks agent (X) for the value of the field F at its location. The query consists of the couple Y, F (see Fig. 6.2b).

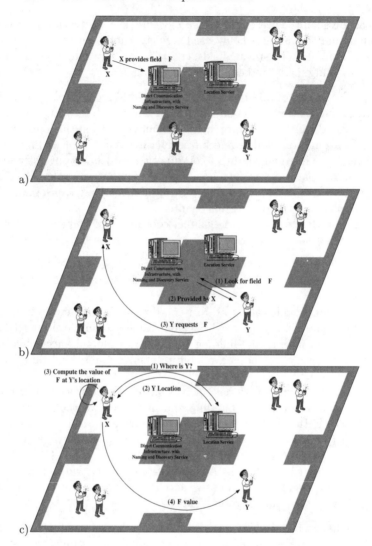

Fig. 6.2. Implementing Co-Fields on top of a direct coordination infrastructure.

3. Upon receiving the query, agent X queries the museum location service to infer the location of agent Y and the distance between them.
4. On the basis of the building floor plan and of the computed locations and distance, the agent X replies to Y by sending the value of field F at the Y's location and the value of field F in Y's one-hop neighborhood. Such values are organized in a properly accessible data structure (see Fig. 6.2c).
5. Eventually, agent Y receives the data structure. Then, it can compute the application-specific coordination field and decide about further actions.

6. The above communication protocol must be repeated whenever the field distribution changes or the inquiring agent (Y) moves.

From this implementation it is rather easy to see that direct coordination models and infrastructures are not really suitable in implementing field-based abstractions and in supporting field-based coordination. The naturally uncoupled communication enforced by fields can be recreated upon a direct coordination model only by roughly mimicking it by rather complex naming and discovery protocols.

Moreover, a more natural (i.e., straightforward) field implementation would require an external distributed repository for storing field values and for codifying field propagation in a distributed way, i.e., by means of a hop-by-hop propagation algorithm as described in the previous chapter. If such a distributed infrastructure is not available, as in the case of middleware infrastructures relying on a single (or on a limited number of) naming and discovery service, implementing field propagation becomes very tricky and requires an artificial evaluation of the value of a field, by estimating location and distances as described above.

6.2 Co-Fields with Shared Data Spaces

Most middleware infrastructures relying on a shared data space coordination model implement data spaces in terms of tuple spaces [43], as described in Chap. 3. The overall architecture of the middleware can then adopt one of these two solutions:

1. *Conceptually centralized.* The mainstream deployment of shared tuple space models consists in a single conceptually centralized (but possibly implemented as physically distributed) globally accessible tuple space or, in some cases, in a limited number of independent but yet globally accessible tuple spaces (as, e.g., in JavaSpaces [39] and TSpaces [39, 83]). Agents can globally access this tuple spaces from everywhere to publish and retrieve data.
2. *Conceptually distributed.* Several other recent proposals (e.g., MARS [22], LIME [112], and TUCSON [121]) focus on conceptually distributed tuple spaces. These models assume that the environment is enriched by a number of independent tuple spaces, typically accessible only from a locality. Agents can disseminate information on tuple spaces in their surroundings, to be possibly collected and exchanged afterward.

Although the first approach is closer to the general idea of *shared data space*, in this section we focus on the latter. In fact, a set of distributed tuple spaces is a very suitable environment in which to realize the field idea. Tuple spaces can naturally contain the local instances of fields and multiple agents can propagate and access fields there, in a completely uncoupled way.

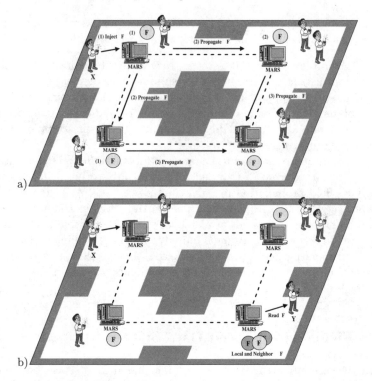

Fig. 6.3. Implementing Co-Fields on top of a middleware infrastructure based on multiple independent tuple spaces

To ground the discussion, we present an implementation of Co-Fields upon a fixed network infrastructure exploiting the services of the MARS coordination infrastructure based on programmable tuple spaces [22]. MARS adds to the classic tuple space model [43] the possibility of programming reactive behaviors triggered by tuple operations. In other words, MARS can be programmed so that when a specific tuple is inserted the infrastructure performs some operations. The described implementation relates to early experiments actually conducted within our research group to test the Co-Fields approach.

Focusing again on the case study scenario, MARS tuple spaces have been allocated on IP nodes acting as wireless access points deployed across the museum building. Users, carrying wireless mobile devices, connect to the MARS tuple spaces in their range. Each tuple space contains a standard tuple with the physical coordinates of the tuple space itself. A user agent running on the mobile device of a tourist periodically queries all tuple spaces in its range for those tuple coordinates, and then maintains a reference only to that tuple space whose coordinates are closest to the ones of the tourist – as provided by the localization mechanism (see below).

MARS tuple spaces are networked with each other, in a topology resembling the museum floor plan, and can access neighbor MARS servers with standard tuple space operations (e.g., a MARS server can insert a tuple in one of its neighbor MARS servers). Different topologies mapping different floor plans can be realized simply by providing each host with only the IP addresses of its virtual neighbors in the intended topology, and having the resulting network being used by the MARS servers to communicate.

Each MARS tuple space has been programmed to react to a new tuple being inserted in it by recursively inserting a modified version of the tuple in neighbor tuple spaces, carefully avoiding loops or backward propagation. This mechanism enables the MARS infrastructure to propagate hop-by-hop a tuple across the building. For example, each MARS server could be programmed to react to the income of a tuple like (TYPE="RoomField", NAME=any, VAL=any) by inserting in neighbor spaces (avoiding loops and backward propagation) the same tuple with the VAL field increased by one. The result is a field-like distributed data structure (implemented by means of tuples) spread across the building and having its VAL entry reflecting the hop distance from the source (see Fig. 6.3a).

Moreover, each MARS tuple space has been programmed to periodically read tuples being stored in its neighbor spaces and to store those tuples locally, adding to the tuple an entry specifying the coordinates of the server from which the tuple has been taken. This is to facilitate agents in computing the gradient of a field. In fact, each agent, by querying the MARS server to which is connected, can determine how a specific tuple (representing a field) changes in the neighborhood. For example, by reading the tuples (TYPE="RoomField", NAME="Room1", VALUE=3) and (TYPE="RoomField", NAME="Room1", VALUE=2, FROM="Room4"), the agent can know that the room field associated with Room 1 is decreasing toward Room 4, and moves toward that location to reach the room (see Fig. 6.3b).

For the sake of testing, a simple localization mechanism based on RFID tags has been set up to locate agents (i.e., PDAs enriched with RFID tag readers access RFID tags, storing coordinate information, are spread in the building) [93].

From this description, it should be clear that an infrastructure based on conceptually distributed data spaces (i.e., a set of disjoint tuple spaces), is a particularly fertile ground on which to build the field abstraction. Still, the pull-based (proactive) mechanism promoted by tuple-based coordination models [43], even when coupled with reactive programmability of tuple spaces as in MARS [22], somewhat clashes with the reactive inspiration at the heart of the field-based coordination approach. In particular, a further set of features supporting push-based (reactive) mechanisms (such as in publish-subscribe systems) should be introduced, also to enable the field-based implementation to properly perceive and react to environmental dynamics.

6.3 Co-Fields with Event-Based Infrastructure

Middleware infrastructure supporting event-based (publish/subscribe) inter-action models can be realized and deployed in a number of different ways [35]. The choice of a specific solution may notably affect the way in which the Co-Fields model can be implemented on top of an event-based infrastructure. In this section, we assume that the museum is provided with a conceptually centralized – but possibly physically distributed – event dispatcher system [23, 26]. The event dispatcher system is in charge of collecting subscriptions from all agents in the system, and of dispatching events to all agents that have subscribed to them. Agents have to connect to the event dispatcher both to register subscriptions and to publish events.

The implementation of the Co-Fields model on top of such an infrastructure relies on two main points: on the one hand, the event dispatcher decouples agent interactions; on the other hand, a special system-level *Field Propagator* agent is introduced with the duty of propagating fields across the museum floor plan. Let us present these concepts in more details.

1. The museum provides a globally accessible event dispatcher and a glob-ally accessible location service that is able to localize agents within the building.
2. A special *Field Propagator* agent run by the museum infrastructure sub-scribes to all the field-related events. This agent has access to the museum floor plan and propagates the field values accordingly (see below).
3. Agents (either associated with the museum rooms or those running on the users' handheld devices) connect the event dispatcher to inject a field by properly generating a specific field-event, or to subscribe to a specific field (see below).

To propagate and read fields, agents have to implement the *inject* and *read* methods. In particular,

1. When an agent (X) injects a field, it publishes the corresponding event to the dispatcher. In particular, we assume that the event is characterized by a tuple (EVENT="Inject", ID="Field Id", PROP-RULE="Propagation Rule", LOC="Location"). EVENT codifies the kind of happening. ID uniquely identifies the field. PROP-RULE expresses how the field should be propagated (i.e., deployed) across the building map. The propagation rule can be codified either by a scripting language or by making use of mo-bile code techniques. Finally, LOC expresses where the source of the field is located. If an agent moves after having propagated a field, it republishes the event with updated location information (see Fig. 6.4a).
2. The *Field Propagator* agent is in charge of deploying a field across the building. It subscribes to all the events in the form (EVENT="Inject", ID=any, PROP-RULE=any, LOC=any). Once such an event is registered, the *Field Propagator* agent computes how the field should be deployed

across the building by applying repeatedly the propagation rule. Then it fires field deployment events to the event dispatcher. These events are in the form (ID="Field Id", VALUE="Field value", LOC="Location"). For each field being injected, the *Field Propagator* agent creates a number of field deployment events equal to the number of relevant places in the building (e.g., one event for each building room and corridor). Each of these events represents the magnitude of the specific field in a specific location in the building (see Fig. 6.4b).

3. Users agents subscribe to the fields that are relevant for their coordination task, specifying their and neighbors' locations in the subscriptions. The event dispatcher notifies them about fields in their surroundings (see Fig. 6.4c).

4. On the basis of the information received, users eventually compute their coordination field and decide for further actions. Upon a movement, users subscriptions have to updated to take into account the new location.

From this implementation it is rather clear that, although an event-based model strongly supports the decoupling between agents' interactions and easily promotes reactive behaviors, the conceptually centralized nature of the event dispatcher (even when implemented in a distributed way) clashes with the distributed nature of fields. Such mismatch forces spurious entities like the *Field Propagator* agent to be introduced.

To conclude, we do not reject the possibility that better implementations than the one we have proposed may be conceived using existing middleware infrastructures. Nor do we reject the fact that specific middleware systems recently proposed, by integrating additional features, can be more suited to support field-based coordination. In any case, it should be rather clear that the best solution to implement and support the Co-Field approach is to define a field-specific middleware infrastructure, properly combining the characteristics of event-based coordination models and of shared data spaces models. This is the rationale at the basis of the definition and implementation of the TOTA middleware infrastructure, presented in the next chapter.

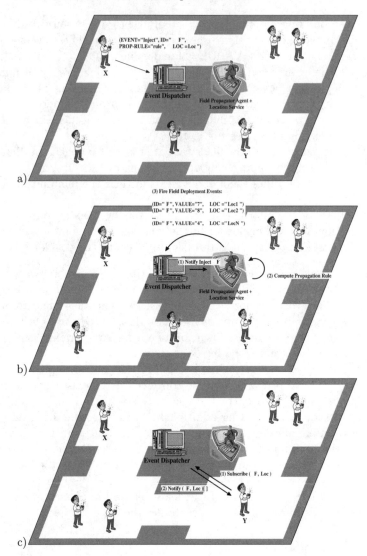

Fig. 6.4. Implementing Co-Fields on top of an event-based middleware infrastructure

7

Tuples On The Air (TOTA)

The choice of implementing the Co-Fields model as an additional layer over an existing middleware infrastructure, although providing for generality and portability, is not the most suitable solution. As illustrated in the previous chapter, the abstraction mismatches between the two layers can introduce computational and communication inefficiency. Therefore, we decided to investigate the possibility of designing and implementing a new middleware infrastructure, specifically conceived to properly support field-based coordination and Co-Fields.

The result of this research is in a middleware, somewhat inspired from our previous research work on tuple-based coordination, that we named TOTA [90, 91]. The acronym TOTA, short for "Tuples On The Air," reflects the fact that fields are implemented in terms of tuples that are capable of propagating in a network as if they were electromagnetic fields propagating in the air. This makes TOTA notably different from traditional shared tuple-based models, in that TOTA tuples are not necessarily associated with a specific node (or with a specific data space), but can propagate in a network according to a variety of propagation patterns, to form a sort of spatially distributed data structure able to express fields, messages to be transmitted/exchanged between agents, or contextual information on the distributed environment.

From the agents' point of view, executing and interacting with the support of TOTA basically reduces to exploiting a simple API to define and inject tuples in the system, perceiving local tuples, and acting accordingly to some application-specific policy. In particular, accessing TOTA tuples can rely on both a proactive scheme, in which agents access the local tuples as if they were accessing a standard tuple space, and on a reactive scheme, in which agents can be notified of locally occurring events such as changes in the locally available tuples and in the structure of the network neighborhood. In this regard, we emphasize that TOTA is not only a special-purpose infrastructure to support field-based coordination. It can also be used as a general-purpose middleware. For instance, by exploiting degenerated tuples that are unable to propagate, TOTA can support standard tuple-based coordination relying on a multiplicity of independent local tuple spaces; by exploiting ephemeral tuples that propagate but do not form a persistent distributed data structure, TOTA can be made to mimick most current event-based middleware infrastructure.

7.1 Overview

From an architectural viewpoint, TOTA is built on a peer-to-peer network of possibly mobile nodes, each running a local version of the TOTA middleware. Each TOTA node holds references to a limited set of neighboring nodes, and it is assumed that communication is limited within this neighborhood. The structure of the network, as determined by the neighborhood relations, is automatically maintained and updated by the nodes to support dynamic changes, whether due to the nodes' mobility or to their insertions or failures. To this end, we assume the system-level capability for nodes to detect events related to changes in the network structure.

The specific nature of the network scenario determines how each TOTA node determines its neighborhood.

In a network scenario without long-range routing protocols being provided, it is rather easy to identify the node's neighborhood with the network's local topology. For example, in a bare MANET scenario, the neighborhood could coincide with the range of the wireless link (e.g., all the nodes within 10 m, for a Bluetooth wireless link). In this case, TOTA nodes will be directly connected to the local network interface to detect nodes in their range either by some periodic broadcasting schema or by catching connection and disconnection events.

In a network scenario with established long-range routing protocols (e.g., the Internet), the definition of the node's neighborhood is less trivial. We can imagine however that in such cases the concept of neighborhood can become an abstraction, not related to the real reachability of a node (e.g., on the Internet IP routing masks network topology), but rather to a more general concept of addressability (e.g., a node can communicate directly with another only if it knows the other node's IP addresses). In this case, a TOTA node can either download from a well-known server the list addresses representing its neighbors. Or it can start an expanding ring search to detect nodes [46, 120, 119] in its proximity.

7.1.1 Distributed Tuples and Fields

Upon the distributed space identified by the dynamic network of TOTA nodes, each agent is capable of locally storing tuples and letting them diffuse through the network. Tuples are injected in the system from a particular node, and spread hop-by-hop accordingly to their propagation rule. In fact, a TOTA tuple is defined in terms of a "content," and a "propagation rule":

T=(C,P)

The content **C** is an ordered set of typed fields representing the information carried by the tuple. Note that this is intended to support a form of informed (or semantic) field-based coordination, as already discussed in Chap. 5 with regard to Co-Fields, in that the content of a TOTA tuple is not constrained to express only a field strength value, but can contain arbitrary information.

The propagation rule **P** determines how the tuple should be distributed and propagated across the network. This includes determining the "scope" of the tuple (i.e., the distance at which the tuple should be propagated and possibly the spatial direction of propagation) and how the propagation can be affected by the presence or the absence of other tuples in the system. In addition, the propagation rule can determine how the tuple's content should change while it is propagated. Tuples are not necessarily distributed replicas: by assuming different values in different nodes, tuples can be effectively used to build a distributed overlay data structure expressing some kind of contextual and spatial information. So, unlike in traditional event based models, propagation of tuples is not driven by a publish-subscribe schema, but it is directly encoded in the tuples' propagation rule and, unlike an event, a TOTA tuple can change its content during propagation.

The spatial structures induced by tuples' propagation must remain coherent despite network dynamism. To this end, the TOTA middleware supports tuples' propagation actively and adaptively: by constantly monitoring the network local topology and the income of new tuples, the middleware lets the tuples repropagate automatically, as soon as appropriate conditions occur. For instance, when new nodes get in touch with a network, TOTA automatically checks the propagation rules of the already stored tuples and eventually propagates the tuples to the new nodes. Similarly, when the topology changes due to nodes' movements, the distributed tuple structure automatically changes to reflect the new topology.

To support tuples' propagation and maintenance TOTA needs a means to uniquely identify tuples in the system in order, for example, to know whether a particular tuple has been already propagated in a node or not. A tuple's content cannot be used for this purpose, because the content is likely to change during the propagation process. To this end, each tuple will be marked with an id (invisible at the application level) that will be used by TOTA during the tuples' propagation and maintenance to keep track of the tuple. A tuple's id is generated by combining a unique number relative to each node (e.g., the MAC address, or a very high random number casted at bootstrap) together with a progressive counter for all the tuples injected by the node. Moreover, as we will see later, the tuple id allows a fast (hash-based) accessing schema to the tuples.

Given these features, it is clear that TOTA distributed tuples are a perfect tool to implement the concept of fields, to enrich fields with arbitrary semantic information (by setting the tuples' contents properly), and more in general to distribute any type of contextual information in a dynamic network scenario.

7.1.2 The Case Study in TOTA

Let us consider again the museum case study. We recall that we assume that the museum is properly instrumented with a reasonably dense number of wireless devices associated, e.g., with museum rooms and corridors as well as with art pieces, and that tourists are provided with wireless-enabled PDAs. We suppose here, that all these devices are TOTA nodes, i.e., are running a local version of TOTA, and connect with each other in an ad hoc network, to define the structure of the TOTA networks. Moreover, we make the following assumptions (most of them had been already specified with regard to Co-Fields):

1. The topology of the ad-hoc network formed by TOTA nodes mimics the museum's topology (i.e., floor-plan). This means in particular that we assume that there are no network links between physical barriers (like walls). To achieve this property, we can assume either that the devices are able to detect and drop those network links crossing physical barriers (e.g., relying on signal strength attenuation or some other sensor installed on the device) [131, 5] or that the museum building is preinstalled with a network backbone – reflecting its floor plan topology – to which other nodes connect [95].
2. All the TOTA devices are connected only to nearby ones: there are no long-range, wired backbones in the network.

These assumptions tend to have the network reflect the map of the physical space in the building. Thus a tuple propagated in the TOTA network will assume a configuration (i.e., a shape) coherent with the building plan.

As an additional hypothesis, we assume that

3. Devices are provided with a localization device [50] enabling them to know where other neighbor devices are located. Further details about this topic are in the next subsection.

To start understanding how TOTA actually works, we concentrate on two specific representative problems: (i) how tourists can gather and exploit information related to an art piece they want to see; and (ii) how they can be supported in planning and coordinating their movements with other, possible unknown, tourists (e.g., to avoid crowd or queues, or to meet together at a suitable location).

The first problem we face is that of enabling a tourist to discover the presence and the location of a specific art piece.

TOTA makes this very simple, and let us envision two possible solutions. As a first solution, each art piece in the museum can propagate a tuple having as a content C its description, its location, and a value specifying the hop distance of the tuple from its source (i.e., of the art piece itself; see Fig. 7.1, "Art Piece Tuple").

Then, any tourist, by simply checking his local TOTA tuple space, can discover where the art piece is located. Then, by following the tuple backward (i.e., following downhill the gradient of the "distance" field), the tourist can easily reach the tuple's source without having to rely on any *a priori* global information about the museum plan.

As an alternative solution, we could consider that art pieces do not propagate any tuple a priori, but they can sense the income of tuples propagated by tourists – describing the art piece they are looking for. Art pieces are programmed to react to these events by propagating backward to the requesting tourists a tuple containing their description and their own location information. In particular, such query and answer tuples could be defined as depicted in Fig. 7.1, "Query Tuple" and "Answer Tuple." It is worth noting that, since TOTA keeps the tuple shape coherent despite node movements, the Query Tuple creates a gradient leading to its source even if the source moves. Thus answers can reach a tourist while he is moving (see Fig. 7.2a, b)).

With regard to the motion coordination domain, the "meeting" service whose aim is to help a group of tourists dynamically find each other and move toward the most suitable room for a meeting (already discussed in Chap. 5), can be easily enforced with TOTA. Even if several different policies can be thought related to how a group of tourists should meet, here we will concentrate on having a group of tourists that wants to meet in the room that is between them (their barycenter or center of gravity). To this purpose each tourist involved in the meeting can inject the tuple described in Fig. 7.1, "Meeting Tuple." Then, any tourist can follow downhill the tuple propagated by the closest other tourist in the meeting group. In this way all the tourists "fall" toward each other, and they meet in their barycenter room (see Fig. 7.2c). It is interesting to notice that, as tourists move following downhill the gradient of the meeting tuple, they perturb the network topology and thus the tuples' shape, even the one they are actually following. However, the ripples being created in the tuple's distributed structure tend to be behind the agents; thus they do not affect their motion.

7.1.3 Spatial Concepts in TOTA

The type of context-awareness promoted by TOTA, as that of field-based coordination, is strictly related to spatial awareness. In fact, by creating an overlaid, distributed data structure, TOTA tuples intrinsically provide a notion of space in the network. For instance, a tuple incrementing a value in its content as it propagates identifies a sort of "structure of space" defining the network distances from the source.

This kind of structure of space provides context-spatial awareness to application agents. For example, in the above museum application, this information

Art Piece Tuple

```
C=  (description, location, distance)
P=(propagate to all peers hop by hop, increasing the
''distance'' field by one at every hop)
```

Query Tuple

```
C = (description , distance)
P =(propagate to all peers hop by hop, increasing the
''distance'' field by one at every hop)
```

Answer Tuple

```
C = (description, location, distance)
P = (propagate following downhill the ''distance'' of the
associated query tuple, incrementing distance value by one
at every hop)
```

Meeting Tuple

```
C= (tourist_name, distance)
P=(propagate to all peers hop by hop, increasing the
''distance'' field by one at every hop)
```

Fig. 7.1. High-level description of the tuples involved in the museum case study. **Art Piece Tuple** is the tuple proactively injected in the network by an art piece to notify other agents about itself. **Query** and **Answer Tuples** are the tuples respectively used by an agent to look for specific art pieces, and used by art pieces to reply. **Meeting Tuple** is the tuple injected in the network by the meeting agents

has been used to route messages between tourists and art pieces, and to guide tourists' movements.

TOTA also allows dealing with spatial concepts in a much more flexible way. Although at the primitive level the space is the network space and distances are measured in terms of hops between nodes, it is possible to exploit a much more physically grounded concept of space. This may be required by several pervasive computing scenarios in which application agents need to interact with and acquire awareness of the physical space. For instance, one can bind the propagation of a tuple to a portion of the physical space by having the propagation procedure – as the tuple propagates from node to node – check the local spatial coordinates, so as to decide whether to further propagate the tuple or not.

In order to bound agents' and tuples' behavior to the physical space, TOTA nodes must be provided with some kind of localization mechanism [50]. A variety of solutions can be conceived for this purpose:

- A *GPS-like* localization mechanism can provide absolute spatial information (e.g., absolute latitude and longitude of a node in the network). An actual GPS (Global Positioning System) getting spatial coordinates from

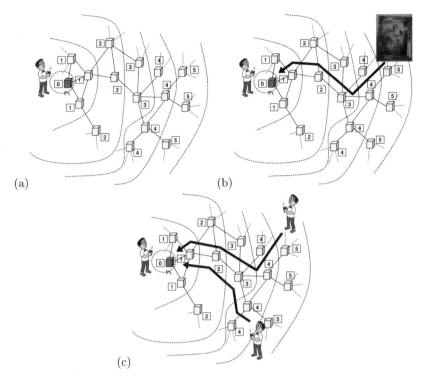

Fig. 7.2. (a) An agent propagates a QUERY field to look for specific information. (b) A suitable art piece propagates an ANSWER field that propagates downhill following the QUERY field. (c) Meeting application: for ease of illustration two agents are directed toward the leftmost agent, that does not move; actually, all three agents would collapse toward each other

satellites naturally belongs to this category. Beacon-based signal triangulation is another example of this category (nodes get their coordinates in an absolute coordinate frame defined by the beacons [105]). RFID tags, distributed in an environment and identifying specific locations or being loaded with absolute coordinates, can be used by TOTA nodes equipped with an RFID reader to infer their absolute actual location [93].

• A *RADAR-like* localization mechanism provides local information (e.g., relative distances and orientations between nodes). An actual radar or sonar device belongs to this category (radio and sound waves reflected by neighbor devices enable them to infer their distance and orientation). A videocamera installed on a node can serve the same purpose (processing the image coming from the camera, a node can infer where other nodes are). Network roundtrip time and signal strength attenuation may also serve this purpose.

The kind of localization mechanism available strongly influences *how* nodes can express and use spatial information. GPS-like mechanisms are more suitable at defining "absolute" regions. For example, they allow us to easily create tuples that propagate across a region defined by means of the coordinates of its corners (e.g., propagate in the square area defined by (0,0) and (100,100)). RADAR-like mechanisms are more suitable at defining "relative" regions, where for example tuples are constrained to travel north from the source or within a specified distance. Further details on these concepts will follow later.

It is interesting to report that spatial concepts play an important role in a variety of different proposals in the area of pervasive computing. For instance, in Spatial Programming [17], a programming language to program and coordinate a vast number of devices dispersed in an environment is proposed. There, the idea is to identify a number of spatial regions relevant for a given application and to access pervasive devices through the mediation of these regions (e.g., "this message is for all the devices on Main Street"). To this end, the definition of the regions is performed by adopting GPS devices and by using distributed data structures similar to TOTA tuples, called Smart Messages [16] .

Moreover, other than in the physical space, one could think of mapping the nodes of a TOTA network in any sort of virtual or logical space. In these cases, TOTA must be supported by an appropriate routing mechanism allowing distant peers to be neighbors in the virtual space. Such virtual spaces are particularly useful and enable the definition of advanced applications such as content-based routing, as in CAN [120] and Pastry [129]. As will be described in the next chapter, TOTA concretely supports the definition of these kinds of applications. Also, in this case it is interesting to report that similar principles are at the core of the Multilayered Multi Agent Situated System (MMASS) model [6]. In MMASS, agents' actions take place in a multilayered environment. Each layer provides agents with some contextual information supporting agents' activities. The MMASS environment is thus a hierarchy of virtual spaces built upon one another, where lower layers provide the routing infrastructure for upper ones.

7.2 The TOTA Middleware

7.2.1 Architecture of TOTA Nodes

The internal architecture of each TOTA node is constituted by three main parts (see Fig. 7.3): (i) the TOTA API is the main interface between the application agents and the middleware. It provides functionalities to let an application agent inject new tuples in the system, retrieve tuples, and place subscriptions in the event interface. (ii) The EVENT INTERFACE is the component in charge of asynchronously notifying the application about subscribed events, like the income of a new tuple, or about the fact that a new node has been connected to/disconnected from to the node's neighborhood. (iii) The TOTA ENGINE is the core of TOTA: it is in charge of maintaining the TOTA network by storing the references to neighboring nodes and of managing tuples' propagation by sending and receiving tuples. In particular, this component is in charge of sending tuples injected from the application level, and of applying the propagation rule of received tuples to repropagate them accordingly. In addition this component monitors network reconfiguration, the income of new tuples, and possibly external events, to update and repropagate already stored tuples with the aim of maintaining their structural coherency. Finally, at the core of the TOTA ENGINE, each TOTA middleware is provided with a local tuple space to store the tuples that reached that node during their propagation.

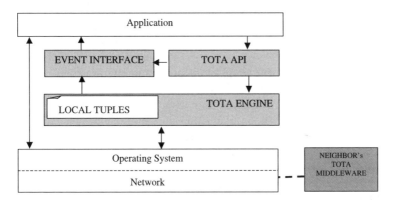

Fig. 7.3. The TOTA middleware architecture

7.2.2 TOTA Implementation

From an implementation point of view, we developed a first prototype of TOTA running on laptops and on HP IPAQs 36xx equipped with the 802.11b wireless card, Familiar LINUX [36], and J2ME-CDC (Personal Profile) [61]. IPAQs connect locally in the MANET mode (i.e., without requiring access points) creating the skeleton of the TOTA network. Tuples are propagated through multicast sockets to all the nodes in the one-hop neighborhood. The use of multicast sockets is driven by the need to improve communication speed by avoiding the 802.11b unicast handshake. By considering the way in which tuples are propagated, TOTA is very well-suited for this kind of broadcast communication. We think that this is a very important feature, because it will allow implementing TOTA in the future on really simple devices (e.g., micromote sensors [114]) that cannot be provided with sophisticate communication mechanisms. The use of Familiar LINUX is driven by the need to easily access low-level network information related to connection and disconnection events, and the strength of wireless connections, as required for the implementation of the TOTA event-based engine.

At the time of the writing, our laboratory owned only a dozen IPAQs and laptops on which to run the system. Since the effective testing of TOTA would require a larger number of devices, we have implemented an emulator to analyze TOTA behavior in the presence of hundreds of nodes. The emulator, developed in Java, enables examining TOTA behavior in a MANET scenario, in which nodes topology can be rearranged dynamically either by a drag and drop user interface or by simulated autonomous nodes' movements. The strength of our emulator is that, by adopting well-defined interfaces between the emulator and the application layers, the same code "installed" on the emulated devices can be installed on real devices. This allows us to test applications first in the emulator, and then to upload them directly to a network of real devices (see Fig. 7.4). Moreover, the implemented emulator also enables a "mixed" testing mode, in which one or more real IPAQs can be mapped into nodes of the simulation. In this mode, all the IPAQ communication is diverted into the simulation, providing the illusion that the real IPAQs are actually embedded in a large-scale network. This enables us to test interesting applications in which a user with a PDA can interact both with real network peers and with simulated ones.

Since our focus is to test TOTA-supported field-based coordination activities in a wide array of different scenarios (other than in pervasive computing), a great deal of care has been taken to allow our emulator to seamlessly integrate with other available emulators. For instance, we managed to integrate our TOTA emulator within a modular robot simulator, within an emulator for urban traffic control, and within the engine of well-known videogames (see also the end of Chap. 4) [99, 124, 48, 51, 62, 123].

7.3 TOTA Programming Model

Developing applications upon the TOTA middleware basically implies knowing

1. what are the primitive operations provided by the TOTA API to interact with the middleware;
2. how to specify tuples and their propagation rules;
3. how to exploit the above to code agent coordination.

These topics are going to be analyzed in the rest of this section.

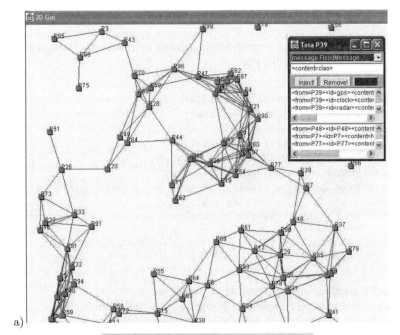

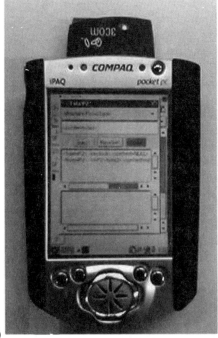

Fig. 7.4. TOTA emulator. (a) A snap shot of the emulator. The snap shot shows the 2D representation of the TOTA network. Moreover, the P39 TOTA GUI pops up when double clicking on the node. (b) The same code running on the emulator can be uploaded into an IPAQ. Note the same GUI as before

7.3.1 The TOTA API

TOTA is provided with a simple set of primitive operations to interact with the middleware (see code in Fig. 7.5).

```
public void inject (TotaTuple tuple);
public Vector read (Tuple template);
public Vector readOneHop (Tuple template);
public Tuple keyrd (Tuple template);
public Vector keyrdOneHop (Tuple template);
public Vector delete (Tuple template);
public void subscribe (Tuple template, ReactiveComponent comp,
                       String rct);
public void unsubscribe (Tuple template, ReactiveComponent comp);
```

Fig. 7.5. The TOTA API

inject is used to inject the tuple passed as an argument in the TOTA network. Once injected, the tuple starts propagating according to its propagation rule (embedded in the tuple definition). The *read* primitive accesses the local TOTA tuple space and returns a collection of the tuples locally present in the tuple space and matching the template tuple passed as parameter. The *readOneHop* primitive returns a collection of the tuples present in the tuple spaces of the node's one-hop neighborhood and matching the template tuple. The *keyrd* and *keyrdOneHop* methods are analogous to the former two, but instead of performing a pattern matching on the basis of the tuple content, they look for tuples with the same middleware-level ID as the tuple passed as argument. The *delete* primitive extracts from the local middleware all the tuples matching the template and returns them to the invoking agent. In addition, *subscribe* and *unsubscribe* primitives are defined to handle events. These primitives rely on the fact that any event occurring in TOTA (including arrivals of new tuples, connections and disconnections of neighbor TOTA nodes) can be represented as a tuple. Thus, the *subscribe* primitive associates the execution of a reaction method in the agent in response to the occurrence of events matching the template tuple passed as first parameter. Specifically, when a matching event happens, the middleware invokes on the agent a special *react* method and passes to it, as parameters, the reaction string and the matching event. The *unsubscribe* primitive removes all the matching subscriptions.

It is worth noting that, despite the fact that all the TOTA read-like methods are non-blocking, it is very easy to realize blocking operations using the event-based interface. An agent willing to perform a blocking *read*, for example, has simply to subscribe to a specific tuple and wait until the corresponding reaction is triggered to resume its execution.

Moreover, the middleware is provided with two methods whose access is restricted to tuples only (see code in Fig. 7.6). The *store* method is invoked by a tuple to be stored in the local tuple space, while the *move* method is invoked by a tuple to be broadcasted in the local one-hop neighborhood.

To clarify the above concepts let us consider the simple application agent of Fig. 7.7). That agent performs three simple actions: it injects a "Hello World" tuple, it looks for another tuple in its tuple space, and finally it subscribes to a tuple and reacts to the income of that tuple, by simply printing out a string.

```
public void store (Tuple t);
public void move(TotaTuple t);
```

Fig. 7.6. Store and move methods. They are not part of the main API, they are only used within tuples code

```
public class ToyAgent implements AgentInterface {
 private TotaMiddleware tota;
 /* agent body */
 public void start() {
  /* create a tuple and inject it*/
  FooTuple foo = new FooTuple("Hello World!");
  tota.inject(foo);
  /* define a template tuple */
  FooTemplTuple t = new FooTempTuple();
  /* read local tuples matching the template */
  Vector v = tota.read(t);
  /* subscribe to changes in tuples matching t*/
  tota.subscribe(t,this,"");
 }
 /* code of the reaction to the subscrption */
 public void react(String reaction, String event){
  System.out.pritnln(event);
 }
}
```

Fig. 7.7. Toy Agent. This agent performs three simple actions: it injects a "Hello World" tuple, it looks for another tuple in its tuple space, and it subscribes to a tuple and reacts to the income of that tuple by printing out a string

7.3.2 Specifying TOTA Tuples

Other than the TOTA API, a suitable approach is required to specify the TOTA tuples that are going to be used in an application. Indeed, specifying tuples is possibly the key issue in TOTA to properly and flexibly support field-based coordination. TOTA tuples have been designed by means of objects belonging to specific tuple classes. The object state models the tuple content, while the tuple's propagation has been encoded by means of a specific *propagate* method. Following this schema, an abstract class *TotaTuple* has been provided as the base of a general framework for tuple classes specification (see code in Fig. 7.8).

```
abstract class TotaTuple {
protected TotaInterface tota;
/* instance variables represent tuple fields */

/* this method inits the tuple, by giving a reference
to the current TOTA middleware */
public void init(TotaInterface tota) {
this.tota = tota;
}
/* this method codes the tuple actual actions */
public abstract void propagate();
/* this method enables the tuple to react
to happening events */
public void react(String reaction, String event)
{
}}
```

Fig. 7.8. Main structure of the TotaTuple class

In TOTA, a tuple does not own a thread, but it is actually executed by the middleware (i.e., the TOTA ENGINE) that runs the tuple's *init* and *propagate* methods. Tuples, however, must remain active even after the middleware has run their code. This is fundamental because their self-maintenance algorithm – see later in Subsect. 7.4 – must be executed whenever the correct condition appears (e.g., when a new peer connects to the network, the tuples must propagate to this newly arrived peer). To this end, tuples can place subscriptions to the TOTA EVENT INTERFACE, as provided by the standard TOTA API. These subscriptions let the tuples remain "alive," enabling them to re-execute their propagation method upon triggering conditions.

A programmer can create new tuples by subclassing the *TotaTuple* class. However, to facilitate this task, we developed and made available a complete class hierarchy for tuples (see Fig. 7.9) from which the programmer can simply inherit to create custom, application-specific tuples. Classes in this hierarchy already take care of implementing propagation and maintenance rules with regard to a vast number of circumstances.

The tuple class hierarchy includes the classes *StructureTuple*, *MessageTuple*, *HopTuple*, *MetricTuple*, and *SpaceTuple*. In the following, we are going to describe in detail these classes of the hierarchy, showing how they can be exploited.

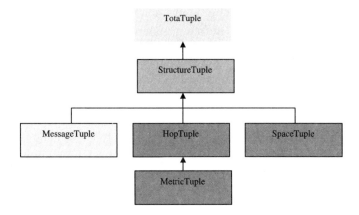

Fig. 7.9. The TOTA tuples' class hierarchy

StructureTuple

The only child of the *TotaTuple* class is the class *StructureTuple*. This class is a template to create distributed data structures over the network with a basic propagation rule. However, propagated *StructureTuples* are still not self-maintained. This means that if the topology of the network changes, tuples are left untouched. This kind of tuple can be used, for example, to implement fields in applications where the network infrastructure is relatively static and thus there is no need to constantly update and maintain the tuple shape because of network dynamics.

The *StructureTuple* class inherits from *TotaTuple* and implements the superclass method *propagate* realizing a propagation schema that is at the core of the whole tuples class hierarchy (see code in Fig. 7.10; note that, being *final*, it cannot be overloaded).

The class *StructureTuple* implements the methods *decideEnter*, *decidePropagate*, *changeTupleContent*, and *makeSubscriptions* so as to realize a breadth-first, expanding ring propagation. The result is simply a tuple that floods the network without changing its content:

- When a tuple arrives in a node (either because it has been injected or because it has been sent from a neighbor node) the TOTA middleware executes the *decideEnter* method that returns true if the tuple should enter the node (i.e., it should propagate in that node) and actually execute there, and false otherwise. The standard implementation returns true if the

```
public final void propagate() {
  if(decideEnter()) {
   boolean prop = decidePropagate();
   changeTupleContent();
   this.makeSubscriptions();
   tota.store(this);
   if(prop)
    tota.move(this);
}}
```

Fig. 7.10. Propagate method in the StructureTuple class

middleware does not already contain that tuple (i.e., the default is that a tuple propagates everywhere).

- If the tuple is allowed to enter a node, the method *decidePropagate* is run. It returns true if the tuple has to be further propagated in other nodes, and false otherwise. The standard implementation of this method always returns true, enabling the tuple to propagate to all the peers recursively.
- The method *changeTupleContent* changes the content of the tuple. The standard implementation of this method does not change the tuple content.
- The method *makeSubscriptions* allows the tuple to place subscriptions in the TOTA middleware. As stated before, in this way the tuple can react to events even when they happen after the tuple has completed its execution, typically to perform self-maintenance operations. The standard implementation does not subscribe to anything.
- After that, the tuple is inserted in the TOTA tuple space by executing *tota.store(this)*. Again, without this method the tuple would propagate across the network without leaving anything behind. Thus no distributed data structure would be ever formed.
- Finally, if the *decidePropagate* method returned true, the tuple is propagated to all the neighbors by the command *tota.move(this)*. The tuple will eventually reach neighboring nodes, where it will be executed again. It is worth noting that the tuple will arrive in the neighboring nodes with the content changed by the last run of the *changeTupleContent* method.

Programming a TOTA tuple to create a distributed data structure basically reduces to inheriting from the above class to define any content for tuples and to overloading the four methods specified above to customize the tuple propagation and self-maintenance behavior.

Here, in the following, we present some examples to show the expressiveness of the introduced framework. These are not tuples in the TOTA tuples class hierarchy; they are examples of how a programmer could use the hierarchy to create application-specific tuples. Specifically, we are going to show two examples of tuples: (i) *NMGradient* and (ii) *TimeDecayingFloodTuple*.

The *NMGradient* is a tuple that floods the network and has an integer *hop* as content, whose value is incremented by one at every network hop. This implements a sort of basic field with a strength which increases moving farther form the source. To code this tuple one has basically to (i) place the integer hop in the object state, (ii) overload *changeTupleContent*, to let the tuple increase the hop value counter at every propagation step, and (iii) overload *decideEnter* so as to allow the tuple to enter in a node not only if there is no tuple yet in the node – as in the base implementation – but also if there is a tuple with a higher hop count. This allows the tuple to enforce the breadth-first propagation assuring that the hop count truly reflects the hop distance from the source (see code in Fig. 7.11).

The *TimeDecayingFloodTuple* is a tuple that floods the network and has an integer value as content. The integer value remains constant as the tuple spreads in the network. However, it decays with time, causing tuple deletion once the value reaches zero. To code this tuple one has basically to (i) place the integer counter in the object state, (ii) overload the *makeSubscriptions* method, to let the tuple subscribe to the peer internal clock associating the *TIME* reaction to every clock tick, and (iii) finally, in the react method, decrease the integer value and delete the tuple as soon as the value reaches zero (see code in Fig. 7.12).

```
public class NMGradient extends StructureTuple {
 public int hop = 0;

 public boolean decideEnter() {
  super.decideEnter();
  NMGradient prev =(NMGradient)tota.keyrd(this);
  return (prev == null ||
          prev.hop > (this.hop + 1));
 }
 protected void changeTupleContent() {
  super.changeTupleContent();
  hop++;
}}
```

Fig. 7.11. The *NMGradient* (i.e., Not Maintained Gradient) is a tuple that floods the network and have an integer hop-counter that is incremented by one at every hop

The rest of the hierarchy of Fig. 7.9 has been built in the same way. Programmers can inherit from the hierarchy by further customizing a tuple's propagation to match a specific application's requirements.

MessageTuple

MessageTuples are used to create messages that are not stored in the local tuple spaces, but just flow in the network as sorts of "events." The basic

```
public class TimeDecayingFloodTuple extends StructureTuple {
 private int value = 300;
 public void makeSubscriptions() {
  SensorTuple st = new SensorTuple("TIME","*");
  tota.subscribe(st, (ReactiveComponent)this,"TIME");
 }

 public void react(String reaction, String event) {
  if(reaction.equalsIgnoreCase("TIME")) {
   value = value -5;
   if(value <= 0) {
    tota.delete(this);
    return;
}}}}
```

Fig. 7.12. The *TimeDecayingFloodTuple* is a tuple that floods the network with an integer value. The integer value remains constant as the tuple spreads in the network. However, it decays with time, causing tuple deletion once the value reaches zero

structure is the same as *StructureTuple*, but a default subscription is in charge of erasing the tuple after some passed time. Note that it would not be possible to simply remove the *tota.store()* method from the propagate method, because previously stored values are used to block the tuple's backward propagation. To this end the tuple's value can be deleted only after the tuple "wave front" has passed. It is worth noting that setting the time before deletion is not trivial. If the tuple propagates in a breadth-first manner, it can simply be set to the time the tuple "wave front" takes to proceed two hops away. However, if the tuple is propagated to a specific direction and the network topology is closed in a circular track, this can lead to a message that continues circulating trough the network endlessly. For this reason, in such asymmetrical situations *MessageTuples* must be used really carefully.

Message tuples could be fruitfully applied as a communication and event propagation mechanism. These tuples, in fact, could embed in their propagation rule a routing policy, without requiring the presence of specific routing agents to properly forward them. Moreover, it is easy to implement with these tuples several different communication patterns like *unicast* or *multicast*. Finally, by combining these tuples with *StructureTuples*, it is easy to realize a publish-subscribe communication mechanism, in which *StructureTuples* create subscriptions paths, to be followed by *MessageTuples* implementing events.

It is worth noting that this kind of interaction pattern is exactly the one exploited in the information retrieval application (i.e., *second* solution) in the museum case study (see "Query Tuple" and "Answer Tuple" in Fig. 7.1).

Here, in the following, we present some examples to show the expressiveness of the introduced framework. Specifically, we are going to show two examples of tuples: (i) *UnicastTuple* and (ii) *DownhillTuple*.

The *UnicastTuple* is a tuple that models a unicast message directed to a specific destination. Since, at the middleware level, TOTA promotes only one-hop broadcast communication, the unicast facility has to be coded within the tuple. A *UnicastTuple* does not implement routing algorithms and it is intended to reach a node directly connected (i.e., one hop) to the source. To code this tuple one has basically to: (i) place in the object state a string representing the destination address, (ii) overload the *decideEnter* method so as to allow the entrance only if the node is the intended destination. Looking at the code, it is worth noting that entrance is allowed also in the source node. This is to allow the tuple to be injected in the TOTA network in the first place (see code in Fig. 7.13).

The *DownhillTuple* is a tuple that propagates by following downhill the trail left by another tuple. Specifically, the *DownhillTuple* follows downhill another tuple whose content is an integer value typically increasing with the distance from the source (e.g., *NMGradient*). To code this tuple one has basically to overload the *decideEnter* method to let the tuple enter only if the value of the tuple being followed (e.g., *NMGradient*) in the node is lower than the value on the node from which the tuple comes (see Fig. 7.14).

Note that if there are multiple paths going downhill, the tuple follows downhill each of them. This can be a limit, in some scenarios, because it wastes bandwidth. However, it improves robustness since it is able to cope with network link failures. Eventually, it would be very easy to base this tuple on the above *UnicastTuple* to avoid multipath propagation.

```java
public class UnicastTuple extends MessageTuple {
 public String destIP = new String();

 public boolean decideEnter()
 {
  boolean cond0,cond1,cond2;
  cond0 = super.decideEnter();
  cond1 = tota.toString().equals(this.getSourceFromId());
  cond2 =  (StaticUtilities.
             peerNameResolver(tota.toString()).
             equalsIgnoreCase(destIP));
  return cond0 && (cond1 || cond2);
 }
 public void setDestinationIP(String destIP)
 {
  this.destIP = destIP;
}}
```

Fig. 7.13. The *UnicastTuple* is a tuple that models a unicast message directed to a specific destination

```
public class DownhillTuple extends MessageTuple {
 public String name;
 public int oldVal = 9999;
 NMGradient trail;

 public DownhillTuple() {
  trail = new NMGradient();
  trail.setContent("ciao");
 }
 public boolean decideEnter() {
  super.decideEnter();
  int val = getGradientValue();
  if(val < oldVal) {
   oldVal = val;
   return true;
  }
  else
   return false;
 }
 /* this method returns the minimum hop-value of the
 NMGradient tuples matching the tuple to be
 followed in the current node */
 private int getGradientValue() {
  Vector v = tota.read(trail);
  int min = 9999;
  for(int i=0; i<v.size(); i++) {
   NMGradient gt =
   (NMGradient)v.elementAt(i);
   if(min > gt.hop)
    min = gt.hop;
  }
  return min;
}}
```

Fig. 7.14. The *DownhillTuple* is a tuple that propagates by following downhill the trail left by another tuple. Specifically, the *DownhillTuple* follows downhill another tuple whose content is an integer value typically increasing with the distance from the source (e.g., *NMGradient*)

HopTuple

This kind of tuple inherits from *StructureTuple* to create distributed data structures that self-maintain their structure in an automatic way, to reflect changes in the network environment (see Fig. 7.15).

Similarly to the previous *NMGradient* in Fig. 7.11, this class overloads the *decideEnter* method so as to allow the entrance not only if the tuple is not in the node yet – as in the base implementation – but also if there is a tuple with a higher value for the hop variable. This allows the tuple to enforce

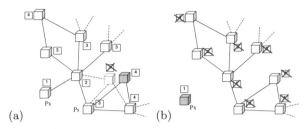

Fig. 7.15. *HopTuples* self-maintain despite topology changes. (a) The tuple on the gray node must change its value to reflect the new hop distance from the source Px. (b) If the source detaches, all the tuples must auto-delete to reflect the new network situation

the breadth-first propagation, assuring that the hop variable truly reflects the actual hop distance from the source. Moreover, this class overloads the empty *makeSubscription* method of the *StructureTuple* class, to let these tuples react to changes in the network topology, by adjusting their values to be consistent (after some delays) with the true hop distance from the source (i.e., the integer hop counter value is adjusted in response to network dynamics). A detailed description of how does the self-maintenance algorithm works will be presented later in this chapter.

Self-maintained tuples like *HopTuples* are fundamental to enable field-based coordination also in the presence of dynamic networks. For instance, tuples to be employed in motion coordination, like the meeting tuples in the case study (see Fig. 7.1, "Meeting Tuple") have to be compulsorily realized by self-maintained tuples, to ensure the adaptive acquisition of up-to-date information. From a software engineering point of view, the value of self-maintained tuples is that programmers have simply to take care of agents injecting proper tuples in the system, without worrying at all about how agents could deal with the network dynamism: all the burden is moved away from the agents and encapsulated in the self-maintenance algorithms of the tuples.

To clarify the above concepts and to show again the expressiveness of the TOTA tuples, we are going to give two other examples of tuples: (i) *BoundedTuple* and (ii) *FlockingTuple*, both derived by inheritance from *HopTuple*.

A *BoundedTuple* is simply a tuple whose integer content reflects the distance from the source and that is propagated only within a limited distance (RANGE) from the source. Since the hop variable is maintained in the superclass *HopTuple*, coding this tuple is trivial. One has basically to overload the *decideEnter* method to enable the entrance only if the hop value is below the specified distance value (see code in Fig. 7.16).

A *FlockingTuple* creates a data structure that has a minimum at a specific distance (RANGE) from the injecting agent.

The name of this tuple comes from the fact it can be employed to realize an interesting application allowing a group of agents to maintain a specific grid formation [14], as from Chap. 5. To implement such a coordinated behavior with TOTA, we can have each agent generate a tuple *(FlockingTuple)* whose value assumes the minimal value at a specific distance from the source, the distance expressing the intended spatial separation between agents. The final shape of this field approaches the function depicted in Fig. 5.4(top) in Chap. 5. *FlockingTuples* are always updated to reflect peers' movements. To coordinate movements, peers have simply to locally perceive the generated tuples and follow them downhill. The result is a globally coordinated movement in which peers maintain an almost regular grid formation (see Fig. 5.4(bottom) in Chap. 5).

Coding this tuple is trivial; one has simply to (i) place in the object state an integer representing the flock value, and (ii) overload the *changeTuple-Content* to let the tuple assume the intended value of this flock value as the tuple propagates. The normal hop variable is still maintained in the superclass *HopTuple* (see code in Fig. 7.17).

```
public class BoundedTuple extends HopTuple {
  private static final int RANGE = 3;
  public boolean decideEnter() {
    boolean b1 = super.decideEnter();
    boolean b2 = (hop <= RANGE);
    return b1 && b2;
}}
```

Fig. 7.16. A *BoundedTuple* is simply a tuple whose integer content reflects the distance from the source and that is propagated only within a limited distance (RANGE) from the source

```
public class FlockingTuple extends HopTuple {
  private static final int RANGE = 3;
  public int value = RANGE;
  protected void changeTupleContent() {
    super.changeTupleContent();
    if(hop <= RANGE)
      value --;
    else
      value ++;
}}
```

Fig. 7.17. A *FlockingTuple* creates a data structure that has a minimum at a specific distance (RANGE) from the injecting agent

MetricTuple and SpaceTuple

In some application scenarios, and possibly even in the museum case study, it can be helpful to ground tuple propagation to actual physical distances rather than to network distances (e.g., 300 m NORTH from the source, rather than 30 network hops from the source). To this end, a common shared coordinate system must be established over the network. Relying on such a coordinate system, nodes are provided with a common knowledge of where the NORTH is and what the physical distance between them is.

Metric and *Space* tuples allow the creation of common shared coordinate systems across the TOTA network. In particular, both these tuples have three float numbers (x, y, z) as a content. Once one of these tuples is injected in the network, it propagates changing its content so that (x, y, z) reflects the coordinates of the node in a coordinate system centered where the tuple was first injected (see Fig. 7.18).

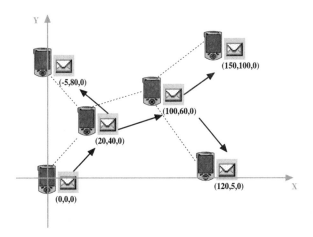

Fig. 7.18. *Metric* and *Space* tuples create a shared coordinate system, centered at the node that injected the tuple

The current implementation of *Metric* and *Space* tuples supports either the presence of a GPS-like device or a RADAR-like device (see Subsect. 7.1.3).

The implementation of *Metric* and *Space* tuples, given the availability of a GPS-like device, is straightforward. Once injected, the tuple will read the injecting node GPS coordinates and will initialize its content to $(0, 0, 0)$. Upon reaching a new node, it will change the content to the GPS coordinates of the new node translated back by the injecting node coordinates. Tuple update proceeds similarly: when a node moves (not the source one), the tuple locally changes its content by accessing the new GPS information.

The implementation of *Metric* and *Space* tuples, given the availability of a RADAR-like device, is more complicated. Here the goal is to create a tuple class that combines the local coordinate systems, built by the RADAR-like devices, into a shared coordinate system, with the center in the node that injected the tuple.

To explain how this can be achieved let us consider Fig. 7.19. The tuple $(0, 0, 0)$ travels from P1 to P2 and it changes its content there. Specifically, it subtracts from its old value the coordinates of P1 as sensed by the RADAR-like device in P2. Thus $(0 - (-100), 0 - (-20), 0 - 0) = (100, 20, 0)$. It is worth noting that, in the figure, all the private coordinate systems are aligned. So combining them is just a matter of adding the coordinates. However, this perfect alignment is unlikely to happen and slightly more complex (geometric) combination will be required. Further propagation hops (from P2 to P3, and form P2 to P4) proceed analogously.

Tuple update proceeds similarly: once these tuples have been propagated, if a node moves (not the source one), only its tuple local value is affected, while all the others are left unchanged. In fact, the other's physical positions with respect to the source do not change. Upon a movement *Metric* and *Space* tuples read the RADAR and adjust their values accordingly (see Fig. 7.20).

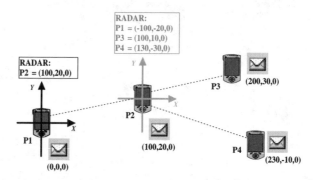

Fig. 7.19. *Metric* and *Space* tuples create the shared coordinate system, by having each node change the content of the tuples on the basis of the coordinates provided by the RADAR-like device

To understand the difference between *Metric* and *Space* tuples, it is fundamental to focus on what happens when the source moves. In theory all the tuple instances must be changed because the origin of the coordinate system has shifted. This is exactly what happens in *MetricTuple* where the origin of the coordinated system is anchored to the source node. This of course can lead to scalability problems, especially if the source is highly mobile. What happens if also the source updates its value locally, without further propagating? In this case, the origin of the coordinate system remains where the tuple

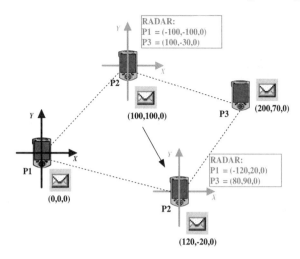

Fig. 7.20. Self-maintenance in *Metric* and *Space* tuples: since the tuple on P3 does not change position with respect to the tuple source, it does not change its content. P2 updates its content on the basis of the new RADAR reading

was first injected, even if no nodes are in that position. The coordinate system is maintained by the network, but not affected by it. This is the *SpaceTuple* implementation.

To further clarify the above concepts and to show again the expressiveness of our abstractions, we are going to show two other examples of tuples: (i) *DistanceTuple* and (ii) *FlockMetricTuple*.

A *DistanceTuple* is a tuple that holds the spatial distance from the source (note that the variables x, y, z are maintained in the *MetricTuple* and *SpaceTuple* classes). In the example, *DistanceTuple* inherits from *MetricTuple* and so it represents the distance from the source, even when the source moves. However, if the same tuple would have inherited from *SpaceTuple*, then it would have expressed the distance from the point at which it had been originally injected (see code in Fig. 8.6), ignoring later movements of the source.

A *FlockMetricTuple* encodes in its shape the flock field described in Fig. 5.4(left). This tuple can be conveniently used to maintain a flock formation in the above three robots application. In fact, the robots can locate at specific distances from each other on the basis of their real physical distances rather than some network hop distances (see code in Fig. 7.22).

7.3.3 Programming Agents

The last step involved in programming a TOTA application is coding the agents that specify the required TOTA tuples to enforce specific coordination tasks and that then use the TOTA API to inject such tuples in the system

```
public class DistanceTuple extends MetricTuple {
 public int value = 0;
 protected void changeTupleContent() {
  super.changeTupleContent();
  value = (int)Math.sqrt((x*x)+(y*y)+(z*z));
}}
```

Fig. 7.21. A *DistanceTuple* is a tuple that holds the spatial distance from the source

```
public class FlockMetricTuple extends MetricTuple {
 private int a = 30;
 public int value = 0;
 protected void changeTupleContent() {
  super.changeTupleContent();
  int d = (int)Math.sqrt((x*x)+(y*y)+(z*z));
  value = (d*d*d*d) - 2*(a*a)*(d*d); // d^4 - 2a^2d^2
}}
```

Fig. 7.22. A *FlockMetricTuple* encodes in its shape the flock field described in Fig. 5.4a

and/or read them. Here we give two detailed examples about how to program agents in the museum case study.

The tuples that our example agents use are the *NMGradient* and the *DownhillTuple* presented in the previous section (actually, the very first line of *NMGradient* should be changed to inherit from *HopTuple*, so as to be maintained despite the movements of the source agent).

Gathering Contextual Information

Let us firstly focus our attention on the task of gathering contextual information. Following the second approach sketched in Subsect. 7.1.2, we consider the solution in which art pieces (i.e., agents running within art pieces in the embedded museum infrastructure) are programmed to sense the income of query tuples propagated by tourists (i.e., by their agents) and to react by propagating backward to the requesting tourists their location information. These agents are coded by the *ArtAgent* and the *QueryAgent* represented in Fig. 7.23 and Fig. 7.24, respectively.

In more detail, a *QueryAgent* of a tourist looking for information about the *da Vinci's Monna Lisa* performs just two simple operations: it injects in the network a tuple of class *NMGradient* with a content string representing the name of the searched painting. Then it subscribes to the income of all the *DownhillTuples* (which are assumed to describe the searched art piece and its location) having as the first content field "Monna Lisa." The associated reaction *displayReaction* is executed on receipt of such a tuple to simply print out the content of the received event tuple in the user interface.

Correspondingly, each *ArtAgent* is identified by a description representing the art piece it stands for (e.g., "Monna Lisa"). *ArtAgent* subscribes to
the local income of those *NMGradient* tuples querying for the art piece they
represent. The reaction to the income of such a tuple event is to inject a
DownhillTuple that simply follows backward the query tuple to reach the
QueryAgent issuing the request.

```
public class ArtAgent implements AgentInterface {
 private TotaMiddleware tota;
 /* this is the piece of art description and location */
 private String description, location;
 /* agent body */
 public void start() {
  /* subscribe to the query */
  NMGradient query = new NMGradient();
  query.setContent(description);
  tota.subscribe(query,this,"answerQuery");
 }

 /*code of the reaction, here it injects the
 answer tuple. The answer will be coded by a
 DownhillTuple following the query.*/
 public void react(String reaction, String event) {
  NMGradient query = Tuple.deserialize(event);
  DownhillTuple answer = new DownhillTuple(query.content);
  answer.setContent(description+" "+location);
  tota.inject(answer);
}}
```

Fig. 7.23. Agent example: *ArtAgent*

Meeting

With regard to the meeting application, the algorithm followed by *Meeting-
Agents* (see code in Fig. 7.25) is very simple: agents have to determine the
farthest peer, and then move (or better, to suggest their user where to go)
by following downhill that peer's presence tuple, coded in the form of an
NMGradient tuple. To this end, each agent injects an *NMGradient* to notify
other agents about its location. Then, it will read the *NMGradients* injected
by the other agents, extract the one corresponding to the farthest agent, and
display the direction to go to follow the tuple downhill. In this way, agents
will eventually meet at their center of gravity.

```
public class QueryAgent implements AgentInterface {
 private TotaMiddleware tota;
 /* agent body */
 public void start() {
  /* inject the query */
  NMGradient query = new NMGradient();
  query.setContent("Monna Lisa");
  tota.inject(query);
  /* subscribe to the answer: the answer will be
  conveyed in a DownhillTuple */
  DownhillTuple answer = new DownhillTuple();
  answer.setContent("Monna Lisa *");
  tota.subscribe(answer,this,"display");
 }

 /* code of the reaction, here it
 simply prints out the result */
 public void react(String reaction, String event) {
  if(reaction.equalsIgnoreCase("display ")) {
   gui.show("Monna Lisa:" + event);
}}}
```

Fig. 7.24. Agent example: *QueryAgent*

```
public class MeetingAgent extends Thread
                          implements AgentInterface
{
 private TotaMiddleware tota;

 public void run() {
  /* inject the meeting tuple to
  participate the meeting */
  NMGradient mt = new NMGradient();
  mt.setContent(peer.toString());
  tota.inject(mt);
  while(true) {
   /* read other agents' meeting tuples */
   NMGradient coordinates = new NMGradient();
   Vector v = tota.read(coordinates);
   /* evaluate the gradients and select the
   peer to which the gradient goes downhill */
   GenPoint destination = getDestination(v);
   /* suggest the user to move downhill following
   meeting tuple */
   gui.show(destination);
}}}
```

Fig. 7.25. Agent example: *MeetingAgent*

7.4 Performances and Experiments

The effectiveness of the TOTA approach is of course related to costs and performances in managing TOTA distributed tuples. Specifically, the following fundamental questions arise: what is the cost of propagating tuples? How much burden self-maintenance adds to the system? Is the process scalable? How should the different parts of the system account for the costs involved in TOTA operations? These questions are indeed very general ones: other than assessing the effectiveness of TOTA, answering them may provide insights on the general feasibility of deploying field-based applications in much more detail than what we have done at the end of Chap. 5.

As answers to these questions, we present some of the most relevant experiments we performed with the TOTA middleware. In particular, the *overhead* subsection deals with overhead and scalability concerns, while the *accounting* subsection illustrates the main operations and system parts responsible for the TOTA overhead.

7.4.1 Overhead

With regard to overhead costs, it is most important to assess whether the overhead on a node is related to (i.e., increases with) the dimension of the network or not. If the answer to this question is negative, then the system is truly scalable: a node performs well independently of the size of the network in which it is embedded; if it is affirmative, then any implementation of the model is probably doomed to failure: the system performances degrade with an increase in network size.

The cost of propagating a tuple, relying on a multi-hop mechanism, is something inherently scalable. Each node will have to propagate the tuple only to its immediate neighbors. The size of the network does not matter since the global effort to spread the tuple is fairly partitioned between the constituting nodes.

The scalability of tuples' maintenance is less clear. To be independent of the network size, maintenance operations must be confined within a locality from where something happened that broke the tuple structure (e.g., a network topology change). If it so, concurrent events (e.g., topology changes) happening at distant points of the network do not add up. If on the contrary maintenance operations always propagate across the whole network, distant concurrent events add up and the system does not scale.

In the rest of this subsection we are going to present the results we found with regard to the different tuples in the hierarchy of Fig. 7.9. However, before we proceed, a caveat is needed: the following considerations and performances refer only to classes in the hierarchy. It is clear that, by subclassing one of these tuples, a programmer can overturn the tuple's behavior and possibly introduce complex cascading events that degrade performances.

Structure and Message Tuple

These tuples are not maintained, so once propagated, they do not add any burden to the system. It is also worth noting that with regard of tuples like the *TimeDecayingFloodTuple* described in Subsect. 7.3.2, which adds a custom reaction, the answer is still positive, since a change in the tuple (i.e., time) affects only the tuple itself, and so it is obviously confined. The same consideration holds also for the delete operation inherent in message tuples.

HopTuples

With regard to *HopTuple*, establishing whether maintenance operations are locally confined is more complicated. Tuples' maintenance operations are required upon a change in the network topology, to have the distributed tuples reflect the new network structure. This means that maintenance operations are triggered whenever, due to nodes' mobility or failures, new links in the network are created or removed. In this context our question becomes, are the tuples' maintenance operations confined to an area neighboring the place in which the network topology had actually changed? This means that if, for example, a device breaks down (causing a change in the network topology), only neighboring devices should change their tuples' values. The size of this neighborhood is not fixed and cannot be predicted a priori, since it depends on the network topology (a detailed description of how the self-maintenance algorithm works is presented later).

What is the impact of a local change in the network topology in real scenarios? To answer this question we exploited the implemented TOTA emulator, and were able to derive results depicted in Fig. 7.26.

The graph show results obtained by a large number of experiments, conducted on different networks. We considered networks having an average density (i.e., average number of nodes directly connected to another node) of 5.7, 7.2, and 8.8 respectively (these numbers come from the fact that in our experiments they correspond to networks composed of 150, 200, and 250 peers over the same area – the density increases because peers are more packed). In each network, a tuple, incrementing its content at every hop, had been propagated. Nodes in the network moved randomly, continuously changing the network topology. The number of messages sent between peers to keep the tuple shape coherent were recorded. Fig. 7.26a shows the average number of messages sent by peers located in an x hop radius from the origin of the topology change, while Fig. 7.26b shows the same values, but in these experiments only the source of the tuple moved, changing the topology.

The most important consideration we can make looking at these graphs is that, upon a topology change, a lot of update operations will be required near the source of the topology change, while only few operations will be required far away from it. This implies that, even if the TOTA network and the tuples being propagated have no artificial boundaries, the operations to keep their

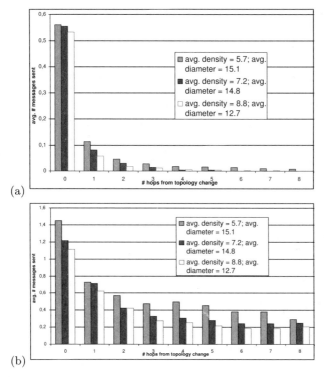

Fig. 7.26. Experimental results: locality scopes in tuple's maintenance operations emerge in a network without predefined boundaries. (a) Topology changes are caused by random peer movements. (b) Topology changes are caused by the movement of the source peer

shape consistent are strictly confined within a locality scope (Fig. 7.26). This fact supports the feasibility of the TOTA approach in terms of its scalability. In fact, this means that, even in a large network with a lot of nodes and tuples, we do not have to continuously flood the whole network with updates, eventually generated by changes in distant areas of the network. Updates are almost always confined within a locality scope from where they took place.

These results are even more significant if compared to the average network diameter (averaged over the various experiments). Considering the experimental results in Fig. 7.26, it is easy to see that the number of operations required to maintain a tuple falls close to zero well before the average diameter of the network, thus confirming the goodness of our results.

Metric and Space Tuple

With regard of these tuples, determining if their self-maintenance operations are confined is rather easy. In Subsect. 7.3.2 we said that a Metric tuple's maintenance is confined to the node itself for all the nodes apart from the source, while it spreads across the whole network if the source moves. So the answer for Metric tuples is partially negative and for this reason they must be used carefully, maybe with custom rules in their propagation rules limiting a priori their scope, or by triggering update operations only if the source node moves by a certain amount (e.g., triggering update only if the source moves at least 1 m). The answer for a Space tuple, in contrast, is a clear affirmative since maintenance is strictly locally confined. All the above considerations are good hints for the feasibility of the model, showing that it can scale to different application scenarios.

7.4.2 Accounting

While performing testing and experiments, it is very important to understand how the different parts of the system contribute to the gross amount of the operations. Specifically, we focus on two important measures.

In every peer-to-peer system, like TOTA, there are two kinds of operations that can be attributed to a node: those caused by the application on that node and those required to support other peers' operations (e.g., forwarding another peer's messages). In our opinion, the ratio between these two is a fundamental measure for the evaluation of a P2P system.

In testing TOTA, we found out that a large number of operations is caused by the pattern matching access to tuples. Basically, pattern-matching is the single most important operation performed by TOTA. In fact, it is invoked either by read operations or by the event interface while matching an event against subscriptions. For this reason another important measure is the ratio between pattern-matching operations and other operations (e.g., sending messages, creating tuples, etc.).

To find out these ratios we exploited our simulator. Specifically, we set up a TOTA network with 100 nodes. We installed an agent on every node performing a TOTA-intensive application (each agent injects several tuples and keeps on reading for incoming tuples). We then examined the trace of operations happening on each node [72], stripping out those operations related to the simulator itself rather than the TOTA middleware (e.g., simulator GUI operations). Finally, we averaged the different traces to find out the trace of operations performed by an *average* node. On the basis of this trace, we counted how many operations were initiated by the agent on the node and how many by neighbors nodes, and how many operations were about pattern-matching and how many about the rest of the TOTA API. The results of the above ratios are in Fig. 7.27.

We can see that TOTA clearly promotes an altruistic P2P approach. Looking at Fig. 7.27a, it appears that almost half of the operations are performed to support other node's activity. On the one hand, in our opinion, this again supports scalability. The burden of a global operation is evenly distributed across the network. On the other hand, it can be source of problems in those

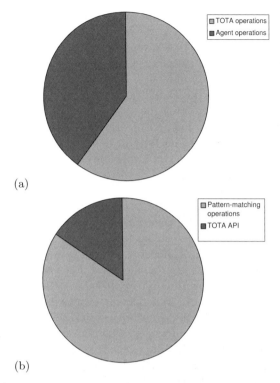

Fig. 7.27. (a) Agent operations vs. TOTA operations. (b) API operations vs. pattern matching

scenarios where an individual node may wish to save resources and not collaborate with others (e.g., in a sensor network a node may wish to save battery energy by not helping neighbors). In our opinion, Fig. 7.27b is more related to the current implementation of the system, rather than to the abstract TOTA model. A great percentage of pattern-matching operations reveals the importance of this operation in the current implementation, and calls for optimized algorithms to deal with this kind of operation.

7.4.3 Details on Hop Tuple's Self-Maintenance

One of the most important algorithms in our model is the one allowing *Hop tuples* to self-maintain their shape despite network dynamism. For obvious scalability reasons, and to be well-suited to our model, we would like such an algorithm to be completely distributed.

Let us consider the case of a tuple incrementing its integer content by one at every hop, as it is propagated far away from its source. Given a local instance of such a tuple X, we will call Y X's *supporting tuple* if Y belongs to the same distributed tuple as X (recall that TOTA marks all the tuples with an unique ID), Y's distance from X is one hop, Y's value is equal to X's value minus one. With such a definition, X's supporting tuple is a tuple that could have created X during its propagation. Moreover, we will say that X is in a *safe state* if it has a supporting tuple, or if it is in the node that first injected the tuple (i.e., its hop value = 0). We will say that a tuple is not in a safe state if the above condition does not apply (i.e., it has no supporting tuple, and its hop counter is greater than 0). Each local tuple can subscribe to the income or the removal of other tuples of its type in its one-hop neighborhood. The basic idea is that a tuple that is not in a safe state should not be there, since no neighbor tuple could have created it. Upon a removal, each tuple reacts by checking if it is still in a safe state.

In the case in which a tuple is not in a safe state, it erases itself (after some time) from the local node. This eventually causes a cascading deletion of tuples until a safe state tuple can be found, or the source is eventually reached, or all the tuples in that connected sub-network are deleted.

In the case in which a tuple is in a safe state, the removal of a neighbor tuple triggers a reaction in which the tuple propagates to that node. It is worth noting that this mechanism is the same as when a new node is connected to the network. Similar considerations apply with regard to tuple arrival: when a tuple senses the arrival of a tuple having a value higher than its own plus one, it means that, because of nodes' mobility, a shortcut leading to the source has been created. In such a situation the tuple can propagate to the new node to overwrite the previous tuple, fixing the tuple's shape.

This set of mechanisms it is enough to make *Hop* tuples self-maintain. To prove the validity of this algorithm we will show its correctness with regard to four special cases (see Fig. 7.28). The rationale behind these four special cases is found by answering the following questions: does the network topology change imply a link creation or removal? Is the changed link the only one connecting two networks or are there others? It is rather clear that the four possible yes/no answers to these questions (four special cases) can be generalized to cover all the other possibilities. The four special cases proving the correctness of the *Hop* tuple's self-maintenance are reported in Fig. 7.28. In Fig. 7.28a the link between A and B breaks down. Since the tuple on B has no supporting tuples, it is not in a safe state anymore. Thus it deletes itself. After that, the tuple on C does not see any supporting tuples; thus it deletes itself. This applies recursively to the bottom of the network. After that, the distributed tuple is in a consistent state with respect to the new topology. In Fig. 7.28b a new link between A and B is created. The tuple on A propagates to B and then recursively to the bottom of the network. In Fig. 7.28c the link between A and B breaks down. As in case (a) this causes a cascading deletion until a safe state tuple is reached. In this example, the safe state tuple is in node D. When this tuple sees that the tuple on C gets deleted it can propagate toward C, fixing the gap. The propagation applies recursively to the bottom of the network, adjusting the distributed tuple. In Fig. 7.28d a new link is created between C and D. The tuple on D finds in its neighbor a tuple with value greater than its own plus one (i.e., $n + 2 > k + 1$). Thus, it propagates to C, overwriting the tuple on C. This process applies recursively until the correct node is found (i.e., where the two branches of the tuple seamlessly merge: $n + 1 = k + 2$).

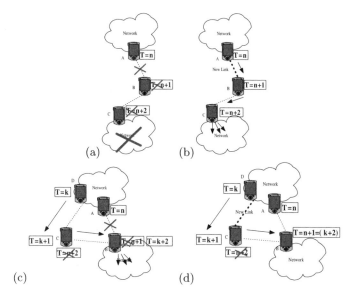

Fig. 7.28. Hop maintenance in four special cases

Clearly, if the network constantly changes its topology faster than the time required by the maintenance algorithm to complete, the process could never converge. However, the self-maintenance algorithm ensures that, once the network stabilizes, the algorithm eventually makes the overlay distributed tuple converge to a consistent state.

In addition to the above considerations, it is important to remark that the above algorithm suffers from the critical race problem depicted in Fig. 7.29. The figure shows a simple network where a *Hop* overlay tuple (called T) has been spread and deployed by the top node (T = 0 at the source). In (a) the link between the top node and the rest of the network breaks down. This makes the bottom subnetwork detached from the source of the tuple and this should lead to the complete deletion of the tuple in the bottom subnetwork. In (b) and (c) the tuple starts deleting with the cascading mechanism described above. In (d), however, it can happen that the tuple on Y (supported by the tuple on X that did not have the time to delete) propagates to Z. In fact, the tuple on Y perceives the missing value in Z as a hole in the overlay, and so it tries to adjust it. This is a problem because it starts a spurious propagation

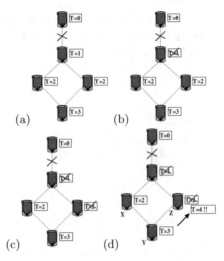

(a)   (b)

(c)   (d)

Fig. 7.29. From (a) to (d), a sequence of self-maintenance operations that create bad cycles

cycle that can possibly last forever, consuming resources, and preventing the overlay tuple to eventually converge to the correct distribution.

The basic approach to overcome this problem is to introduce delays in the overlay tuple operations. There are two possible implementations of this idea: (i) A node seeing a deletion must wait for the other neighbor nodes to possibly delete the tuples. Only after that time can it try to propagate the tuples. (ii) A node that is not in a safe state must wait to delete itself in order not to create "space" for cycles to transit. Cycles can start, but they terminate if no space is left for propagation (i.e., the distributed tuple is already around everywhere).

We opted for the latter approach in order to reduce the time an agent must wait before receiving an updated tuple (although the tuple it receives may temporarily be corrupted by cycles).

Let us explain the adopted mechanism in detail. We set an artificial delay before giving the chance to a tuple to delete itself. During that time, the tuple goes in a "zombie" (i.e., pre-delete) state that has two main properties: (i) the tuple is no longer a supporting tuple, and (ii) the tuple cannot further propagate. Since the tuple is no longer supporting anything, it can initiate cascading (pre-)deletion. Such pre-deletions extinguish cycles since the tuple in a "zombie" state cannot propagate further. After the delay, the tuple in the "zombie" state actually deletes, and the overlay tuple updates its distribution, avoiding cycles.

The setting of a fixed-delay parameter in a distributed system is always troublesome. However, in our case it is not critically important to carefully set a correct value. If the *correct* value is set, the cycles are eliminated without wasting time. If the set value is greater than the correct one, the system still works, but some time is wasted (i.e., tuples wait more than necessary before deleting). If the set value is lower than the correct one, the system still works: cycles can restart, but each time they are smaller and have less time to cycle. Thus after few iterations they are eliminated anyway.

7.5 Ongoing Activity

Apart from low-level implementation issues (e.g., up to now, TOTA completely lacks of any kind of security policy to rule accesses to distributed tuples and their updates), a criticism that can apply to TOTA is the lack of an effective underlying general methodology, enabling engineers to map a specific coordination policy into the corresponding definition of tuples and of their shape (see also Subsect. 5.3.6).

In pursuing this long-term goal, our research focuses on trying to achieve a wide range of self-organized behaviors by adopting field-based coordination and the TOTA middleware. If we succeed, such abstractions and the lessons learned, during the process, will possibly become the embryo of an engineering methodology suited to develop self-organizing and autonomic multiagent applications in TOTA.

In the next section we present some advanced applications in radically different areas, i.e., (i) content-based access to information in MANET, (ii) control algorithms for metamorphic modular robots, and (iii) a speculative sensor network application.

The fact that the abstractions promoted by TOTA seem suitable in managing such diverse scenarios, is a good result by itself and a good starting point for future researches.

Part IV

Advanced Applications

8

Content-Based Information Access and Coordination

Field-based coordination and TOTA, by their very nature, tend to promote a sort of location-oriented contextual model and location-based methods to access data and contextual information, and to coordinate agent activities.

At its most basic, a simple field monotonically increasing its strength as it propagates farther from the source (and the corresponding basic $HopTuple$ in TOTA) provides information about the distance from the source and some direction on the location of that source. Starting from this, it is possible to define, e.g., fields and TOTA tuples that have a limited propagation scope, thus representing information accessible only from a locality. Or one can select a specific direction of propagation for a field/tuple, thus making it represents information accessible only from agents located at specific locations from the source. In general, field-based coordination and TOTA appear intrinsically suited to coordinate activities in space (whatever specific space abstraction is adapted in a specific application context) and to promote a location-dependent approach to coordination and information access.

However, in several application scenarios, the need to access information and interact in a global way, based on *what* information and interactions actually mean to the application, rather than on *where* information and interacting agents are located, arises. That is, information access and interactions should rely on the actual *content* of the information or of the data involved in interactions. As a trivial example, a user interested in retrieving the MP3 of "Hey Jude" from the Internet does not care at all about the location of that file (e.g., where it is located, on what IP, and by what user). What matters is the content of the file.

In this chapter we tackle the problem of analyzing how content-based information access (and more in general content-based coordination) can be supported in Mobile Ad-hoc Networks (MANETs). Content-based information access methods have been widely studied in the area of Internet-scale peer-to-peer computing [120, 129, 140], to provide functionalities such as the one sketched in the above trivial example. A few works have addressed this topic in the area of MANETs [118, 119], and have proposed specific mechanisms and strategies to provide effective ways to enforce content-based information access in MANETs in a robust and adaptive self-organizing way.

Here, rather than presenting novel mechanisms and strategies, we show that the spatial, location-oriented, abstractions promoted by field-based co-ordination and TOTA are suited to effectively implement in a simple way the content-based strategies proposed so far for MANETs.

8.1 Content-Based Information Access in Mobile Ad Hoc Networks

In most actual application scenarios, the key interest in having the component devices of a MANET (or of a sensor network) interact with each other derives primarily from the data and information the various devices hold. The identity of the individual nodes storing the data tends to be much less relevant than the actual data they hold. Accordingly, interaction models and information access should be content-based, in the sense that they should provide access to information on a content basis rather than on the identity or on the location of the device in which information is actually stored [17, 55]. More in general, content-based information access is a key basis for achieving context-awareness and for enabling interactions in dynamic and decentralized network scenarios, where identity of nodes and their positions cannot be known a priori.

8.1.1 Geographical Hash Tables

An effective solution to this problem, in the area of dynamic mobile networks, has been proposed: geographical hash tables (GHT) for information access [118, 119].

In GHT-based approaches, the specific node that will be devoted to store given information is determined by the correspondence of the physical location of the node with the content of the information itself (indicated, e.g., by a keyword or a list of keywords). All data with the same general content (i.e., indicated by the same keywords) is routed to the same network node (not necessarily the node that originally gathered the data). This is achieved by having the list of keywords hashed – by a predefined hash function H – to a particular physical location,

$$H(KW_1, KW_2, \ldots, KW_n) = (X, Y),$$

and by routing the data to the node closest to that physical location. For this purpose some kind of localization mechanism and a geographic routing algorithm [18, 75, 81] can be conveniently used. Localization has the purpose of assigning to the nodes of the network some coordinates related to some coordinate frame. A geographic routing algorithm is a mechanism that takes advantage of the established coordinate frame to route messages to a specific

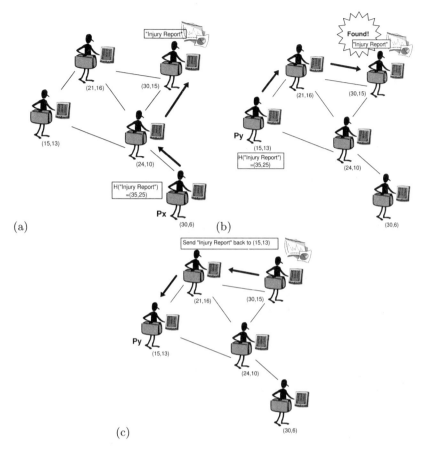

Fig. 8.1. Content-based information access in a rescue scenario. (a) Px dispatches an "injury report" describing the injured people found. It evaluates H("injury report") that results in (35, 25). It then sends the report to the node closest to that location (b) Py looks for "injury report" by querying the only node that could possibly have it: the one at H("injury report")=(35, 25). (c) The peer closest to (35, 25) receives the query and replies with a message routed back to the coordinates of the inquiring node

location in the coordinate frame or, in the case in which no nodes exist at that exact location, to the node closest to it.

Geographic routing algorithms inherently support communication decoupling in that senders and receivers are decoupled by the coordinate frame. For example, a sender can send a message to an unknown receiver located at a specific location and the message will be received by whoever is closest to that location. Content-based requests for information based on geographical hash tables extend this schema: information is sent to the location derived from the hashing function applied to the list of keywords; a request for information, described by a specific list of keywords, is sent to the node at the location indicated by the hashing of that list. In this way, information and requests meet in a rendezvous node without any kind of flooding being involved (see Fig. 8.1) and without the producer of information being aware of the nodes that are interested in it. Such uncoupling, as already stated in this book, is of paramount importance in modern large-scale and dynamic network scenarios.

In addition, geographical routing algorithms and geographical hash tables are intrinsically adaptive and robust, in that it does not really matter if the network changes its topology or if the node at a specific location moves or disappears: the routing of data is only interested in the node closest to the target location, no matter what this node is and no matter how far from the exact location it is.

8.1.2 Applications and Issues

Content-based information access is well-suited in a lot of MANET scenarios. In fact, to provide nodes with an uncoupled and anonymous communication mechanism with which to exchange information in a scalable and efficient way is a key point for several emerging scenarios.

In the pervasive computing scenario described in Fig. 8.1, for example, the members of a rescue team (e.g., the guides of a museum in charge of dealing with a fire alarm) can be made aware of relevant information (e.g., "there are people injured in this wing of the museum!") in a totally uncoupled way, without even knowing each other. Simply, whenever an injury has to be reported, it can be hashed to a specific location (based on a specific "injury report" keyword) and stored at the node closest to the resulting hashed location; whenever members of the team want to know if there are injury reports, they can hash a query with the appropriate keyword to have it reach the proper location, and eventually discover if there are any. Such a mechanism allows, for example, members of the team to move in the museum, members to disappear, or new members to join the team, without preventing the possibility of fruitfully exchanging relevant information.

Other than the request-response information access mechanism depicted in Fig. 8.1, content-based information access also allows us to realize publish-subscribe (event-based) mechanism [35] rather easily. To realize this mechanism, components could post subscriptions to specific places in the network (by the above-described hash-based mechanism). Events would be routed (by the same hash function) to the node that holds related subscriptions. There, possible matches between subscriptions and events would be computed. The results would be sent back to the actual subscriber node. With regard to the case study, such a kind of mechanism would allow us to realize reactive behaviors. For example, a member of the rescue team could be notified by requests for help made by others. Other interesting and articulated applications of these ideas, applied to a peculiar sensor network scenario, are reported in Chap. 10.

Besides the application, it is important to understand that content-based information access decouples node interactions at the cost of introducing an overhead. Specifically, nodes are requested to act as points of rendezvous according to their position in the physical space. This implies that, when a node moves from one region to another, it possibly needs to migrate data associated with its old location to other nodes that eventually become closer to that location, and, vice versa, it can potentially obtain new data from nodes in the new region. Moreover, if nodes are not distributed uniformly in the geographical space spanned by the network, the scheme can lead to load imbalance with some nodes responsible for much more information than others.

Internet-oriented content-based mechanisms to access information [120, 129] solve this problem by introducing a virtual geographical space, built as an overlay over the physical network, on which it is possible to map nodes and the outcomes of the hash function (an approach known as Distributed Hash Tables, or DHT) . This approach can work because the virtual space, as a physical geographical space, decouples content-based information access from the actual locations and identities of nodes. Thus, if a node moves in the physical space, it may remain still in the virtual one, and if nodes are clustered in the physical space, they may be evenly distributed in the virtual one. It is, however, fundamental to understand that it is feasible to realize such a kind of virtual space only if a long-range multi-hop routing protocol is available. Such a long-range routing protocol allows distant peers in the physical space to be neighbors in the virtual one. On the Internet, of course, TCP/IP well serves this purpose. In contrast, the situation in MANETs may be different and long-range routes may be very hard to maintain. Moreover, to the best of our knowledge, all the Internet-based systems assume the presence of only a single huge virtual space on which to perform content-based information access. All the nodes connect to that virtual space, and the possibility that multiple spaces can coexist in the network is disregarded. In a MANET scenario, however, it is likely that separate disjoint groups of nodes will start a content-based information access application. If these groups come together, their MANETs will coalesce, and it will be profitable if also their content-based information access applications do the same. Now, while merging physical spatial coordinates requires only updating the co-domain of the hash function (it may also require large amount of data to be relocated), merging virtual spaces may require complex algorithms. Despite all these difficulties, in our future work, we plan to conduct experiments on the overhead involved in maintaining a virtual space over a MANET.

8.2 Content-Based Information Access in TOTA

The basic idea of the GHT schema can be easily implemented in terms of field-based coordination, and in particular by exploiting the services of the TOTA middleware. Specifically, this involves two key stages: firstly, agents running on MANET nodes have to set up the proper framework required to support their interactions, including a coordinate frame and a hashing function; secondly, they exploit such a framework to actually perform content-based information access.

8.2.1 Setting up the Framework

When a group of nodes, running autonomous agents, come together forming a MANET and want a content-based access to shared information, the following "bootstrap" operations are required:

1. Agents need to self-organize a common coordinate frame and place themselves there in a coherent way (neighbor nodes must be nearby). This can be done by exploiting a sequence of propagation of TOTA tuples that enable electing a limited number of beacon nodes, and subsequently by exploiting TOTA tuples that enable all the nodes of the system to triangulate their distances from the beacons.
2. Agents must be provided with a geographic routing algorithm, to be used to send messages to nodes located at specific points of the coordinate frame. Specific classes of TOTA tuples can be defined relying on propagation rules that make tuples propagate following specific directions, i.e., direct them toward specific coordinates.
3. Agents need to build a common shared hash function that maps shared information (e.g., file names or strings in general) to specific locations of the established coordinate frame. This can be achieved by having nodes agree – by proper exchange of TOTA tuples – on geographical bounds for the hashing function.

8.2.2 Access to Information

Once the above framework has been established, supporting content-based information access by GHT is rather trivial. It basically involves interactions between three types of agents: *PubAgents* in charge of publishing information, *QueryAgents* in charge of looking for information, and *AnswerAgents* in charge of responding to other agents' queries.

4. A *PubAgent*, willing to publish information, will inject into the network an *Info* tuple like the one described in Fig. 8.2. This tuple will have as content the information being published and a list of keywords describing the information. The propagation rule of this tuple first applies the hash

function to the list of keywords to determine where the tuple should finally go. Then, it applies the geographic routing algorithm it embeds to realize the actual routing. When the destination node is finally reached, the tuple just settles (see Subsect. 8.3.4).

5. When a *QueryAgent* looks for specific information, it injects a *Query* tuple, having as content the list of keywords describing the data it is looking for and also the location of the inquiring node (see Fig. 8.2). This tuple is routed with the same hash-based mechanism to the only node that could possibly have the information described by the list of keywords.

6. Upon the receipt of a *Query* tuple (having the node as its final destination), an *AnswerAgent* answers by injecting an *Answer* tuple (see Fig. 8.2) having as content "NOT FOUND" if the node does not store an *Info* tuple having the same keywords as those of the received *Query* tuple, while having as content the information contained by the matching *Info* tuple, if it is present.

7. The *Answer* tuple, also created with the location of the inquiring node, travels across the network to reach the inquiring node.

```
Info Tuple
C = (information, keywords)
P = (propagate using geographic routing algorithm to the node
closest to coordinates H(keywords))

Query Tuple
C = (keywords, source_location)
P = (propagate using geographic routing algorithm to the node
closest to coordinates H(keywords))

Answer Tuple
C = (information, reply_location)
P = (propagate using geographic routing algorithm to the node
closest to coordinates ''reply_location'')
```

Fig. 8.2. Tuples involved in content-based information access

8.3 TOTA Implementation Details

Given the above description, it should be clear that the nontrivial issue for supporting content-based information access is to set up a proper framework supporting actual content-based access to information. Once the framework has been set up correctly, the rest becomes straightforward. To this end, in the following, we will focus on how to perform the initial steps so as to provide a flexible and robust ground for the rest of the application. Specifically, we are going to deal with (i) How agents actually establish their coordinates. (ii) How the geographic routing algorithm is actually implemented. (iii) How to set up the hash function. (iv) What happens upon network reconfigurations – either due node movements or failures. All of these features are important and only a correct implementation can produce a truly robust and adaptive system for content-based information access.

The actual use of the system can then rely on the execution of agents (*PubAgents, QueryAgents, AnswerAgents*) that only slightly differ from the agents already discussed in the previous chapter, for which reason their detailed description will be skipped.

8.3.1 Coordinate Triangulation

The first task the agents need to undertake is to create a common shared coordinate system and to located themselves in there. Clearly, this task critically depends on the information available to the agents. For example, if they are provided with a GPS device, the task becomes trivial – just read the GPS! If the agents are provided with a radar-like localization device, providing the coordinates of only neighbor nodes, the task is easy as well. In fact, an agent could inject a TOTA *Metric* or *Space* tuple in the network and let it create a global coordinate system (see Subsect. 7.3.2 and Fig. 7.19).

In contrast, if the agents lack of any kind of localization device, the problem becomes rather difficult and its solution is an exemplary application of self-organization and coordination. In the latter case, in fact, localization can rely on the (geometrically intuitive) fact that the position of a point on a surface can be uniquely determined by measuring its distance from at least three nonaligned reference points ("beacons"), by a process of "triangulation" [105]. TOTA makes this process very simple:

1. All the agents start running a particular leader-election algorithm that elects the node in the middle of the network (i.e., the network barycenter – or center of gravity). This algorithm takes advantage of the fact that, given n points in space, their barycenter is the point that minimizes the sum of the distances to all the n points. Agents, provided with only local (one-hop) perception of their environment, can measure each other's distances by relying on TOTA *HopTuples*. In fact, an agent receiving a *HopTuples* having value n, can roughly infer that the source of the tuple is about at a distance of $n(wireless - link - range)$. This enables agents to determine the barycenter using the completely distributed algorithm described in Fig. 8.3. In the following, to ground the discussion, we will provide a pseudo-code implementation of the discussed algorithms. Pseudo-code has been chosen to avoid the verbosity of real code. Converting such pseudo-code in Java is straightforward using the TOTA primitives.

2. Once the barycenter has been elected, it injects another *HopTuple* in the network. Nodes that do not see any neighbor node having a value of this *HopTuple* greater than their own, are on the perimeter of the network (see code in Fig. 8.4). These nodes will be the beacons in charge of initializing the coordinate system.

3. Since a node can determine its location by measuring its distance from at least three nonaligned reference points ("beacons"), by a process of "triangulation." Each beacon "arbitrarily" locates (see code on Fig. 8.5) at specific coordinates. Then it injects a *HopTuple*, marked with the beacon coordinates, allowing other devices to estimate their distance from it. After a number of beacons have propagated their ranging signals, other nodes can apply a triangulation algorithm to infer their coordinates (see Fig. 8.5).

It is worth noting that, as pointed out in [105], the precision of such a coordinate system critically depends on the density of the network. However, for the purpose of enabling content-based access, precision is not so important and mostly topological relations matter (i.e., nodes neighbor in the network must be neighbors in the coordinate system). Moreover, according to experiments conducted in [118], the use of a coordinate system built only upon mere network topological features, can actually improve the performances of content-based access. Also, since *HopTuples* are automatically maintained by the TOTA middleware, the coordinate system remains up-to-date and coherent despite network dynamism. If upon a node movement the topology of the network changes, the tuples' maintenance triggers an update in the coordinate system, making the latter robust and self-healing.

8.3.2 Geographic Routing

Once network nodes are located in a coordinate system, the routing problem seems to become trivial. A tuple, by adopting a geographic routing algorithm, could basically take advantage of node locations to move greedily, following simple Euclidean considerations, to reach, at every hop, a node closer to its destination (see Fig. 8.6).

More specifically, once injected, a tuple could inspect its local neighborhood looking for the node whose coordinates are closest to its destination and then migrate there. Unfortunately, the above picture it is too simplistic a tuple and dead ends (i.e., false minima in the coordinate system) are likely to arise. These dead ends happen in those situations in which a tuple arrives at a node, but then does not find any neighbor closer to the intended destination. In such cases, the tuple should stop acting greedily, travel a bit backward (thus getting farther from the destination) and look for alternative paths (see Fig. 8.7).

To overcome this problem, the solution mainly adopted [18, 75, 81] is to move past the local minima by applying a graph traversing algorithm, to the

```
01: // sum of distance evaluated up to now
02: totCount = 0
03: // number of gradients received
04: totGrad = 0
05: // inject tuples to rend variables
06: // visible to neighbors
07: tota.inject(new Tuple("count", totCount))
08: tota.inject(new Tuple("tot",totGrad))
09: // inject distance tuple
10: tota.inject(new HopTuple(uniqueNumber))
11: Vector readV = tota.read(new HopTuple())
12: if readV.size() != totGrad
13:   totGrad = readV.size()
14:   tota.inject(new Tuple("tot", totGrad))
15:   go to 11
16: else
17:   // read other totGrad
18:   Tuple otherTotGrad = new Tuple("tot")
19:   Vector ot = tota.readOneHop(othetTotGrad)
20:   for every i in ot
21:    if totGradient!=ot[i].totGrad
22:      go to 11
23:    end if
24:   end for
25: end if
26: // Have received all the gradients
27: totCount = sumOfGradientsValue(readV)
28: for every node in neighbor
29:   if neighborTotCount < totCount
30:    return NOT_BARYCENTER
31:   end if
32: end for
33: return BARYCENTER
```

Fig. 8.3. Barycenter election

planar graph [42] obtained by locally pruning links in the network. The idea is the one depicted, in more detail, in Fig. 8.8 and described in the following:

1. Tuples start propagating following plain Euclidean considerations. However, when a tuple finds itself at a minimum of the coordinate system, it switches to a, let us call it, "circumnavigate" propagation mode.
2. Since most graph traversing algorithms works only in planar graphs, the first thing a tuple has to do is to prune (i.e., avoid using) some of the network links in the host node neighborhood. This can be easily done by enforcing a planarization algorithm as proposed in [18, 75]. This locally

```
01: HopTuple g = new HopTuple(CENTER)
02: if node == BARYCENTER
03:  tota.inject(g)
04: end if
05: // compare my gradient value with
06: // neighbors one
07: LOCAL_VAL = tota.read(g)
08: N_VAL[] = tota.readOneHop(g)
09: if(VAL > max(N_VAL[]))
10:  return PERIMETER_NODE
11: else
12:  return INNER_NODE
13: end if
```

Fig. 8.4. Perimeter election

```
01: // each beacon injects a gradient
02: // identified by a random number
03: if node == PERIMETER_NODE
04:  id = castRandomNumber()
05:  HopTuple g = new HopTuple(id)
06:  tota.inject(g)
07:  // beacons locate themselves on the
08:  // coordinate system, starting from
09:  // the one the cast the lower value
10:  Vector v = tota.readOneHop(g)
11:  val = getMinValue(v)
12:  if(val == id)
13:   tota.delete(g)
14:   MY_COORD = triangulate()
15:   tota.inject(new HopTuple(MY_COORD)
16:  end if
17: end if
18  // main triangulation
19: v = tota.read(new HopTuple(COORD))
20: MY_COORD = triangulate(v)
```

Fig. 8.5. Core localization

```
public class GreedyEuclideanTuple extends MessageTuple {
 public int destX, destY; // x,y intended destination
 public int currX, currY; // x,y current location
 public GreedyEuclideanTuple(int x, int y) {
  destX = x;
  destY = y;
  /* each node stores its coordinate in a LocTuple.
  LocTuple can be created by subclassing TOTA Metric
  and Space tuples */
  LocTuple loc = tota.keyrd(new LocTuple());
  currX = loc.x;
  currY = loc.y;
 }
 public boolean decideEnter() {
  super.decideEnter();
  // get the location of the visited node
  LocTuple loc = tota.keyrd(new LocTuple());
  int newX = loc.x;
  int newY = loc.y;
  // previous distance from the destination
  int oldd = (curX - destX) * (curX - destX) +
           (curY - destY) * (curY - destY);
  // new distance from the destination
  int newd = (newX - destX) * (newX - destX) +
           (newY - destY) * (newY - destY);
  if(newd < oldd) {
   currX = newX;
   currY = newY;
   return true;
  }
  else
   return false;
}}
```

Fig. 8.6. A *GreedyEuclideanTuple* is a tuple that moves, at every hop – following simple geometrical considerations – to a node closer to its intended destination

transform the MANET in a planar network, and logically divides the network into a set of adjacent "faces."

3. Suppose now that the tuple wants to travel from a vertex s to a vertex t of the network in Fig. 8.8(c). First it needs to calculate the line segment st joining s to t. Then it navigates across the face crossed by st. The tuple can navigate across a face, provided with only local information, by always choosing the leftmost link from the direction from which it comes (right-hand rule [18, 75, 81]).

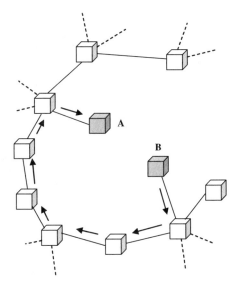

Fig. 8.7. The routing between nodes A and B cannot follow simple Euclidean consideration. Packets need to circumnavigate the network to reach their destination.

4. The above step is repeated either until no other faces, crossing st, can be found or until the tuple can revert to the Euclidean routing propagation (this propagation mode is only intended for escape from a dead end).
5. In the end, once the tuple reaches the last face (F3 in Fig. 8.8), it routes to the node of that face closest to t. Further details on this algorithm are in [18, 75, 81].

It is worth noting that, in this implementation, the route to the destination is computed dynamically as the tuple travels across the network. In fact, the route derives actually from the hop-by-hop execution of the tuples' propagation algorithm. This implies that if, during propagation, the underlying coordinate system changes, then the tuple takes into account such a new coordinate system on the fly (i.e., at the next propagation hop). Given that, the self-healing properties of this routing algorithm derive from the underlying adaptive coordinate system. If because of network dynamism the topology of the network changes, then the established coordinate system will change to account for the new topology, and the routing algorithm will be automatically retuned to the new situation, even for those tuples that were already in transit.

8.3.3 Hash Function Construction

Given the above coordinate system and the geographic routing mechanism, nodes can easily send messages to anywhere in the network. To enable content-

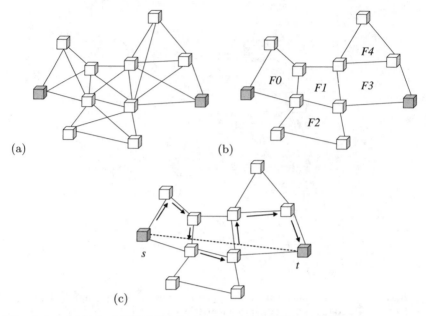

Fig. 8.8. (a) Original MANET; (b) Planarized MANET; (c) Right-hand routing

based information access, they need a mechanism (hash function) to map strings (i.e., keywords) into network locations. Independently of how the hash function is built, it is fundamental that nodes agree on a plausible co-domain for that hash function. This co-domain must represent roughly the range of coordinates covered by the network, so that any given string will be hashed to a point near an arbitrary network node. To this purpose, nodes can conveniently exploit the following algorithm (see code in Fig. 8.9) to determine a bounding box for the whole network exploiting only local information. It is worth noting that small errors in this algorithm just produce small imbalances in the way information is spread across the network, without undermining the application. This is because, if the hash function co-domain is slightly misplaced with respect to the network's actual distribution, there will be nodes (especially the ones at the border of the network) assigned to larger portions of the coordinate frame. However, this algorithm could also be placed "into the loop", i.e., executed iteratively upon a change in the underlying coordinate system.

8.3.4 Dealing with Network Reconfigurations

Although the majority of problems related to possible network reconfigurations are dealt with the self-healing properties of the coordinate system, a last fundamental step is required. *Info* tuples (see Fig. 8.2) must always remain

```
01: Point here = getLocation()
02: Point[] neigh = getNeighLocation()
03: if isNOTInBoundingBox(here,neigh)
04:   // perimeter node
05:   tota.inject(new FloodTuple(here))
06: end if
07: Vector v = null
08: while(v = tota.read(new FloodTuple())
09:   // network bounding box is computed by
10:   // considering the greatest and the
11:   // lowest coordinates being received
12:   netBBox = computeNetworkBBox(v)
13: end while
14: setupHash(netBBox)
```

Fig. 8.9. Algorithm to set up the parameters of the hash function

active and ready to migrate again, if upon node movements, there appears a node closer to the tuple's intended final destination. In fact, if another node becomes closer to the tuple destination, the self-healing geographic routing will send queries for the tuple to that node. Now, if the *Info* tuple has not migrated, the node will answer incorrectly that the information required is not available since it is in charge for the information hashed in that location, but does not store the corresponding *Info* tuple. To this end, *Info* tuples will contain also the code making the required migration happen automatically, as soon as a node closer to their intended destination appears in the neighborhood.

8.4 Concluding Remarks

In this chapter we presented a possible implementation of content-based routing based on TOTA. We emphasize that our goal was not to present new techniques, but to show that the TOTA middleware is capable of dealing with and supporting even this kind of complex application.

Still, we think it is fair to briefly review those other approaches that can enable content-based routing. These could possibly serve both as a benchmark to performance evaluation and as a source of ideas to eventually refine our application.

A number of recent proposals address the problem of defining content-based interaction mechanisms in mobile and P2P computing scenarios. Most of the proposals introduce novel "overlay network" architectures, and define the specific algorithms for building such networks, reorganizing them in response to dynamic network changes, and routing data and requests across them. Most of these proposals focus on the problem of Internet-scale peer-to-peer routing (e.g., CAN [120] and Pastry [129]), and others on more specific P2P scenarios (e.g., GHT [119] and [118]). However, to the best of our knowledge, none of these proposals provide a configurable framework with which to define and customize the structure of the overlay network and the associated policy. TOTA can provide this feature by a simple and intuitive programming model, and can make it possible to define, say, libraries of tuples with which to implement any needed content-based policy for data and service access.

Smart Messages (SMs) [17], rooted in the area of active networks, is an architecture for computation and communication in large networks of embedded devices. Communication is realized by sending "smart messages" in the network, i.e., messages which include code to be executed at each hop in the network path. SM shares with TOTA the general idea of putting intelligence in the network by letting messages (or tuples) execute, hop-by-hop, small chunks of code to determine their propagation. The main difference between SM and TOTA is that in SM messages tend to be used as lightweight mobile agents, roaming across the network, and performing different tasks. In TOTA, tuples are mainly passive entities that tend to form self-maintained distributed data structures guiding other agents in their task. Content-based routing had been realized in SM, with some restrictive hypotheses: nodes are provided with a GPS device providing absolute coordinates, and the network topology is assumed to be free from dead ends, making routing based on Euclidean considerations always effective.

The research projects Anthill [3] and SwarmLinda [98] both use algorithms based on distributed data structures spread in the network by mobile software agents to enable file sharing in Internet-scale peer-to-peer applications. Agents spread the data structure as they randomly move across the network. As a result, paths are created between peers that share similar files, thus enabling a fast content-based navigation in the network of peers. Although, to the best of our knowledge, content-based routing has not been implemented in such systems, the trails laid down by the agents could be used to realize content-based access to information.

In conclusion of this chapter, we think that field-based coordination and the TOTA middleware represent suitable models and tools to deal with content-based information access. This is not the full story: content-based access is just an example of a larger class of applications in which agents' interactions are decoupled by making use of spatial abstractions. Our feeling is that the field-based approach and TOTA can be applied successfully in several of these spatial applications [94].

9

Self-Assembly in Mobile and Modular Robots

In this chapter, we put TOTA at work in a totally different application area, i.e., self-assembly robotics. In particular, we intend to show how field-based coordination – as supported by TOTA – can be effectively exploited for orchestrating spatial movements in two different robotics scenarios:

1. a swarm of simple mobile computational particles (i.e., minimal robots), that need to coordinate their independent movements in space so as to have the swarm as a whole assume a specific global shape (e.g., recall the pipe-repairing spray application in Subsect. 2.1.1, or the T1000 robot in the *Terminator 2* movie);
2. a modular robot, made up of interconnected autonomous computer-based components (i.e., actuators), connected to each other with joints providing a limited degree of freedom in movements. The components need to coordinate the way in which the joints are bent so as to let the modular robot assume specific shapes and flexibly reshape to enforce a specific motion gait (recall Subsect. 4.2.2).

The above two scenarios are representative of the fundamental questions at the very basis of this book: (i) how does one engineer robust coordinated behaviors in a system made up of a large number of components that are interconnected in local, irregular, and time-varying ways? (ii) How does one translate prespecified global goals (e.g., global shapes or global motion gait) into the local interactions of vast numbers of parts (e.g., individual particle movements or bending of single joints)?

Earlier in this book (Chap. 4) we have already anticipated how biologically inspired mechanisms such as morphogen gradients and hormones (both of which can be assimilated to fields) can be effectively exploited for that purpose. Here, morphogen gradients and hormones will be translated into TOTA tuples to be applied for enabling adaptive self-organization of spatial shapes in swarms of simple particles and of gait control in modular robots.

9.1 Shape Formation in Swarms of Mobile Autonomous Robots

The first application scenario we are going to consider is self-assembly of spatial shapes (or "morphogenesis") in swarms of very simple computational particles, i.e., mobile robots with minimal capabilities [89]. The assumption of minimal capabilities, while possibly simplifying the future implementation of such robots (we consider simulated scenarios only), is also finalized by making the goal more challenging: having a swarm assume a specific spatial shape cannot rely on any sophisticated feature of robots, but must necessarily rely on the power of the adopted interaction model.

In the rest of this section, we firstly characterize our approach in detail, also in comparison with related approaches. Then, we report a number of experiments about a number of spatial shapes we have been able to enforce in a self-organized way with the use of field-based coordination and TOTA.

9.1.1 Our Approach

To be compliant with foreseeable future nanotechnology scenarios, other than with a more challenging scenario, we focus on swarms in which robots have very minimal capabilities. Specifically, we assume that

1. Robots are autonomous (i.e., have a separate thread of execution and control) and equally programmed (i.e., they run the same code). Differentiation in their activities – if needed – must be established at runtime.
2. Each robot is provided with a random number generator enabling symmetry breaking and robot identification (with high probability; e.g., cast ten random numbers and let them be the robot id).
3. Robots can freely move on a 2-D plane, even walking through each other. This hypothesis relies on the fact that, in this scenario, we disregard low-level motion details. Robots' movement, depending on the specific hardware, will be realized with various mechanisms (e.g., wheeled robots, robots moving by exploiting their direct contact [133], etc.).
4. Robots interact by wireless connections. Each robot is provided with a short-range wireless communication device enabling the robot to broadcast messages in its neighborhood and to receive messages sent by other robots. This allows each robot to know how many other robots are in its neighborhood (e.g., every robot periodically broadcasts "I am here" messages to be received by neighbor robots).
5. Robots do not have other capabilities other than the ones listed above. In particular, they do not perceive the location (neither direction nor distance) of other robots', they do not have any kind long-range communication mechanism, nor can rely on a global accessible data space or base station.

From a methodology point of view, we will focus on robots exploiting TOTA to self-organize their respective positions. Each robot will be provided with a local TOTA middleware to act as a TOTA node. By exploiting the TOTA middleware and their wireless network, robots constitute the TOTA network. Robots will iteratively propagate and sense TOTA tuples representing morphogen fields, and then will move according to the tuples they locally sense. Specifically, in our approach the tuples being propagated will represent a "constructive" description of the shape we want to obtain. Complex shapes will be obtained by robots incrementally deploying tuples and moving to intermediate positions.

9.1.2 Related Approaches

In the last few years, several approaches and algorithms for shape formation in robot swarms have been proposed. However, these approaches either assume more sophisticated capabilities for robots or have to adopt more complicated solutions to achieve what we are able to achieve in a simple way with TOTA.

One of the first approaches proposed about formation of a shape using autonomous mobile robots is [142]. In this work, several algorithms have been proposed to form shapes like circles and polygons with robots that are able to determine the positions of all the other robots, without any kind of communication, but by only observing other robot positions and movements. In our opinion, these hypotheses are not applicable to micro or nanorobots in that scalability, battery consumption, line of sight problems, cost of global localization, etc., all call for a strictly local and simpler perception of the environment.

A similar approach is presented in [151], where robots are able to detect signals from other robots in a limited area, and to compute the distance and direction of the signal sources. Shapes like a 2D circle or a 3D cone can be obtained using one or more fixed signal sources, called beacons, and by having robots move away from or toward beacons. In our approach, and in stark contrast with most of the others, robots are not able to compute distance and direction of the signal sources. This is justified by the idea that it will not be easy to provide nanorobots with complex radar-like devices.

In [38] robots only use local sensing and do not share a common coordinate system. Every robot is provided with an unique ID that is broadcasted at regular time intervals. Other robots can detect this signal and also infer from the signal itself the relative location of the source. Different formations are specified by forcing each robot to maintain a certain angle and distance from others. Specifically, robots can create formations like lines, columns, diamonds, and wedges and pass from one formation to another dynamically. The algorithm has been simulated and also implemented on real robots. However, this approach also requires robots to acquire a detailed knowledge about the location of nearby robots.

The method proposed in [47] relies on the creation of a shared coordinate system over a robot network. This is motivated by the fact that, once provided with a shared coordinate system, robots can easily assume any kind of spatial configuration, expressed by means of the coordinates of the points to be reached. Each robot lives in a 2D grid and sees the locations of all other robots with respect to its own private coordinate system. Starting from an arbitrary initial configuration in which the robots occupy distinct points, all the robots will meet at a certain location. Robots elect that location as the origin of a common shared coordinate system. Then, the robots will perform a series of voting procedures to agree on direction and orientation of each axis. This process is very interesting, and a comparison with this idea will be treated separately in the next subsection.

In [71] a method is presented to organize the growth of a 2D structure in a swarm of mobile robots. Robots are autonomous, can only sense their local environment, and are largely interchangeable. Each robot is defined by a state value and a lookup table of transition rules. A transition rule specifies a condition under which a robot will connect itself to one of its neighbor robots. Connections, as prescribed by the lookup table, take place on the basis of a robot's internal state. Robots move randomly in a 2D square lattice around an initial robot, called seed, and when the conditions of a transition rule are met they attach themselves to neighbor robots.

A similar approach is proposed in [25], where robots build a 3D structure using building blocks of different types and following building rules. Robots move randomly in a 3D lattice around an initial building block. They can sense the presence of building blocks or other robots within the local 3x3x3 lattice. When a robot finds a building block, it can pick it up and carry it toward the growing structure. Then, if the robot perceives a suitable environmental configuration (a match in its building rules), it deposits the block, making the structure grow.

These two approaches are very close in spirit to the one we propose, and future investigation on their potential integration is on our research agenda. However, our perception is that, relying only on strict local rules without the possibility of mediated multi-hop, long-range interactions – like the ones enabled by TOTA tuples – severely constrains the kind of patterns that can be achieved and the possibility to engineer such patterns.

The approach presented in [135] enables robots to create regular spatial distributions like hexagonal and square lattices. Each robot is like a particle with a mass and it is subject to "artificial physical" forces enabling robots, detecting only nearby robots' distances, to spread in the space, creating regular lattices. This approach is clearly a field-based one and, thus, it is strongly related to ours. However, it misses identifying the possibility of shaping more complex fields than simple gravitational-like fields, thus limiting the variety of spatial patterns they are able to enforce in a robot swarm.

The approach proposed in the Amorphous Computing project [102], for the self-organization of spatial patterns in a smart paper made up of a multitude of simple computational particles, is the one more directly related to our approach. There, particles capable of communicating only with their local neighborhood, can shape 2D patterns on the paper by having particles propagate field-like data structures and by changing their internal state on the basis of the locally sensed fields. The main differences from our approach are that particles cannot move on the paper (a spatial shape is determined by the spatial distribution of particles in a given state and not by the movement of particles), and that particles can initially know in which part of the paper (a corner, a side, etc.) they are located.

9.1.3 A Possible Objection

Algorithms to create a shared coordinate system on a network of mobile devices on the basis of mere network connectivity information have only been recently proposed [103, 105]. Moreover, as discussed in the previous chapter, they can be rather easily implemented with the TOTA middleware. So, a question arises: since a swarm of mobile robot can be assimilated to a MANET, why not build a shared coordinate system for the swarm, and use it to direct robots in the forming of a specific spatial shape?

Something similar has indeed been done in other proposal [103, 141], and it is in principle straightforward to implement:

1. Robots can be provided with an $f(x, y)$-like description of the 2D shape to form;
2. They can set up a shared coordinate system;
3. Then, they can move to the closest (x,y) within the shape and attempt to stay – within the shape – as far as possible from each other (to gracefully fill the shape).

Although this approach would allow us to build any kind of shape with great accuracy, we disregard it for the following reasons:

1. Building a coordinate system from mere connectivity requires a highly dense network of nodes (something like 15 other nodes in each node's wireless communication range). Lower densities can cause an exponential loss of precision in the coordinate system and, thus, in the formation of the shape, since such a density for robots cannot be guaranteed in every application scenario and in every area of a network.
2. Upon nodes' movement, the coordinate system should be rebuilt every time. In some MANET scenarios the movements of nodes can be occasional or slow, thus making feasible the continuous update of the coordinate system by, e.g., TOTA self-maintenance of tuples. However, when the very application goal is to move the components of a MANET (i.e., of the robots in a swarm), having to rely on a continuous update of a shared coordinate system may impose too much overhead, and it is likely to saturate the robots' available bandwidth.

3. Coding a complex shape in an $f(x, y)$-like representation can turn out to be really difficult, and likely to require notable memory for robots to locally store it.

Given that, we decided to avoid relying on a shared coordinate system and have robots self-organize a global spatial shape only with the proper propagation and sensing of different types of TOTA tuples.

9.1.4 Experiments

Here we present a variety of exemplary spatial patterns that we have been able to obtain by self-organization with the use of TOTA tuples implementing fields. All the experiments have been performed by using the TOTA emulator described in Chap. 7.

Center of Gravity

In this example, robots run a distributed field-based algorithm to cooperatively identify the robot closest to the barycenter (i.e., center of gravity) of the swarm. Such a kind of algorithm has been already presented in the previous chapter, since it is also used for establishing the shared coordinate system used for content-based information access. However, given its importance in this scenario also, we present it again, in more detail.

Electing a barycenter is a kind of leader-election algorithm. Specifically, given n points in space, their barycenter is the point that minimizes the sum of the distances to all the n points. Agents, provided with only local (one-hop) perception of their environment, can measure each other's distance by relying on a TOTA *HopTuple*. In fact, an agent receiving a *HopTuple* having value n, can roughly infer that the source of the tuple is at a distance of about $n \cdot (wireless - link - range)$.

More in detail, each robot propagates a TOTA *HopTuple*. Each robot senses the TOTA *HopTuple* propagated by all the other robots and adds their values together; let us call the resulting value B. B is the sum of distances to all the other robots, so the robot having the minimum B is the barycenter. Since B decreases monotonically to the barycenter, each robot can understand whether it has B as minimum or not, by simply comparing its value of B with that of the neighbor robots. If no neighbor has a lower value, the robot is the barycenter.

The pseudo-code implementing this algorithm with TOTA is in Fig. 8.3. Some snapshots of robots achieving this task in our simulator are in Fig. 9.1.

Circle

In this example, robots run a distributed algorithm to cooperatively assume a circular shape. The algorithm is indeed very simple.

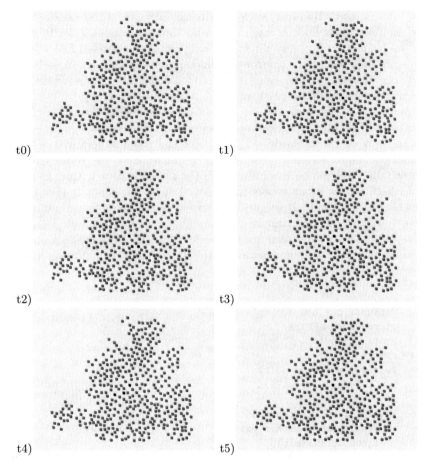

Fig. 9.1. From t0 to t5, different stages in the discovery of the barycenter. It is worth noting that, because of tuple propagation delays, more that one barycenter can arise during the process. However, after some time, the algorithm converges and only one barycenter is elected

First, each robot has to run the barycenter algorithm described above. The resulting barycenter robot (call it the CENTER) will serve as the circle center. The CENTER propagates a TOTA *HopTuple* named CIRCLE. All the other robots sense the CIRCLE tuple, and if they sense a value greater than R (the intended radius of the circle to be obtained) they move following downhill the CIRCLE tuple.

A question may arise with regard to this algorithm: how can simple robots that cannot have any location information properly move following the CIR-CLE tuple downhill? In fact, a robot can receive the information that there is another robot in its neighborhood having a CIRCLE tuple with a local value lower than its own. However, such information appears to be useless if the robot does not know how to reach that robot: since it cannot know in which direction that robot is, every direction being equally plausible. The solution to this problem is to have the robot randomly choose a direction to be followed. The direction will be eventually inverted if the robot finds out that the gradient is not actually decreasing, i.e., that the guess is wrong.

However, it is fair to report that it is possible that some robots get lost in this process. This happens if upon a wrong guess the robot gets disconnected from the rest of the network. At this point the robot is left without any information about where the rest of the world is! Here the robot can try to invert the direction to reconnect with the network. But if this does not happen because the other robots have moved away, the robot is lost and is left wandering randomly. However, these unfortunate events turned out to be extremely rare in our experiments.

The pseudo-code implementing the circle algorithm with TOTA is in Fig. 9.2. Some snapshots of robots achieving this task in our simulator are in Fig. 9.3.

```
01: HopTuple c = new HopTuple(CIRCLE)
02: if robot == CENTER
03:   tota.inject(c)
04: end if
05: Vector v = tota.read(c)
06: c = (HopTuple)v.get(0);
07: if c.hop > R
08:   Vector w = tota.readOneHop(c)
09:   HopTuple min = getMinimum(w)
10:   followDownhill(min)
11:   go to 05
12: else if c.hop == R
13:   moveAwayFromCrowd()
14:   go to 05
15: end if
16: end if
```

Fig. 9.2. Circle shape: pseudo-code

Ring

In this example, robots run a distributed algorithm to cooperatively assume a ring shape.

This algorithm is very similar to the circle one. Once the circle has been formed, robots that find themselves on the perimeter of the circle (i.e., that

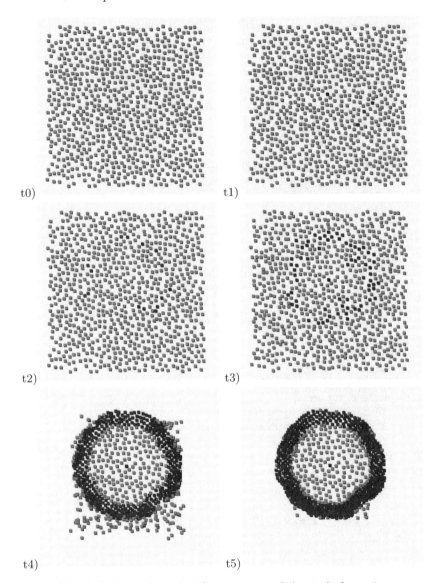

Fig. 9.3. From t0 to t5, different stages of the circle formation

perceive a value R for the value of the CIRCLE tuple), start propagating a TOTA *HopTuple* named RING. This TOTA *HopTuple* attracts robots to the middle of the circle, creating the void inside the ring. Specifically, if a robot senses the RING tuple with a value greater than T (the intended thickness of the ring to be formed), it starts following the RING tuple downhill.

The pseudo-code implementing this algorithm in TOTA is in Fig. 9.4. Some snapshots of robots achieving this task in our simulator are in Fig. 9.5.

```
01: HopTuple c = new HopTuple(CIRCLE)
02: HopTuple r = new HopTuple(RING)
03: if robot == CENTER
04:   tota.inject(c)
05: end if
06: Vector v = tota.read(c)
07: c = (HopTuple)v.get(0);
08: if c.hop == R
09:   tota.inject(r)
10:   return
11: else if c.hop != R
12:   Vector w = tota.read(r)
13:   if w.size == 0
14:     goto 12
15:   endif
16:   r = (HopTuple)w.get(0)
17:   while r.hop >= T
18:     Vector neigh = tota.readOneHop(c)
19:     HopTuple min = getMinimum(neigh)
20:     followDownhill(min)
21:   end while
22: end if
23: end if
```

Fig. 9.4. Ring shape: pseudo-code

Making Lobes

In this experiment, we tried to break the circular symmetry of previous experiments and let irregular shapes with lobes emerge in the swarm.

The idea to create lobes is to apply the circle algorithm and to identify a mechanism to deform the circle. To this end, it is worth noting that in the circle algorithm a circle is created because the TOTA *HopTuple* CIRCLE spreads in every direction uniformly, i.e., it increases its value by one at each and every hop, in all directions along which it is propagated. In this way, all

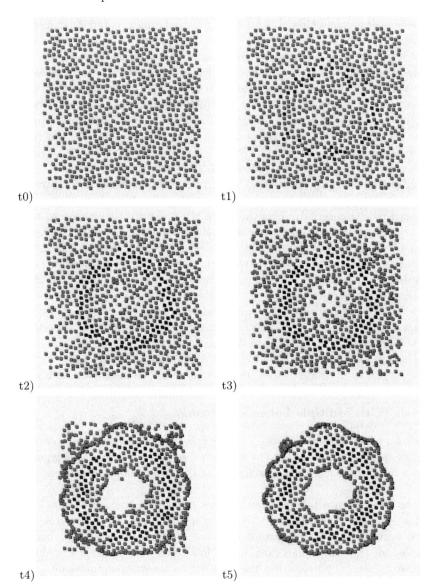

Fig. 9.5. From t0 to t5, different stages of the ring formation

the robots sensing a value of R for this tuple are almost equidistant from the center.

What if, in certain regions of the swarm, the value of the CIRCLE tuple would increase slower? Of course, the tuple would reach the value R farther from the source. Consequently, those robots perceiving that tuple and trying to dispose themselves in a position in which the tuple has a value R, would not end up in the actual perimeter of the circle: a lobe would be formed in those regions of the swarm where the tuple has increased more slowly and where it has reached the value of R farther from the center.

A possible idea to identify regions in which to make lobes emerge is to have robots sense how many robots they have in the neighborhood (something that even our very minimal robots can do, by perceiving from how many robots they can receive a signal). This can be used to identify the density of robots in a region, and to have lobes emerge in the denser regions. In particular, if a robot perceives a local number of neighbors (i.e., a local density) exceeding a specified threshold, that robot forwards the CIRCLE tuple without increasing its value. This let the CIRCLE tuple increase slower and thus the lobe to appear. Of course, it may not be possible to identify a priori where such lobes will appear, because this depends on the initial configuration of robots: even a small imbalance in the initial density of nodes, amplified as nodes get attracted to the circle, can lead to the emergence of a lobe in a specific region.

The pseudo-code implementing this algorithm in TOTA is in Fig. 9.6. Some snapshots of robots achieving this task in our simulator are in Fig. 9.7.

Shapes With Multiple Lobes – Polygons

In this set of experiments, we built on the previous one and tried to control the number and position of lobes to be created, so as to obtain regular polygon-like shapes (e.g., three lobes for a triangle-like shape, four lobes for a square-like shape, etc.).

The idea to control the number of lobes is again rooted in a leader-election mechanism. We want to design an algorithm to elect n leaders on a circle. These leaders must be equidistant from one another. Once this has been accomplished, the leaders can execute the lobe algorithm described in the previous section (i.e., propagating the CIRCLE tuple without increasing it), to create n lobes equidistant from one another.

The idea for the leader-election algorithm is very simple: (i) each node runs the circle algorithm; (ii) once a circle has been created nodes on the perimeter start casting random numbers; (iii) each node casting a number greater than a specified threshold becomes a leader – the threshold is chosen so that it is very unlikely that two nodes becomes leaders shortly one after another; (iv) the leader starts propagating a TOTA *HopTuple* named ELECT, that propagates only in the circle perimeter region; (v) nodes receiving the ELECT tuple stop casting random numbers, and if the received ELECT tuple value overcomes another specified threshold L, they become leaders; (vi) each leader sets the

```
01: HopTuple c = new HopTuple(CIRCLE)
02: if robot == CENTER
03:  tota.inject(c)
04: end if
05: value = getTupleValue(CIRCLE)
06: if value > R
07:  followDownhillTuple(CIRCLE)
08: else if value == R
09:  moveAwayFromCrowd()
10: end if
11: else
12:  followUphillTuple(CIRCLE)
13: end if
14: if numNeighbours() > criticalDensity1
15:  /* do not increase the field upon tuple propagation-forwarding */
16:  setTupleIncValue(CIRCLE, 0)
17: end if
18: if numNeighbours() < criticalDensity2
19:  /* restore default increase upon tuple propagation-forwarding */
20:  setTupleIncValue(CIRCLE, def)
21: end if
```

Fig. 9.6. Shape with lobes: pseudo-code

ELECT tuple value to 0 and continues its propagation; and (vii) once the ELECT tuple is fully propagated there should be almost $(circle - length)/L$ equidistant leaders on the circle. Thus L is a parameter controlling which polygon will emerge.

The pseudo-code implementing this algorithm in TOTA is in Fig. 9.8. Some snapshots of robots achieving this task in our simulator are in Fig. 9.9.

9.1.5 Performance Evaluation

Validating our approach in terms of performance basically amounts to verifying (i) that it is reasonably scalable and (ii) that the assumption of minimal capabilities is not too penalizing. The results are presented in Fig. 9.10 and refer to a virtual time that adopts as unity '1' the time taken to propagate a gradient between neighbor robots. Referring to an actual time requires assumptions on hardware and motion speed that are not relevant here. With regard to point (i), we have verified that our approach scales linearly with the number of robots: the time for a swarm of randomly placed robots to reach a stable configuration increases linearly with the number of robots. With regard to point (ii) we have limited our attention to verifying that the impact of the assumption of nondirectional sensing is not too penalizing. We have compared the time required by robots to self-organize into specific shapes with and with-

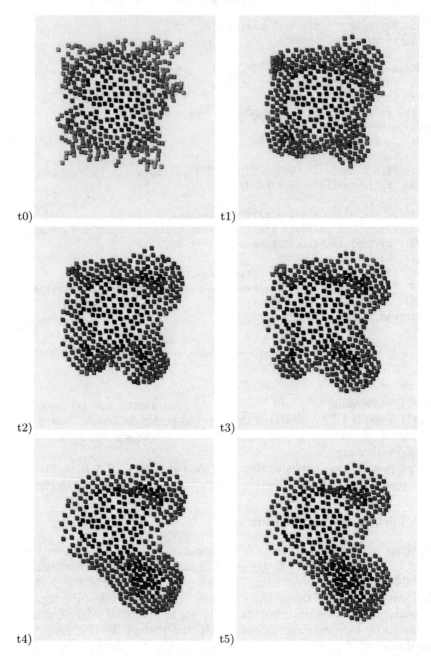

Fig. 9.7. From t0 to t5, different stages of the circle with lobes formation

```
01: if robot == CENTER
02:   injectTuple(CIRCLE, 10)
03: end if
04: if getTupleValue(CIRCLE) == R
05:   if hasTuple(ELECT)
06:     if getTupleValue(ELECT) > dist
07:      iAmLeader();
08:      injectTuple(ELECT)
09:      setTupleIncValue(CIRCLE, 0)
10:     end if
11:   else if nextRandom() > threshold
12:      iAmLeader();
13:      injectTuple(ELECT)
14:      setTupleIncValue(CIRCLE,0)
15:     else
16:      go to 04
17:     end if
18:   end if
19: else if getTupleValue(CIRCLE) > R
20:   if getTupleValue(ELECT) == 1
21:     setTupleIncValue(CIRCLE, 0)
22:   end if
23: end if
24: end if
25:
26: value = getTupleValue(CIRCLE)
27: if value > R
28:   followDownhillTuple(CIRCLE)
29: else if value == R
30:   moveAwatFromCrowd ()
31: end if
32: go to 26
```

Fig. 9.8. Polygons: pseudo-code

out the capability to perceive the direction in which a morphogen gradient is decreasing. The result is that the overhead caused by robots wandering randomly to properly detect in which direction to go is very limited, independent of the specific shape to be obtained and independent of the overall number of robots in the system. Comparing our approach with other approaches based on robots with more powerful capabilities (i.e., global sensing and a priori knowledge of the geometrical shape to obtain) is simply meaningless. In fact, the notably better performances that these approaches would obviously exhibit would be obtained at the price of notably increasing the robots' complexity, size and price.

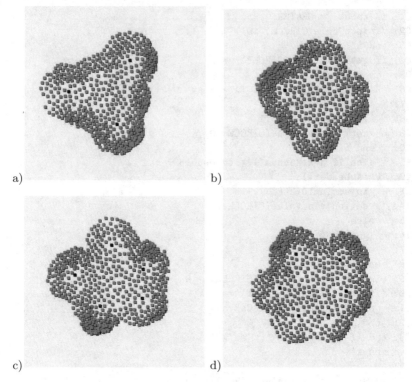

Fig. 9.9. Different polygon shapes obtained by multiple lobes: (a) Triangle; (b) Quadrilateral; (c) Pentagon; (d) Hexagon

9.1.6 Open Issues

The above experiments have shown the power of field-based coordination and of TOTA in supporting self-organizing shape formation in swarms of simple mobile robots. We are aware that the spatial shapes we have presented are indeed simple. Nevertheless, they represent the basic starting point from which to compose more complex manifolds involving circles, polygons, areas with holes (as in the circle), areas in which irregular features emerge (as in the lobes).

Unfortunately, effective methodologies to support developers in understanding what fields (i.e., what TOTA tuples) one must exploit and how to achieve such complex composite spatial shapes are still to be fully identified – see also Subsect. 5.3.6. However, as already stated in Chap. 7, this is a general open issue of field-based coordination and of adaptive self-organizing systems.

A specific issue of robot swarms worth investigating relates instead to the understanding of how the integration of additional capabilities in robots (e.g.,

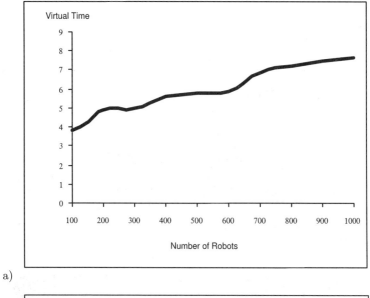

a)

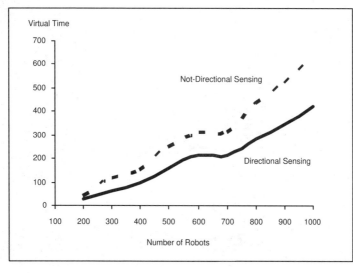

b)

Fig. 9.10. Performance evaluation. (a) Identification of the barycenter. The time required to elect a barycenter grows linearly with the number of robots. (b) Ring formation. The time required for the shaping of robots into a ring grows linearly with the number of robots. Furthermore, the assumption of nondirectional sensing is not highly penalizing, if compared with the results achieved by robots capable of directional sensing

direction and distance sensing) could be exploited to its best in the context
of field-based coordination.

9.2 Gait Control in Modular Robots

The second, somewhat related, scenario we have considered to evaluate the
effectiveness of field-based coordination and of TOTA, is modular robots control.

As already introduced in Subsect. 4.2.2, a modular robot is a collection
of simple autonomous actuators connected with each other, with few degrees
of freedom in their relative movements. The key problem in the control of a
modular robot is to design distributed control algorithms to be executed by
the actuators that – interacting with each other and changing their relative
positions – have to have the robot assume global coherent shapes or global
coherent motion patterns (see Fig. 9.11).

Fig. 9.11. Modular Robot: a robot adopting a caterpillar gait to climb a porous
material. Photo taken from [159]

Some of the most innovative approaches to control a modular robot (already discussed in Subsect. 4.2.2) adopt the biologically inspired idea of hormones [133]. Hormone signals are actually sort of field-like messages, spread
across the robot and triggering the individual actuator's bending. For example, a "head" module in a modular robot (see later) can inject in the robot

a sequence of hormone signals. All the other modules can be programmed to react to the income of such signals by bending their actuator by a specified angle. A motion gait would be encoded by means of a specific sequence of hormones to be injected in the robot and by means of specific reactions triggered by these hormones, changing the bending angles.

In our experiments, we have (successfully) tried to implement hormones in terms of TOTA tuples. To perform these experiments, we connected our TOTA simulator with a simulator for 3D modular robots available at [99]. This program can simulate the behavior of various types of modular robots, taking into account both the characteristics of the joints connecting different parts of the robot and the physical forces acting on the robot (e.g., gravitation), and offers a 3D view of the robot's actual configuration and movements.

Distributed algorithms to control the robot can be implemented with this simulator. Specifically, each module of the robot is provided with an API enabling us to drive the module actuator, and to sample and possibly change the way in which the robot is connected to the other modules.

To connect this simulator with the TOTA one, we created an object having access both to the TOTA API and to the modular robot API. This object "runs," at the same time, in the TOTA simulator and in the modular robot simulator, connecting the two.

9.2.1 Our Approach

The main subject of our research has been the chain-type modular robot (although we later report also about an experiment with a "legged" robot). In our experiments, we assumed that the robot is composed of very simple equal modules (i.e., joint actuators). Each module has a "front" side and a "back" side. On each side there are two docking points and an infrared (IR) network link. The two docking points enable a module to physically connect with other ones. This is of course fundamental to actually building the chain constituting the modular robot. The IR link enables communication between connected modules (see Fig. 9.13).

Each module runs the TOTA middleware and an agent in charge of driving the module joint. In a chain-type modular robot, modules connect by their IR links in a chain-type network, resembling the robot topology.

An agent, installed on a module, looking at the active IR links, is able to infer whether it is the "head," the "tail," or a part of the "body" of the robot. Specifically, the "head" agent is the one with only the back IR link active, the "tail" agent is the one with only the front IR link active, a "body" agent is one having both the IR links active.

The process of assessing whether an IR link is active or not can be based on "ping" messages and can be executed iteratively to take into account topological reconfigurations and module breakdown.

From a methodology point of view and in very general terms, our setup consists in codifying a motion gait by means of a *GaitTuple* TOTA tuple. Such a tuple has the structure depicted in Fig. 9.12.

```
Abstract GaitTuple
C = (..., angle)
P = (propagate hop-by-hop, changing the content so as
to encode in the "angle"-distributed data structure
the shape the robot has to assume)
```

Fig. 9.12. Structure of the abstract *GaitTuple*. This tuple encodes in its distributed shape (i.e., angle field values) the form we want the robot to assume

When an agent installed on a module senses the income of a tuple of this kind, it reacts by bending the module joint by the angle specified in the tuple. So, for example, if in a robot composed of N modules a tuple having in its content a fixed angle of about $(360/N)°$ is spread, the robot closes into a loop.

More specifically, our approach is based on the following key points.

1. The head agent injects in the network (i.e., in the robot modules) a specific GaitTuple, representing the shape (or a step of the gait) the robot has to assume.
2. The tuple propagates from the head to the tail letting the robot bend accordingly.
3. When the tail receives the tuple, it injects another tuple (a *MessageTuple* with constant value) for the purpose of notifying the head that the Gait Tuple completed its travel.
4. When the head receives the above tuple it can inject another *GaitTuple* implementing the second configuration the robot has to assume (i.e., second step in a motion gait). Or, alternatively, the *MessageTuple* can automatically trigger a change in the content of the *GaitTuple* to let the robot assume the second configuration.
5. The process continues iteratively.

9.2.2 Related Approaches

The research on CONRO modular robot [133] (already introduced in Subsect. 4.2.2) directly inspired our experiments. Basically, all we did was to rephrase their concept of hormone signals in terms of TOTA tuples. To this end, we emphasize again that our goal, in this scenario, is not to devise new control mechanisms to drive the modular robot, but to test if the TOTA approach is general enough to be applied also in this scenario. It is however worth noting that our approach actually slightly extends the original hormone-based approach. In [133], hormones are passive ("dead") data structures, and agents,

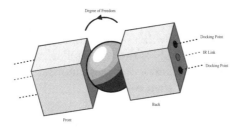

Fig. 9.13. A single module composing the modular robot. In our research we focus on simple module having just two docking points and two IR network links one for each side (front and back) of the module.

running on modules, are expected to inject different hormones to achieve, for example, a complex motion gait. In our approach, TOTA tuples are active and can change while being stored in the modular robot. Exploiting this feature, even a complex gait can be obtained by using just one TOTA tuple that changes to let the robot assume different configurations.

In [13], each module of the modular robot runs a simple finite state automaton in which state transitions are driven by the local state, the state of neighbor modules, their locations, and some external information. Communications are limited to the immediate neighborhood and a limited number of bits are exchanged at each time step. The goal is not to create an exact predefined shape, but a structure with the correct properties (structural, morphological, etc.). Any stable "emergent" structure that exhibits the desired properties is considered satisfactory, with no regard for the "optimality" or details of the resulting geometry. This approach is very similar to ours, although our goal is to actually create engineered shapes and gaits, and not just purely emergent ones.

Another thread of research, in modular robots, involves conceptually centralized control mechanisms [160]. In these approaches, a control table, specifying how each module must bend its actuator, is compiled off-line and then uploaded into the modules. The main advantage of this approach is that it allows us to design even complex motion gaits rather easily. The main drawback is that the control table is built for a specific robot configuration, and if the robot changes (e.g., new modules get connected), the table must be rebuilt from scratch. The research in this area is mainly oriented to devising new languages to build the control table. One of the most advanced proposals is PARSL (Phase Automata Robot Scripting Language) [99]. PARSL is a scripting language based on XML syntax, designed to express motion gaits for chain-type modular robots. In PARSL it is possible to design a motion gait by means of abstract "waves of activity" traveling across the robot. Such high-level description is then automatically compiled to create the control table.

9.2.3 Experiments

In the rest of this section we will use our approach to create two motion gaits in a chain-type modular robot: the "caterpillar gait" (that lets the robot proceed by mimicking the motion of a snake) and the "rolling gait" (that lets the robot close in a loop, and then roll).

Caterpillar Gait

To implement the caterpillar gait, the head agent starts the movement by injecting a caterpillar tuple (i.e., a TOTA tuple of the class *CaterpillarGait-Tuple*). The general structure of such a tuple is depicted in Fig. 9.14, it propagates across the robot letting it bend accordingly.

Once the tail agent receives the tuple, according to the general description given above, it injects another tuple to notify the head that a new step is ready to be executed.

At this point, the head agent updates the *Caterpillar GaitTuple* accordingly to the Table 9.15 and injects it again. Once spread, this tuple lets the gait proceed by another step.

Useful insights to understand how the caterpillar gait works and how the Table 9.15 has been compiled can be found in Fig. 9.16.

The code implementing the *CaterpillarGaitTuple* tuple can be found in Fig. 9.17. This process is iterated letting the whole robot move performing the caterpillar gait (see Fig. 9.18).

```
CaterpillarGait Tuple
C = (state, angle)
P = (propagate hop-by-hop, storing on intermediate
nodes changing the content accordingly to the table
in Fig. \ref{fig:caterpillar-table}. If on the head node and upon the rece
of a gait-tuple, re-apply propagation)
```

Fig. 9.14. The structure of the *CaterpillarGaitTuple* tuple

Current State	New State	New Angle
INIT	A	+45°
A	B	+45°
B	C	−45°
C	D	−45°
D	A	+45°

Fig. 9.15. This table shows how the content of the *CaterpillarGaitTuple* changes

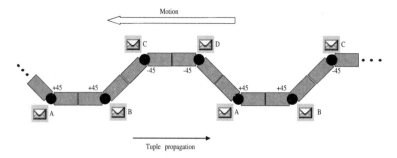

Fig. 9.16. The caterpillar gait works by letting a pattern of activity travel along the robot, letting it going forward

```
public class CaterpillarGaitTuple extends MessageTuple {
 /* constant declaration as in caterpillar gait table */
 /* tuple sates: INIT, A,B,C,D and respective angles
 degA,degB,degC,degD are defined */

 public int state = INIT;
 public int angle = 0;

 protected void changeTupleContent()
 {
  switch(state)
  {
   case INIT : state = A;
               angle = degA;
               break;
   case A    : state = B;
               angle = degB;
               break;
   case B    : state = C;
               angle = degC;
               break;
   case C    : state = D;
               angle = degD;
               break;
   case D    : state = A;
               angle = degA;
               break;
  }
 }
}
```

Fig. 9.17. The code realizing the *CaterpillarGaitTuple* TOTA class

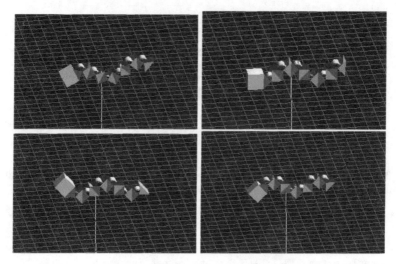

Fig. 9.18. Some stages of a caterpillar gait, in a chain-typed modular robot, composed of six actuators

Rolling Gait

The idea of this gait is to let the robot close in a loop and then roll. Unfortunately, the modular robot simulator we employed does not allow structures with loops. Structures with loops are overconstrained. The simulation does not solve the constraint satisfaction problem. The simulation does not detect self-collision either.

To overcome this problem, we let the robot bend in an open loop (something like a 'C' shape) and then roll. Although this complicates the rolling procedure, it allows us to maintain the general approach described before. In fact, we still have a "head" and a "tail" agent that would be otherwise removed if the loop were actually closed (i.e., with only "body" agents).

The *RollingGaitTuple* is the tuple employed to let the robot roll. In general terms, it can have two states, T (turn) and F (flat). Consider, for example, a robot composed of 12 modules and assuming a turning angle of 45°. A tuple spread in the robot with a distributed shape like "FTTFTTFTTFTT" (see Fig. 9.19) closes in a loop. Then, if the tuple changes its content by "rolling" the above string (like the ROL assembler command), the robot performs the rolling gait.

From the single tuple point of view, this consists in changing its content to assume values F - T - T iteratively. It is worth noting that such a kind of content change critically depends on the number of modules composing the robot and the number of turns we want to implement to let the robot close in a loop. For example, three turns of 60° each create a triangular track, four turns of 90° each create a rectangular track, etc. Moreover, it depends on the number of modules involved in each turn. For example, in Fig. 9.19, two modules bend by 45° to create a 90° turn.

Despite all these parameters, it is rather easy to build a general algorithm enabling a tuple to create dynamically, at runtime, the sequence of F and T states it has to cycle (e.g., F - T - T) to enable the rolling gait.

A general description of the *RollingGaitTuple* enabling the rolling gait in the case of a robot composed of 12 modules and assuming four turns of 90° each, split between two modules bending by 45°, is illustrated in Fig. 9.20.

The code realizing the *RollingGaitTuple* can be found in Fig. 9.21. Some snapshots showing the rolling gait in action are in Fig. 9.22.

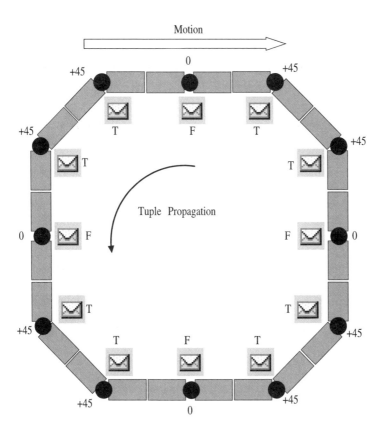

Fig. 9.19. In the rolling gait, the robot moves in one direction by shifting the turning modules (T) to the opposite direction

```
Rolling Gait Tuple C = (state, angle) P = (propagate hop-by-hop,
cycling between the states F - T - T. Set the angle to 45deg if
the state is T. Set the angle to 0 if the state is F)
```

Fig. 9.20. The rolling gait tuple

9.2.4 A Walking Legged Robot

Another experiment we performed on a different type of robot related to a "legged" robot that can move by coordinating legs movements.

The idea of this experiment is to have the modules of the robot connected in a 6-legs configuration (see Fig. 9.23), and then coordinate the actions of these modules so as to let the legged robot walk. In this example, the robot is built from two types of modules (both available from the Polybot simulator [99]): joints and connectors. Among the several possible configurations upon which it is possible to build a legged robot, the one we choose presents three key advantages:

- The adopted configuration is very modular. In order to crate a robot with more legs it is sufficient to add other legs (in multiples of two) at the end of the previous robot.
- The robot is highly flexible. It can swing in pitch and yaw both the backbone and the legs.
- Most importantly for the upcoming discussion, modules have a direction (front-rear) and they can distinguish both the kind of module to which the are attached (i.e., joint or connector) and the orientation of the connection (i.e., pitch-pitch, yaw-yaw, or pitch-yaw), see Fig. 9.24(left). Thus each module can infer its position within the robot. Since connectors have no degrees of freedom – they are passive components – they do not need to localize. In particular it is possible to identify the following six important *roles* for modules: HEAD, SPINE, LEFT-SHOULDER, RIGHT-SHOULDER, LEFT-LEG, and RIGHT-LEG (see Fig. 9.24(right)).

The robot in Fig. 9.23 is in the rest mode. The first tuple we envisioned is the one forcing the robot to stand up (see Fig. 9.25). The code of this *StandUpTuple* tuple (reported in Fig. 9.26) is really simple. It basically forces all leg modules to turn 90°. More precisely, the way in which modules are connected implies that left legs should bend by 90°, while right legs by −90°.

Once the robot is standing up. It can start moving the legs to proceed upward. This again is realized by letting the head of the robot inject another tuple that propagates across the modules. This *WalkerGaitTuple* tuple is very simple: it alternatively lets the left and right robot legs swing 45° forward. The code of this tuple is reported in Fig. 9.27, while some screen-shots of the actual robot movement are presented in Fig. 9.28.

```
public class RollingGaitTuple extends MessageTuple
{
 // number of modules composing the robot
 private static final int N_MODULES;
 // number of turning points
 private static final int N_TURNS;
 // radius of the turn
 private static final int RADIUS ;
 // turning angle in deg
 private static final int TURN;

 public int state = 0;
 public int angle = 0;

 protected void changeTupleContent()
 {
  if(this.getSourceFromId().equals(tota.toString()))
   state = (state + 1)% N_MODULES;

  int mod = Integer.parseInt(tota.toString().substring(1));

  boolean cond = false;
  for(int i=0;i<N_TURNS;i++)
  {
   boolean cond1 =
   ((state+(i*N_MODULES)/N_TURNS) % N_MODULES) == mod;
   boolean cond2 =
   ((state+(i*N_MODULES)/N_TURNS) % N_MODULES) ==
   ((mod + RADIUS)% N_MODULES);
   if(cond1 || cond2)
   {
    cond = true;
    break;
   }
  }

  if(cond)
   angle = TURN;
  else
   angle = 0;
 }
}
```

Fig. 9.21. The code realizing the *RollingGaitTuple* TOTA class

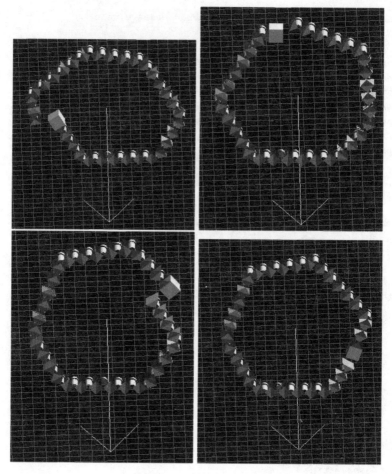

Fig. 9.22. Some stages of a rolling gait in a chain-typed modular robot composed of 32 actuators.

9.3 Final Considerations

In our opinion, robotic self-assembly is a research area that is destined for dramatic growth in the near future. Advances in swarm robotics and in modular robots will lead us to a brand new world in which artificial societies of simple computational particles will self-organize to create artificial organisms made up of flexible computational cells connected with each other, and will populate our everyday environments to (hopefully) put their capabilities at our service.

In this context, field-based coordination will most likely play an important role. Despite the simplicity of the experiments reported in this chapter, we are confident that the capability of field-based coordination (and of TOTA) in

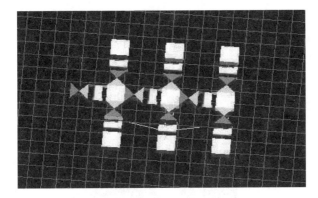

Fig. 9.23. A modular robot arranged in a 6-legged configuration

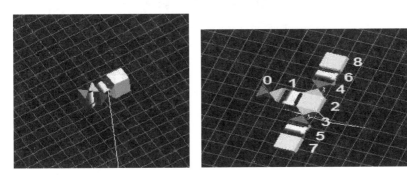

Fig. 9.24. (left) Detail of a robot leg. The pitch-yaw orientation between the two modules allows high flexibility. (right) Different neighbor connections allow each module to estimate its role within the robot (0 = HEAD, 1 = SPINE, 3 = LEFT-SHOULDER, 4 = RIGHT-SHOULDER, 5 = LEFT-LEG, 6 = RIGHT-LEG)

properly supporting biologically inspired interaction models – i.e., morphogen gradients and hormones – will be the key to its future successes. However, we are also aware that the widespread exploitation of field-based coordination will require the identification of proper methodologies to help designers in the development of complex field-based applications and, specifically, in the development of complex self-assembling robotics artifacts.

In addition to that, we must also recognize that additional mechanisms – not dealt with by this book – may have some impact in computational self-assembly and are worth investigating. These include game-theoretic approaches [155] and cellular automata approaches [154, 88].

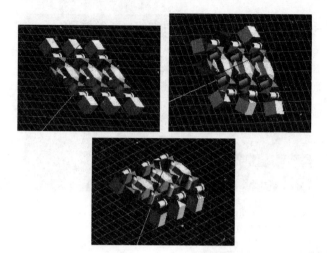

Fig. 9.25. A 4-legged robot stands up

```
public class StandUpTuple extends MessageTuple {

  // bend degree
  private static final int Deg = 90;
  public int angle;

  protected void changeTupleContent()
  {
   int role = (RoleTuple)tota.read(new RoleTuple()).role;
   if (role == RIGHT-LEG) angle = -Deg;
   else if (role == LEFT-LEG) angle = Deg;
   else angle = 0;
  }
}
```

Fig. 9.26. The code realizing the *StandUpTuple* TOTA class.

```
public class WalkerGaitTuple extends MessageTuple
{
 //states
 private static final int FORWARD = 0;
 private static final int REVERSE = 1;

 public int state = FORWARD;
 public int angle = 0;

 protected void changeTupleContent()
 {
  int role = (RoleTuple)tota.read(new RoleTuple()).role;

  if (role == RIGHT-LEG) angle = -45;
  if (role == LEFT-LEG) angle = 45;
  if (role == SPINE) angle = 0;

    if (state == FORWARD)
    {
     if (role == LEFT-SHOULDER) angle = 0;
     if (role == RIGHT-SHOULDER) angle = -45;
     state = REVERSE;
    }
    else
    {
     if (role == LEFT-SHOULDER) angle = 45;
     if (role == RIGHT-SHOULDER) angle = 0;
     state = FORWARD;
    }
 }
}
```

Fig. 9.27. The code realizing the *WalkerGaitTuple* TOTA class.

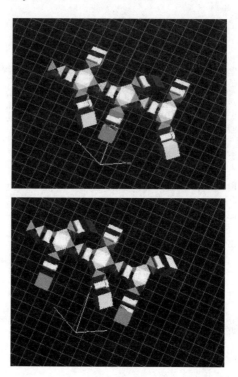

Fig. 9.28. The legged robot walks by coordinating legs movements.

10

The Cloak of Invisibility

Is it possible to create a cloak of invisibility – a flexible artifact that can make anything inside it invisible despite mobility and deformation? Humans have dreamt of what invisibility might mean since the beginning of civilization, and this dream persists in today's literature and culture. However, although more improbable methods of invisibility will remain unrealized, an invisibility cloak could be feasible in the future through technology.

In this chapter, we intend to show that a cloak of invisibility can be – at least conceptually – built by exploiting a huge network of tiny micro-devices (i.e., literally a network of spray computers) and content-based access algorithms like the ones described in Chap. 8 [163].

In particular, our proposal is for a fabric of small computing devices, capable of receiving and retransmitting light emissions in a directional way, and capable of interacting with each other in a wireless amorphous network [20, 102]. While someone or something is inside the cloak, the emissions of the cloak devices make external observers perceive exactly the same light configurations they would have perceived if nothing were in between. Sensors on the rear side of the cloak can receive such configurations and, by distributed coordination, can communicate them to emitters on the observer's side to be retransmitted.

Building a solid wall exhibiting such a property for an observer at a fixed position may be already difficult. Even more challenging problems arise when such a property has to be preserved:

- for any observer in any position;
- for any shape of the cloak;
- despite deformations of the cloak tissue.

This chapter does not have the ambition to present fully fledged solutions to all of the complex issues involved. Still, in the attempt of sketching some promising solutions, with the use also of field-based coordination and TOTA, it brings together a number of technological and algorithmic aspects (related to

Smart Dust technology [114], sensor networks [33], mobile computing and ad hoc networks [33, 118], peer-to-peer and content-based coordination [52, 113], and self-organization and self-localization [102, 164]), showing once and for all the strict relations between apparently diverse emerging scenarios, relations that we identified since the beginning of this book.

For the sake of readability, we present our arguments in an incremental step-by-step way. For each step, we discuss the associated technological and software challenges, and the artifacts you might create after resolving the challenges.

10.1 STEP 1. The Invisible Wall

Let us consider the basic scenario of realizing a rigid flat wall invisible to a single fixed observer at a known position (e.g., centered in front of the wall and at a known distance from it). You could do this simply by having a camera capture everything behind the wall (from the known fixed perspective of the observer) and project it on the front side of the wall.

The alternative we propose, serving as a basic building block toward the definition of the cloak of invisibility (where the constraint of a fixed single observer will be removed), is to build the invisible wall by making use of a network of small computer-based devices. In particular, two kinds of devices are needed:

1. IN devices, sensors capable of perceiving light emissions and of transforming them into digital signals, such as the CCD sensors of a digital camera;
2. OUT devices, capable of emitting light according to specific signals received, such as LCD displays, LEDs, and micro-lasers.

Of course it is possible to conceive devices acting both as IN sensors and OUT emitters.

To realize the wall, the basic principle is to deploy densely packed IN and OUT devices on the two sides of the wall, respectively. We do not consider such devices as placed in a regular – possibly wired – grid (as in cameras and monitors). Instead, we consider the wall randomly filled with unwired devices, to avoid any placement and wiring efforts and to enable us, say, to "paint" or "spray" the wall with transparent glue mixed with sensors and emitters. Such a choice, while it increases flexibility and fault tolerance, requires devices to have short-range wireless communication capabilities (optical- or radio-based) [104] and to be either internally self-powered (e.g., by solar energy or by some sort of light battery), or laid on a conductive substrate feeding them with external power.

Once painted, each of the IN devices must record the information on the light locally incident on the wall, and transmit it to the opposite side of the wall to the corresponding OUT devices, so as to globally reconstruct the image. Such transmissions, due to the short-range communication capabilities

– and not to limit the potential size and thickness of the wall – must occur in a multi-step fashion, by properly routing messages across the network to their destination (see Fig. 10.1(left)). Of course, this requires the two sides of the wall to be seamlessly part of the same network, so that a message can be routed from one side to the other by continuously traveling over the network (e.g., with regard to Fig. 10.1(left), we assume that the gray lateral parts of the wall are filled with devices too).

10.1.1 Software Issues

The possibility of deploying sensors and emitters without any predetermined layout can dramatically cut the costs in building such a wall. However, it complicates software design. In particular, when dealing with the software to control such an artifact, there are two main issues that need to be addressed:

- How can devices determine where they are so as to properly establish the IN and OUT pairs?
- How is data routed across the network from IN to OUT devices?

With regard to the first question, since devices are spread randomly on the wall (e.g., by a painting process), they do not have any a priori knowledge about their position. However, this information is fundamental: each device will in fact find its mate by looking for the device on the opposite side of the wall having the same coordinates.

Of course, the use of GPS technology is ruled out, due to the lack of the required accuracy and due to its costs [50]. The alternative solution could be based on a triangulation algorithm, like the one presented in Chap. 8 (i.e., Subsect. 8.3.1). More concretely, we can suppose that each IN and OUT device runs the TOTA middleware and injects by TOTA the tuples required for establishing a coordinate frame.

Given the availability of a set of coordinates, the same for the two sides of the wall, the second question can now be restated as, how can the data sensed by an IN device at coordinates (XIN, YIN) be routed to the OUT device positioned at the (XIN, YIN) coordinates on the opposite side of the wall? Better, since there is not necessarily an OUT device at exactly the same coordinates (or since such a device can be dead or be temporarily unreachable), how can such data be routed to the OUT device closest to (XIN, YIN)?

The answer, in this case, is rather simple (see Fig. 10.1(right)). Each IN device has to inject a TOTA tuple in the form (see Fig. 10.2) *(XIN, YIN, Color)* representing the image information it has captured at its own coordinates. Such a tuple can then propagate in a directional way, from device to device, toward the closest edge of the wall. Then, once the tuple has reached the opposite side of the wall, propagation proceeds from device to device in the direction toward the (XIN, YIN) coordinates. Propagation stops when the OUT device at the (XIN, YIN) coordinates is reached, or when no emitter

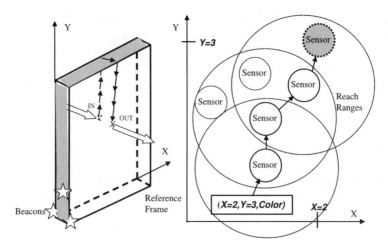

Fig. 10.1. The invisible wall: (left) A global view; (right) Local routing of a tuple toward a specific point

closer to the goal is found in the neighborhood. Note that this kind of propagation can be easily obtained by embedding in the TOTA tuple propagation a geographic routing algorithm like the one described in Subsect. 8.3.2.

```
Wall Tuple
C = (XIN,YIN, Color)
P = (propagate using geographic routing algorithm to the node
closest to XIN, YIN on the opposite side of the wall)
```

Fig. 10.2. Each IN device has to inject this TOTA tuple representing the image information it has captured at its own coordinates. Such tuple can then directionally propagate to the corresponding OUT device

10.1.2 Optical and Hardware Issues

What should be the size of the above devices to provide a reasonable visual rendering? Following the Listings-Donders model of the human eye [41] (see Fig. 10.3) we can define θmin as the minimum angle at which the points A and B are perceived separately . This angle is approximately $1/60°$, the minimum at which two light rays hit two distinct cone cells separated by a cone cell not hit. Thus, considering Fig. 10.3, A and B are perceived separately only if

$$l > d \cdot tan(1/60°) \approx d/3400$$

In order to have a good image the distance between any two devices has to be less than $d/3400$ (e.g., two objects separated by 1 mm are perceived as a single object from a distance of 3400 mm $= 3.4$ m).

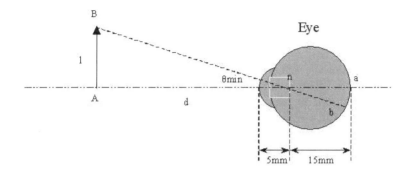

Fig. 10.3. Listings-Donders model of the human eye

For instance, to render invisible a wall of 1 m^2 from a distance of 10 m, 115600 devices on each side of the wall are required. In fact, the allowed maximum distance between two devices to provide the impression of smoothness is $10/3400 = 2.9$ mm. So, each device must be approximately 2.9 mm$^2 \approx 8.4$ mm^2 wide, a linear meter must have at least 340 devices and a square meter 115600 devices (340^2).

The above requirements appear feasible with regard to the state of the art in optical MEMS technologies. For instance, in the context of the Smart Dust project at Berkeley [114, 136] internally powered computer-based sensors and emitters of few mm^2, which could well serve our purpose, have been already realized for a few years.

Even the amount of data to be dealt with by each device and by their wireless communication channels is not challenging. If we assume each device should record and transmit a 24 bit value for the color information (16 million colors) and two 16 bit values representing device coordinates, this results in a 24+16+16=56 bit tuple. These values must be updated 30 times per second as the normal television frequency. In the case of a 1 m^2 wall, with devices at an approximate distance of 2.9 mm, and assuming that the communication range enables a device to connect only to its closest neighbors (a very strict hypothesis), the routing process of a tuple takes 170 steps on average and, in the worst case of centrally located pairs, 340 steps. Thus, devices located at the edge of the wall (the ones dealing with the highest traffic) will be in charge of routing information for all of the 170 other devices on the line between them and the center of the wall. All this considered, the wireless link bandwidth of a single device should be $(170 \cdot 56 \text{ bit}) \cdot 30 \text{ Hz} \approx 286 \text{ kbit/sec}$ to sustain such peaks, low enough to be sustained by modern micro devices.

In any case, we emphasize that we are considering here the very physiological limits of the human eye. For several applications, less strict constraints (and a coarser rendering) may be enough.

10.1.3 Applications

Since it can render the image only from a fixed perspective, the described wall cannot render invisibility: any observer moving around it would not perceive the image, produced by the OUT devices, changing according, making the illusion vanish. Still, a transparent wall can have several potential applications in all those cases where there is the need for observing without being observed (e.g., in therapy and investigation, as well as in entertainment). The advantage with regard to more traditional technologies (e.g., camera-based or magic-mirror-based ones) relates to the fact that its installation is not intrusive, and does not require specific infrastructures or skills.

The described technology would also allow building more interesting artifacts. Specifically, an amorphous network perfectly analogous to the one described in this section could be used to produce a paintable television (or monitor): a television to be sold as a paint that, once applied, starts working as a normal flat screen television. The idea, in that case, is to have a TV signal receiver at one of the edges of the painted wall act also as a beacon for the network coordinate system. Once all emitters are localized, the receiver can transmit tuples in the form $(X, Y, Color)$, to be propagated in the network of emitters to render the TV image.

10.2 STEP 2. The Invisible Object

The real power of invisibility, and of a larger class of related applications, can be effectively enabled only by making it possible to paint invisible objects of any shape, other than on a flat wall, and by enhancing image rendering so as to relax the constraint of the fixed and single point of observation, and to render invisibility to multiple and possibly mobile observers. The idea is that the object gets completely covered by a sensor network so that, for any point of its surface, any ray of light incident from any direction gets properly captured and retransmitted on the opposite side of the surface.

By assuming that one or multiple observers can move around the object and see all its sides, the IN and OUT devices described previously must be integrated together in a single device (or, from a different perspective, they must be both densely painted on the whole surface): in fact, there are no longer separated IN and OUT sides on the object. Moreover, if we want the object to show what is behind it independently of the position of the observers, each

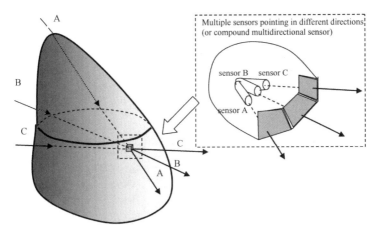

Fig. 10.4. The invisible object

portion of the surface should be able to retransmit different light configurations in different directions, so as to virtually extend all (a reasonable number of) the rays of light incident on the object (see Fig. 10.4). To this purpose, we can consider a device as a compound object capable of acquiring different light information (IN function) and of firing different light rays (OUT function) in different directions. Alternatively, we can consider a device as a unidirectional sensor or emitter. By distributing these unidirectional devices densely on the object surface (with a random orientation, as it would derive from painting), any portion of the surface will have, with high probability, sensor and emitters pointing in all directions. In the following, we mainly consider this latter alternative.

10.2.1 Software Issues

Given the above distribution of devices, implementing invisibility is apparently very similar to the case described in the previous subsection: each IN device must provide light information to the OUT device on the "opposite" side of the object, i.e., to the emitter on the surface which is the closest (in terms of both surface position and orientation) to the virtual extension of the ray of light captured by the sensor. However, in this case, answering the same questions introduced before (how devices determine their position and the IN-OUT pairs, and how data can be routed from IN to OUT devices) is more challenging.

To explain the problems related to the above issues and to present our proposal to solve them, it is important to distinguish between what we call extrinsic and intrinsic coordinates.

Extrinsic coordinates identify the position and orientation of devices with respect to a three-dimensional frame attached to the object (see Fig.

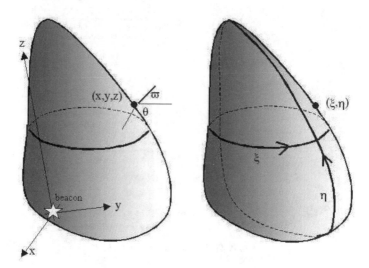

Fig. 10.5. (left) Extrinsic coordinates. (right) Intrinsic coordinates

10.5(left)). The extrinsic coordinates of a device could be represented, for instance, by its (X, Y, Z) coordinates and by the two angles (θ, ω) determining its orientation.

Intrinsic coordinates, instead, specify the positions of devices in the object surface. In other words, they are two-dimensional coordinates (ξ, η) mapped on the surface and establishing a frame on the object's surface (see Fig. 10.5(right)).

Extrinsic coordinates of a device are fundamentally important, in that they unambiguously determine the coefficients of the specific ray of light associated with the device, i.e., the ray of light received and blocked by an IN device, or the ray of light to be reproduced by an OUT device. Thus, an IN-OUT pair has to be established between two devices whose extrinsic coordinates identify the same straight line (i.e., the ray of light to be reproduced). Therefore, each device must know its extrinsic coordinates to establish such a pair. The determination of the extrinsic coordinates of a device in a distributed way from local information can take place by extending the beacon-based localization mechanism – already discussed with respect to the wall of invisibility – to consider the local curvature of the object and the orientation of the devices.

Local curvature can be determined from within the surface in a totally distributed manner by taking into account the following geometric property: while on a plain surface the ratio of the circumference to the radius of a circle is always 2π, on a curved surface this is no longer true. In fact, on a curved surface, the ratio of the circumference to the radius of a circle as measured on the surface decreases as the curvature increases (this is because the measured radius is actually an arc on the surface). Starting from this property, each device can measure the local curvature of the object on which it is located by measuring the circumference and the radius of a small circle centered on itself.

As described in [148], this can operatively take place by using the following algorithm. Each device probes the neighborhood, and determines the number of devices at a given distance (i.e., the circumference) and the number of devices on the shortest path from the central device to a neighboring device (i.e., the radius). Then, examining how far their ratio is from 2π, it can infer the local curvature.

Moreover, each sensor must also be able to determine its orientation with respect to the frame. This information can be obtained by comparing the beacon's orientation with other sensors' orientation, in an recursive manner (as supported by TOTA tuples). For this purpose each sensor must be equipped with a proper device capable of determining relative orientations [50]. It can be observed that determining relative orientations through the above-described procedure depends on the way in which the process spreads from the beacon (in a curve object). Following the Levi-Civita approach [137], we will consider as the valid direction the one obtained considering the shortest path (geodetic) from the beacon (see Fig. 10.6).

Once the above information (both curvature and devices' orientation) has been gathered, the extrinsic coordinates can be easily obtained by a simple variant of the previously described triangulation procedure. Again, it is important to remark that the TOTA distributed tuples provide a natural support to all these operations.

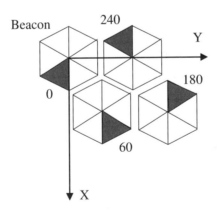

Fig. 10.6. Beacon-based evaluation of orientation

Unfortunately, even once each device knows its extrinsic coordinates (so that IN devices know what rays of light they block and OUT devices know what rays of light they have to reproduce), such knowledge is of no help in establishing the correct IN-OUT pairs that would enable a ray of light to be reproduced. In fact, if an IN device starts propagating a tuple reporting its extrinsic coordinates and the color to be reproduced, $(X, Y, Z, \theta, \omega, Color)$, the information contained in it cannot be exploited to properly route the message toward the corresponding OUT device. In fact, extrinsic coordinates do not tell in any way where a ray of light "entering" the object will "exit" the object, this being dependent on the shape of the object. Without any local knowledge about the global shape of the object (information which is simply impossible to store locally on each device, unless the object is very regular) one can a priori know neither where the tuple should eventually arrive nor the correct direction to the destination. To solve this problem without flooding tuples across the whole network, we need a strategy to route information even without an explicit knowledge of the mates' extrinsic coordinates. This is where intrinsic coordinates come in.

Evaluating intrinsic coordinates is perfectly analogous to the flat wall case and, unlike extrinsic ones, intrinsic coordinates can be effectively exploited to route tuples toward a specific point on the surface, by making a tuple progressively approach the needed destination, as we have already shown for the case of the rigid wall (the fact that, on a closed surface, discontinuities in the intrinsic coordinates inevitably arise, can be easily solved by the routing algorithm). So, to solve the problem of establishing IN-OUT pairs, one could think of somehow exploiting intrinsic coordinates instead of extrinsic ones. The main idea of our proposal is that each device, once it has determined its extrinsic coordinates, can determine the coefficients ($coeffs$) of the straight line that coincides with the ray of light incident on it. Of course, two IN and OUT devices are mates if and only if they compute the same (or very close) $coeffs$. Then we can use a content-based communication mechanism, like the TOTA one, to let opposite sensors interact.

Specifically, let us suppose that all the TOTA devices agree on a continuous hash function H that maps an equation's coefficients in intrinsic coordinates (ξ, η). An IN device A can then send the tuple containing the color information to the device at intrinsic coordinates $H(coeffA)$. An OUT emitter B, by its side, can try collect color information from the device at intrinsic coordinates $H(coeffB)$. Thus, if A and B are mates, the calculated intrinsic coordinates are $H(coeffA) = H(coeffB)$, identifying a unique device closest to those coordinates. This device will act as the rendezvous point of content-based routing (see Fig. 10.7) to establish the pair and exchange the needed information. Of course, the extrinsic coordinates must be carried with the message to deal with hash collisions, i.e., to check the correctness of a forming pair in the case of multiple pairs using the same rendezvous node.

We want again to emphasize that, as shown in the previous sections, the TOTA middleware is ideally suited to support this kind of interaction.

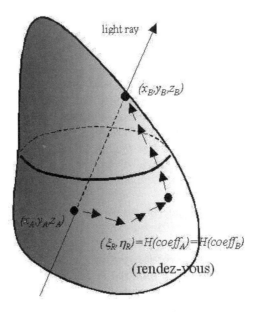

Fig. 10.7. Rendezvous communication

10.2.2 Optical and Hardware Issues

By considering each sensor and emitter as a separate device, the number of (directional) devices involved to render invisible an object may be very high: in fact, the object surface must be densely filled with sensors/emitters oriented toward all the possible directions of the object's outer space. To provide some quantitative data, we can reapply the considerations already made with respect to the wall of invisibility to a sphere of 1 m diameter. Let us consider again for just a moment a single fixed point of observation; in this case, to render invisibility at a 10 m distance, the sphere surface must be covered by approximately 372000 devices, each one 8.44 mm^2 wide. This number again derives by the Listing-Donders model: from a 10 m distance, a device of 8.44 mm^2 is seen as a single point, and it is easy to calculate that there is room for 372000 such devices in a 1 m diameter sphere. When such property has to be preserved for any direction of observations, however, the area of 8.44 mm^2 previously occupied by a single device, has now to include a high number of sensors and emitters pointing in different directions. In particular, as a first approximation, we can say that the creation of a smooth 3D "view" of an object requires that the number of directional sensors/emitters in the 8.44 mm^2 area be at least half of the total number of such areas (i.e., 372000/2=186000). This is because, to acquire/display a coherent image from all the possible points of view in each of the 8.44 mm^2 areas, there must be at least one sensor/emitter to support any of the other sensors/emitters directly visible from a common viewpoint (that is about the number of sensors/emitters in a half of the surface, e.g., a hemisphere). To makes it possible to fill a 8.44 mm^2 area with 186000 sensors and with a similar number of emitters, each of these devices should occupy an area smaller than 5 μm · 5 μ m. A single stand-alone computer-based device of that size is hardly imaginable. Still, one can think of packing in and controlling by a single compound device multiple optical micro devices pointing in different directions. Efforts such as the ones at Texas Instruments (where micro-displays made up of electro-statically actuated mirrors of a few μ have already been produced) and at Philips Research Laboratories [34] (showing the possibility of growing μ-scale LCD cells on any type of surface) demonstrate the potential feasibility of such an approach.

Coming to bandwidth requirements, we can apply calculations similar the ones in the previous section. To code the $(X, Y, Z, \theta, \omega, Color)$ information, each tuple has to carry its extrinsic coordinates to avoid hash collisions, while the intrinsic coordinates required for routing can be dynamically recomputed at each hop – the number of bit required is 24+5 · 16 bit = 104 bit. Considering that each message has to be routed, in the worst case, for 1.57 m (half of a maximum circle in the sphere), an IN-OUT communication occurring through a rendezvous device would require, in the worst case, 3.14 m, i.e., 1082 hops (we assume that the wireless communication range is long enough to transmit over the 8.44 mm^2 area). Thus, for a single directional facet, i.e., for a unidirectional device, the required bandwidth to route 30 messages per second for a maximum worst case of 1082 other devices is 1082 · 104 bit · 30 Hz $\approx$ 3.4 Mbit/sec (although the average bandwidth required by sensors may be lower). By considering packing in a single compound device all the devices contained in the 8.44mm^2 area (i.e., 372000 devices), the bandwidth requirements for a single compound device increase tremendously (approximately 1.2 Tbit/sec). Achieving such a bandwidth in such small devices is indeed very challenging, but not technically impossible, especially when taking into account recent advances in the area of terahertz band technologies [80]. In addition, one could also think of exploiting AI and image-recognition technologies to have sensors track the position of observers and reduce their efforts by rendering invisibility from a limited set of viewpoints.

10.2.3 Applications

The most natural applications of invisible objects are in the military market, e.g., invisible cars and tanks, and in the nonintrusive study of natural ecosystems. Moreover, several other applications can be conceived, by exploiting in different ways the achieved power of invisibility.

By considering painting the internals of an object (e.g., of a room) instead of its external, one can produce realistic immersive virtual reality environments, freeing users from wearing intrusive hardware [113] and from sticking to a specific place in a specifically shaped room [60]. A related application with a great potential market in southern Europe comes from the possibility of producing paintable windows. Tall buildings, very dark inside due to both narrow windows and narrow streets, characterize south European cities. Since local laws forbid changing the structure of these buildings, the only solution to improve the quality of living within them would be to paint virtual windows: from the inside, they would look like real huge windows; from the outside, no changes to the building would be perceived.

More generally, the outlined technology can be effectively exploited to produce visibility despite occluding objects. For instance, one could produce trucks with notable rear visibility by appropriately painting them. Also, one could consider solving the problem of limited visibility on mountain trails by painting portions of the occluding slopes.

10.3 STEP 3. The Cloak of Invisibility

The last constraint we have to remove in order to build the cloak of invisibility (or more generally, a comfortable invisible cloth) is rigidity. The above-described network of devices needs to be deployed on a flexible fabric, that can be deformed according to unpredictable dynamics and shapes, due to both external (e.g., wind) and internal (e.g., movement of the person wearing it) factors. Here, the challenge is that, because of the cloak's movements and folding, devices can change their relative positions and orientations quite rapidly with time.

10.3.1 Software Issues

In contrast with the previous cases, IN-OUT pairs in a flexible cloak must necessarily be continuously reestablished to reflect the cloak's movements. In particular, while the device's intrinsic coordinates remain fixed, extrinsic coordinates may change continuously. For this reason, the routing problem becomes particularly challenging and it must account for the overhead in maintaining an overlay coherent structure over the cloak's amorphous network. To solve this problem, we could envision two different strategies.

As a first strategy, devices could reevaluate their extrinsic coordinates continuously (e.g., 30 times per second) to account for cloak reshaping. The communication would then proceed with the rendezvous approach described in the previous sections. Unfortunately, this strategy imposes a notable computational and communication overhead on devices, leaving little room for the activities related to image rendering.

As an alternative strategy, one could think of relying on at least a small rigid portion of the cloak (e.g., a belt or a necklace) as a central point for geometrical references. Both IN and OUT devices, without being forced to know a priori their extrinsic coordinates, could send a partially undefined tuple (containing only the color information) toward the rigid reference point. While being routed from the source toward the rigid portion of the cloak, each of the intermediate devices could dynamically compute the geometric information related to the path followed by the tuple, and include such information in the tuple itself before propagating it. Once the tuple arrives at the rigid portion of the cloak, it can exploit the information collected during the travel to discover the extrinsic coordinates of the source. At this point, it can apply the hash-based rendezvous mechanism to meet its mate. The drawback of this solution is to produce load imbalances, by concentrating computational and communication activity in (and in the proximity of) the rigid portion of the cloak. We do not ignore the fact that better strategies and algorithmic solutions may exist. Sources of inspiration can be possibly found in the area of mobile ad hoc networks, where the focus is on enabling mobile peers to communicate with each other, despite the continuously changing topology of the network [20].

Independently of the solution being adopted, the self-maintenance of TOTA tuples can be of help to support cloak reshaping, by adapting the structure of fields automatically.

10.3.2 Optical and Hardware Issues

Cloak flexibility does not change the optical and size characteristics of the devices, already outlined in Sect. 10.2. What may change instead is their bandwidth requirement, as induced by the additional communication overhead to support cloak deformations and dynamic reforming of the IN-OUT pairs.

If we consider the first of the solutions proposed (dynamic recomputing of positions and orientations), and optimistically assume that such a solution is computationally feasible, the bandwidth requirements are likely to dramatically increase, due to the iterations of the relocalization process. If we consider the second of the proposed solutions, it appears like the bandwidth requirements do not even double. In fact, before each message can be routed to the appropriate rendezvous place, it has to travel toward the rigid reference point (e.g., the belt). Thus, each message on a flexible cloak travels for a total distance that would be less than twice the distance it would have traveled in the case of a rigid object. However, such considerations must be carefully checked against the load imbalances introduced.

A key issue in which a deformable, wearable, cloak can be advantageous over a wall or a rigid object relates to energy recharging. In fact, even in the absence of external power supply, (i) the inertial forces induced by cloak movements can be used for mechanically recharging the devices and (ii) the thermal energy of the human body can be an alternate source of energy for wearable computing systems (e.g., thermal-body-powered clothes are already available by Infineon Technology).

A final note relates to the cost of such an artifact. It is foreseen that large-scale production of MEMS computer-based systems will reduce their costs, in the near future, well below 1 Euro each [114]. A cloak of invisibility of 3 m^2 would require approximately 372000 compound (multidirectional) devices to be invisible at a 10 m distance, implying an overall cost well below a half million Euros.

10.3.3 Applications

In addition to a cloak, one could build any type of clothing by using the same technology. Their use in military operations and investigation would be definitely of great use, although ethically debatable. We better envision the use of invisibility clothes in fashion and entertainment markets. With regard to fashion, it is possible to think of small (and cheap) portions of clothes and accessories (e.g., T-shirts, bracelets, or necklaces) enriched with invisibility frames. With regard to entertainment, a cloak of invisibility could be effectively used as a tool for augmented and virtual reality games in parks like Disneyland.

Another application we have thought about, but whose feasibility we are by no means convinced about, is internal body monitoring. The idea would be to have a patient drink (or be injected) a set of sensors, and let them distribute in the zone of the body of interest (e.g., the stomach). Then, by an emitter-based cream to be painted on the body of the patient (e.g., the belly), one could see the body's interior, despite the internal movements of the body and of the sensors within it. Should this not be feasible with regard to the human body, it would be probably feasible to visualize other types of "internals" (e.g., an underground river or a complex pipeline) characterized by dynamic internal activity.

As visionary and speculative the cloak of invisibility and the related applications can be, the associated coordination activities can find natural applicability in much more concrete scenarios. With this in mind, we think that the support TOTA gives to all these activities is a good hint about its soundness and its potential extent of applicability.

11

Conclusions

Starting from the recognition that most emerging distributed computing scenarios challenge traditional approaches to distributed systems engineering, this book has outlined the fundamental role that will be played in that context by the choice of a proper coordination model. The design of large-scale, decentralized, open, and dynamic distributed systems, rather than relying on static, architecture-centric design approaches, should focus on the engineering of component interactions, by relying on a flexible and expressive coordination model, able to support context-awareness and adaptive self-organization.

Among several potential candidates, most of which getting inspiration from the models of interactions found in natural systems, field-based coordination appears a very general and usable one. All along the book, we have shown that field-based coordination (and in particular the Co-Fields model as embodied by the TOTA middleware) has several advantages that are likely to facilitate the design and development of adaptive self-organizing multiagent applications.

11.1 Key Advantages

The key advantages of field-based coordination – as they have emerged from this book – can be summarized as follows:

- *Expressive Context-Awareness.* Field-based coordination provides a suitable and expressive means to enforce context-awareness. Fields can convey any kind of contextual information across a distributed system, and can tailor the representation of this information to specific application needs. By means of fields, agents can be provided with locally accessible contextual information that can be used to represent global properties of their context, and that can be used by agents to achieve their goals directly.
- *Simplicity of Programming.* The expressive power of fields directly contributes in simplifying the internal activities of agents. In fact, application-specific fields can be shaped so that agents can immediately recognize what

they have to do, without being involved in complex activities to interpret contextual information and decide how to act.

- *Adaptive Self-Organization.* Fields are used as an indirect interaction mechanism between agents. This uncouples the interacting agents, which do not have to know each other a priori, thus making fields suitable for decentralized and open scenarios. Also, interactions mediated by fields promote a design as a whole perspective: the global behavior of a system (as resulting from the ensemble of the individual agents' behaviors) is driven by the global configuration of the fields distributed in the environment. Thus, an overall self-organized behavior of the system naturally emerges from the continuous feedbacks induced by having agents act on the basis of perceived fields and, consequently, by having them influence the global field configuration. The fact that fields continuously reshape to reflect the current system situation, makes such self-organizing behaviors also intrinsically adaptive.
- *Biologically Inspired Computing.* Although field-based coordination owes to physical inspiration, fields can be effectively used to reproduce a variety of interaction models typical of biological systems that have already found practical applications in several areas. These include pheromone-based coordination, morphogen gradients, and hormones.
- *Semantic Self-Organization.* Most approaches to self-organization assume that agents are very simple components devoted to reacting to specific environmental stimuli, without requiring any cognitive ability. Field-based coordination can support such simple reactive forms of self-organization, but also promotes enriching fields with expressive semantic information to give agents the possibility to exploit their cognitive abilities to autonomously decide how to act, other than by simply reacting. Therefore, field-based coordination may leverage reactive self-organization approaches toward more sophisticated forms of cognitive or semantic self-organization.
- *Effective Modeling.* Field-based coordinated systems can be effectively modeled by the simple and familiar formalism of dynamic systems. This modeling enables us to evaluate the effectiveness of an envisioned field-based solution by simply writing a few differential equations, integrating them with the help of some mathematical software, and visualizing the resulting behavior of the system.
- *Effective Implementation.* Field-based coordination can be implemented by making use of available middleware infrastructures, or it can rely on appropriate middleware infrastructures – like TOTA – explicitly conceived to support field-based coordination in dynamic network scenarios.

The additional fundamental advantage of field-based coordination is its generality. As we have tried to show in this book, field-based coordination can be suitably applied in very diverse application scenarios. At the so called micro scale, field-based coordination can be used to enforce self-assembly and self-configuration in swarms of simple computational devices and in spray computers. At the so-called medium scale, field-based coordination can be used to support self-localization for the nodes of a MANET, geographical routing algorithms, and the coordinated activities of humans and robots in pervasive computing environments. At the so-called global scale, we still require satisfactory experiences, but are nevertheless confident that field-based coordination could find additional practical applications in wide-area distributed computing (e.g., P2P and the Grid). In this regard, it is worth pointing out that researches such as [3, 98] already adopt field-related ideas, at the global scale.

11.2 Open Issues

Despite its notable advantages, several research work is still needed to make field-based coordination a practically usable tool for the extensive design and development of complex self-organizing distributed applications.

Some of the most critical open research issues we have identified include

- *Methodologies.* A critical open issue in field-based coordination (and consequently, in Co-Fields and TOTA) is the lack of an effective underlying general methodology enabling engineers to map a specific application goal into the corresponding definition of fields and their distributed shapes. In very simple application cases, the identification of fields can come rather easily from the problem definition (e.g., to have a group of agents meet, simply make them emit gravitational fields that attract them toward each other); see also Subsect. 5.3.6. In more complex cases, the lack of precise guidelines in identifying fields or in supporting the building of complex field-based coordination patterns from the composition of simple ones, leaves all the responsibility in the skill of designers. In pursuing the long-term goal of identifying suitable methodological guidelines to support designers, we are trying to gain experience with field-based coordination in more and more complex scenarios. The experiences and the lessons learned during this process, together with a documented catalogue of several field-based coordination patterns, will possibly form the embryo of a general-purpose supporting methodology. In any case, we emphasize that the lack of a methodology is not a specific drawback of field-based coordination, but it is a general limitation of all researches in the area of complex self-organizing distributed systems.
- *Tools.* Along with the identification of a proper methodology, designers and developers should be provided with proper tools to make their work of building field-based coordinated applications more efficient and reliable. The modeling tools presented in this book, together with the simulation tools of Co-Fields and TOTA, are only very preliminary results in that direction. More flexible and extremely realistic simulation tools, suitable

to reliably predict the behavior of a prototype system in the target operational environment, are required. Profiling tools must be integrated within, to properly benchmark applications and identify their limitations and bottlenecks prior to actual deployment. Novel decentralized control tools must be invented to enable developers to tune the behavior of a running system without having to stop it, and without undermining its basic capabilities of self-organization. More in general, the results that researchers in the area of complex adaptive systems are continuously producing should be properly documented, as they represent potential sources for the identification of novel tools to improve our capabilities in properly managing complex computational systems.

- *Applications.* Although field-based coordination is indeed a general model to orchestrate the activities in a distributed system, we feel that almost all the applications of this model are somewhat biased toward motion coordination (i.e., following a field spread across the physical space). In this book, we presented lots of applications in which human users follow such fields, others in which messages follow such fields (e.g., for the sake of routing in a network), and others where robots move following such fields; the motion bias is clear. Still, some applications somewhat avoiding this bias are possible; see Subsect. 4.3.4 and Sect. 9.2. We think that exploring how field-based coordination can be applied to non-motion scenarios is a ripe and still open research avenue.

- *Security and Privacy.* This book has mostly disregarded security issues; what field-based coordination may imply in terms of security and privacy is still to be deeply explored. Nevertheless, some preliminary considerations can be made. When fields are propagated in a distributed computing environment to convey contextual and application-specific information and to support the coordinated activities of distributed agents, security and privacy become critical issues. One should be able to prevent third parties from reading private information conveyed by fields, despite the fact that these fields may propagate in various – possibly untrusted – regions of the system. Also, one must avoid modifying the structure of existing fields or the information they convey: the result could be a global alteration of the whole field-based coordinated system. Considering the robotic self-assembly scenario, such a kind of intrusions could be capable of morphing self-assembled robots at will. Both these issues, plus any others still to be identified, are open to research.

- *Relations with Other Approaches.* Other than field-based coordination, a number of additional mechanisms and models – not covered in this book – have been successfully experienced to enforce adaptive self-organization in complex distributed systems. Negotiation mechanisms and agent-based economies [78, 28], interactions based on competitive games [155], cellular automata [154, 88], and the mechanisms of emergence of complex structures in networks [2], all represent interesting alternative approaches. In this book, we have been able to show how field-based coordination can be

used to model several biologically inspired coordination models. How and
to what extent field-based coordination can support the modeling of these
additional approaches, or how it can be somewhat integrated with them,
is still to be explored.

- *Identification of More General Models.* An even more general question is
whether field-based coordination is only the first step toward the identification of a more general and powerful coordination model for the next
generation of distributed computing systems. Of course, if we had an answer, we would have written a different book. Nevertheless, as scientists,
we have the moral obligation to be always unsatisfied with what we have
and to continuously look for better and more general solutions.

11.3 Perspectives

Solving the above issues, and leveraging our currently limited capabilities in
developing and managing very complex and dynamic software systems, will
open up brand new scenarios that, as of today, may appear visionary.

In a not so distant future, we expect the everyday activities of humans will
be supported by an ubiquitous environment of adaptive and self-organizing
computational services, always available to cater dynamically to our needs in
a context-aware manner. The Internet as we know it today will become like an
immense organism of composite, highly distributed, pervasive, and context-
aware services. Such services, by autonomously detecting, understanding, and
exploiting the general context – physical, technological, and social – in which
they operate, will be able to autonomously adapt their characteristics, and to
spontaneously aggregate and orchestrate their activities accordingly. This will
enable a wide range of new activities that are simply not possible or impractical now. Other than computational services, future scenarios will integrate
much more physically grounded notions of services. We will be able to exploit
in ubiquitous way the functionalities provided by clouds of micro-computers
dispersed in the environment, notably increasing our capability of interacting with the environment (e.g., by sensor networks) and possibly capable of
dynamically reshaping the physical environment to our needs (e.g., by self-
assembly materials). Also, we will be supported in our physical actions by
teams of cooperative mobile robots or by flexible modular robots.

In the above scenario, engineers will be provided with tools by which to
design and develop new applications and services that will be able to self-
configure and self-adapt their behavior in reliable and predictable ways. After
deployment, it will be optional for humans to remain in the loop: developers
and users should of course retain the capability of controlling and directing
the behavior of such autonomous self-organizing systems, but they will also
be free to fully rely on their internal self-organizing capabilities.

At the time of this writing, and despite our own personal expectations, we
cannot say for sure if the main drive for the realization of the above vision

will be field-based coordination, a combination of other coordination models and mechanisms, or even a totally different yet to be invented general model. What we know for sure is that there is an exciting research future ahead.

References

1. H. Abelson, D. Allen, D. Coore, C. Hanson, G. Homsy, T. Knight, R. Nagpal, E. Rauch, G. Sussman, and R. Weiss. Amorphous computing. *Communications of the ACM*, 43(5):74 – 82, 2000.
2. R. Albert, H. Jeong, and A. Barabasi. Error and attack tolerance of complex networks. *Nature*, 406:378 – 382, 2000.
3. O. Babaoglu, H. Meling, and A. Montresor. A framework for the development of agent-based peer-to-peer systems. In *Proceedings of the International Conference on Distributed Computing Systems*. IEEE CS Press, Wien, Austria, 2002.
4. J. Bachrach, R. Nagpal, M. Salib, and H. Shrobe. Experimental results for and theoretical analysis of a self-organizing global coordinate system for ad hoc sensor networks. *Telecommunication Systems*, 26(2 – 4):213 – 233, 2004.
5. P. Bahl and V. Padmanabhan. Radar: An in-builiding rf-based location and tracking system. In *Proceedings of the Infocom*. IEEE CS Press, Tel-Aviv, Israel, 2000.
6. S. Bandini, S. Manzoni, and C. Simone. Heterogeneous agents situated in heterogeneous spaces. *Applied Artificial Intelligence*, 16(9 – 10):831 – 852, 2002.
7. Y. Bar-Yam. *Dynamics of Complex systems*. Addison-Wesley, 1997.
8. L. Barabasi. *Linked*. Perseus Press, 2002.
9. J. Beal. A robust amorphous hierarchy from persistent nodes. In *Proceedings of the Conference on Communication Systems and Networks*. ACTA Press, Benalmadena, Spain, 2003.
10. F. Bellifemine, A. Poggi, and G. Rimassa. Jade - a fipa2000 compliant agent development environment. In *Proceedings of the International Conference on Autonomous Agents (Agents 2001)*. ACM Press, Montreal, Canada, 2001.
11. A. Berlin and K. Gabriel. Distributed mems: New challenges for computation. *Computing in Science and Engineering*, 4(1):12 – 16, 1997.
12. A. Birk, S. Coradeschi, and S. Tadokoro. *Proceedings of the Robocup International Symposium*. Number 2377 in LNAI. Springer-Verlag, 2002.
13. H. Bojinov, A. Casal, and T. Hogg. Emergent structures in modular self-reconfigurable robots. In *Proceedings of the Intlernational Conference on Robotics and Automation*. IEEE CS Press, San Francisco, California, USA, 2000.

14. E. Bonabeau, M. Dorigo, and G. Theraulaz. *Swarm Intelligence. From Natural to Artificial Systems.* Oxford University Press, 1999.
15. E. Bonabeau and G. Theraulaz. Swarm smarts. *Scientific American*, pages 72 – 79, 2000.
16. C. Borcea, D. Iyer, P. Kang, A. Saxena, and L. Iftode. Cooperative computing for distributed embedded systems. In *Proceedings of the International Conference on Distributed Computing Systems.* IEEE CS Press, Wien, Austria, 2002.
17. C. Borcea, D. Iyer, P. Kang, A. Saxena, and L. Iftode. Spatial programming using smart messages: Design and implementation. In *Proceedings of the International Conference on Distributed Computing Systems.* IEEE CS Press, Tokio, Japan, 2004.
18. P. Bose, P. Morin, I. Stojmenovic, and J. Urrutia. Routing with guaranteed delivery in ad hoc wireless networks. *Wireless Networks*, 7(6):609 – 616, 2001.
19. D. Braginsky and D. Estrin. Rumor routing algorithm for sensor networks. In *Proceedings of the Workshop on Sensor Networks and Applications.* ACM Press, Atlanta, Georgia, USA, 2002.
20. J. Broch, D. Maltz, D. Johnson, Y. Hu, and J. Jetcheva. A perfomance comparison of multi-hop wireless ad hoc network routing protocols. In *Proceedings of the Conference on Mobile Computing and Networking.* ACM Press, Dallas, Texas, USA, 1998.
21. W. Butera. Programming a paintable computer, 2002. PhD Thesis, MIT.
22. G. Cabri, L. Leonardi, and F. Zambonelli. Engineering mobile agent applications via context-dependent coordination. *IEEE Transaction on Software Engineering*, 28(11):1040 – 1056, 2002.
23. A. Carzaniga, D. Rosenblum, and A. Wolf. Design and evaluation of a wide-area event notification service. *ACM Transactions on Computer Systems*, 19(3):332 – 383, 2001.
24. M. Chricton. *Prey: a Novel.* Harper Collins, 2002.
25. Cooperative multi-robot control architecture. http://www.dynamic-concepts.com.
26. G. Cugola, A. Fuggetta, and E. De Nitto. The jedi event-based infrastructure and its application to the development of the opss wfms. *IEEE Transactions on Software Engineering*, 27(9):827 – 850, 2001.
27. Darpa agent markup language. http://www.daml.org.
28. R. K. Dash, N. R. Jennings, and D. C. Parkes. Computational-mechanism design: A call to arms. *IEEE Intelligent Systems*, 18(6):40 – 47, 2003.
29. N. Davies, K. Cheverst, K. Mitchell, and A. Efrat. Using and determining location in a context-sensitive tour guide. *Computer*, 34(8):35 – 41, 2001.
30. S. Day and P. Lawrence. Measuring dimensions: the regulation of size and shape. *Development*, 127(14):2977 – 2987, 2000.
31. A.K. Dey and G. Abowd. The context-toolkit: Aiding the development of context-aware applications. In *Proceedings of the Conference on Human Factors in Computing Systems.* ACM Press, New York, New York, USA, 1999.
32. K. Edwards and R. Grinter. At home with ubiquitous computing: Seven challenges. In *Proceedings of the International Conference on Ubiquitous Computing.* ACM Press, 2001.
33. D. Estrin, D. Culler, K. Pister, and G. Sukjatme. Connecting the physical world with pervasive networks. *IEEE Pervasive Computing*, 1(1):59 – 69, 2002.

34. R. Penterman et al. Single substrate lcds by photo enforced stratification. *Nature*, 417(6684):55 – 58, 2002.

35. P. Eugster, P. Felber, R. Guerraoui, and A. Kermarrec. The many faces of publish/subscribe. *ACM Computing Surveys*, 35(2):114 – 131, 2003.

36. Familiar linux. http://familiar.handhelds.org.

37. I. Foster. The grid: Computing without bounds. *Scientific American*, 288(4):78 – 85, 2003.

38. J. Fredslund and M. Mataric. A general algorithm for robot formations using local sensing and minimal communication. *IEEE Transactions on Robotics and Automation*, 18(5):837 – 846, 2002.

39. E. Freeman, S. Hupfer, and K. Arnold. *JavaSpaces Principles, Patterns, and Practice*. Addison-Wesley, 1999.

40. A. Fuggetta, G. Picco, and G. Vigna. Understanding code mobility. *IEEE Transactions on Software Engineering*, 24(5):352–361, 1998.

41. J. Fulton. *Howells Textbook of Physiology*. W.B. Saunders, 1946.

42. K. Gabriel and R. Sokal. A new statistical approach to geographic variation analysis. *Systematic Zoology*, 18(3):259 – 278, 1969.

43. D. Gelernter and N.Carriero. Coordination languages and their significance. *Communication of the ACM*, 35(2):96 – 107, 1992.

44. H. Gellersen, A. Schmidt, and M. Beigl. Multi-sensor context-awareness in mobile devices and smart artefacts. *Mobile Networks and Applications*, 7(5):341 – 351, 2002.

45. M. Gleizes, J. George, and P. Glize. A theory of complex adaptive systems based on co-operative self-organisation. demonstration in electronic commerce. In *Proceedings of the Conference on Self-organisation in Multi-agent Systems*. BT conference facility, Milton Keynes, United Kingdom, 2000.

46. Gnutella. http://gnutella.wego.com.

47. N. Gordon, I. Wagner, and A. Bruckstein. Discrete bee dance algorithm for pattern formation on a grid. In *Proceedings of the International Conference on Web Intelligence*. IEEE CS Press, Halifax, Canada, 2003.

48. Green light district. http://stoplicht.sourceforge.net.

49. C. Hess and R. Campbell. A context-aware data management systems for ubiquitous computing applications. In *Proceedings of the International Conference on Distributed Computing Systems*. IEEE CS Press, Providence, Rhode Island, USA, 2003.

50. J. Hightower and G. Borriello. Location systems for ubiquitous computing. *Computer*, 34(8):57 – 66, 2001.

51. S. Holmes. *Focus on MOD programming in Quake 3 Arena*. Premier Press, 2002.

52. A. Howard and M. Mataric. Relaxation on a mesh. In *Proceedings of the International Conference Robots and Systems*. IEEE CS Press, Los Alamitos, California, USA, 2001.

53. A. Howard, M. Mataric, and G. Sukhatme. An incremental self-deployment algorithm for mobile sensor networks. *Autonomous Robots*, 13(2):113 – 126, 2002.

54. T. Imielinski and S. Goel. Dataspace - querying and monitoring deeply networked collections in physical space. *Personal Communications Magazine*, 7(5):4 – 9, 2000.

55. C. Intanagonwiwat, R. Govindan, and D. Estrin. Directed diffusion: A scalable and robust communication paradigm for sensor networks. In *Proceedings of the International Conference on Mobile Computing and Networking*. ACM Press, Boston, Massachusetts, USA, 2000.

56. International conference on autonomous agents and multi-agent systems. http://www.aamas-conference.org.

57. International conference on distributed computing systems. http://www.cis.ohio-state.edu/icdcs04.

58. International conference on software engineering. http://www.icse-conferences.org.

59. International workshop on mobile teamwork support. http://www.infosys.tuwien.ac.at/motion/mts.

60. J. Jacobsson and Z. Hwang. Unreal tournament for immersive interactive theater. *Communications of the ACM*, 45(1):39 – 42, 2002.

61. Java 2 micro edition. http://www.java.sun.com.

62. Java bot for unreal tournament. http://utbot.sourceforge.net.

63. N. Jennings. An agent-based approach for building complex software systems. *Communications of the ACM*, 44(4):35 – 41, 2001.

64. N. Jennings and M. Wooldridge. Agent-oriented software engineering. In *Handbook of Agent Technology*. MIT Press, 2000.

65. Jini. http://www.jini.org.

66. B. Johanson and A. Fox. The event heap: A coordination infrastructure for interactive workspaces. In *Proceedings of the Workshop on Mobile Computer Systems and Applications*. IEEE CS Press, Callicoon, New York, USA, 2002.

67. S. Johansson and A. Saffiotti. Using the electric field approach in the robocup domain. In *Proceedings of the Robocup International Symposium*, number 2377 in LNAI. Springer-Verlag, Seattle, Washington, USA, 2002.

68. N. Johnson, S. Rasmussen, C. Joslyn, L. Rocha, S. Smith, and M. Kantor. Symbiotic intelligence: Self-organizing knowledge on distributed networks driven by human interactions. In *Proceedings of the Artificial Life Conference*. MIT Press, Los Angeles, California, USA, 1998.

69. S. Johnson. *Emergence: the connected lives of ants, brains, cities and sofware.* Scribner Press, 2001.

70. S. Johnson. Wild things. *Wired*, 10(3), 2002.

71. C. Jones and M. Mataric. From local to global behavior in intelligent self-assembly. In *Proceedings of the Conference on Robotics and Automation*. IEEE Press, Taipei, Taiwan, 2003.

72. Jprofiler. http://www.ej-technologies.com/products/jprofiler/overview.html.

73. J. Kahn, R. Katz, and K. Pister. Emerging challenges: Mobile networking for smart dust. *Journal of Communications and Networks*, 2(3):188 – 196, 2000.

74. G. Kaminka, P. Lima, U. Pedro, and R. Rojas. *Proceedings of the Robocup International Symposium*. Number 2752 in LNAI. Springer Verlag, 2003.

75. B. Karp and H. Kung. Gpsr: Greedy perimeter stateless routing for wireless networks. In *Proceedings of the International Conference on Mobile Computing and Networking*. ACM Press, Boston, Massachusetts, USA, 2002.

76. J. Kennedy, R. Eberhart, and Y. Shi. *Swarm Intelligence*. Morgan Kaufmann, 2001.

77. J. Kephart and D. Chess. The vision of autonomic computing. *Computer*, 36(1):41 – 50, 2003.

78. J. O. Kephart and Amy R. Greenwald. Shopbot economics. *Autonomous Agents and Multi-Agent Systems*, 5(3):255 – 287, 2002.

79. O. Khatib. Real-time obstacle avoidance for manipulators and mobile robots. *Journal of Robotics Research*, 5(1):90 – 98, 1986.

80. R. Kohler. Therahertz semiconductor-heterostructure laser. *Nature*, 417(6685):156 – 159, 2002.

81. E. Kranakis, H. Singh, and J. Urrutia. Compass routing on geometric networks. In *Proceedings of the Canadian Conference on Computational Geometry*. University of British Columbia, Vancouver, Canada, 1999.

82. P. Lawrence. *The Making of a Fly: the Genetics of Animal Design*. Blackwell Science, 1992.

83. T. Lehman and al. Hitting the distributed computing sweet spot with tspaces. *Computer Networks*, 35(4):457 – 472, 2001.

84. Q. Li, M. Rosa, and D. Rus. Distributed algorithms for guiding navigation across a sensor network. In *Proceedings of the International Conference on Mobile Computing and Networking*. ACM Press, San Diego, Rhode Island, USA, 2003.

85. K. Lorincz, D. Malan, T. Fulford-Jones, A. Nawoj, A. Clavel, V. Shnayder, G. Mainland, S. Moulton, and M. Welsh. Sensor networks for emergency response: Challenges and opportunities. *IEEE Pervasive Computing*, 3(4):16 – 23, 2004.

86. T. Malone and K. Crowston. The interdisciplinary study of coordination. *ACM Computing Surveys*, 26(1):87 – 119, 1994.

87. M. Mamei, L. Leonardi, M. Mahan, and F. Zambonelli. Coordinating mobility in a ubiquitous computing scenario with co-fields. In *Proceedings of the Workshop on Ubiquitous Agents on Embedded, Wearable, and Mobile Devices*. DEIS, University of Bologna, Bologna, Italy, 2002.

88. M. Mamei, A. Roli, and F. Zambonelli. Emergence and control of macro spatial structures in perturbed cellular automata, and implications for pervasive computing systems. *IEEE Transactions on Systems, Man, and Cybernetics*, 35(3):337 – 348, 2005.

89. M. Mamei, M. Vasirani, and F. Zambonelli. Experiments of morphogenesis in swarms of simple mobile robots. *Journal of Applied Artificial Intelligence*, 18(9 – 10):903 – 919, 2004.

90. M. Mamei and F. Zambonelli. Programming pervasive and mobile computing applications with the tota middleware. In *Proceedings of the International Conference On Pervasive Computing (Percom)*. IEEE CS Press, Orlando, Florida, USA, 2004.

91. M. Mamei and F. Zambonelli. Self-maintained distributed tuples for field-based coordination in dynamic networks. In *Proceedings of the Symposium on Applied Computing (SAC)*. ACM Press, Nicosia, Cyprus, 2004.

92. M. Mamei and F. Zambonelli. Motion coordination in the quake 3 arena environment: a field-based approach. In *Proceedings of the Workshop on Environments for Multi-Agent Systems*, number 3347 in LNCS. Springer-Verlag, New York, New York, USA, 2005.

93. M. Mamei and F. Zambonelli. Physical deployment of digital pheromones through rfid technology. In *Proceedings of the Swarm Intelligence Symposium*. IEEE CS Press, Pasadena, California, USA, 2005.

94. M. Mamei and F. Zambonelli. Spatial computing: The tota approach. In *Self-Star Properties in Complex Information Systems*, number 3460 in LNCS. Springer-Verlag, 2005.

95. M. Mamei, F. Zambonelli, and L. Leonardi. Co-fields: A physically inspired approach to distributed motion coordination. *IEEE Pervasive Computing*, 3(2):52 – 61, 2004.

96. C. Mascolo, L. Capra, and W. Emmerich. An xml based middleware for peer-to-peer computing. In *Proceedings of the International Conference of Peer-to-Peer Computing*. IEEE CS Press, Linkoping, Sweden, 2001.

97. Mathematica. http://www.wolfram.com.

98. R. Menezes and R. Tolksdorf. A new approach to scalable linda-systems based on swarms. In *Proceedings of the Symposium on Applied Computer*. ACM Press, Orlando, Florida, USA, 2003.

99. Modular reconfigurable robotics at parc. http://www2.parc.com/spl/projects/modrobots.

100. F. Mondada, G. Pettinaro, A. Guignard, I. Kwee, D. Floreano, J. Deneubourg, S. Nolfi, L. Gambardella, and M. Dorigo. Swarm-bot: a new distributed robotic concept. *Autonomous Robots*, 17(2 – 3):193 – 221, 2004.

101. R. Nagpal. Programmable self-assembly: Constructing global shape using biologically-inspired local interactions and origami mathematics, 2001. PhD Thesis, MIT.

102. R. Nagpal. Programmable self-assembly using biologically-inspired multiagent control. In *Proceedings of the International Conference on Autonomous Agents and Multi-Agent Systems*, pages 418 – 425. ACM Press, Bologna, Italy, 2002.

103. R. Nagpal, A. Kondacs, and C. Chang. Programming methodology for biologically-inspired self-assembling systems. In *Proceedings of the Spring Symposium on Computational Synthesis*. AAAI Press, Stanford, California, USA, 2003.

104. R. Nagpal and M. Mamei. Engineering amorphous computing systems. In *Methodologies and Software Engineering for Agent Systems*. Springer-Verlag, 2004.

105. R. Nagpal, H. Shrobe, and J. Bachrach. Organizing a global coordinate system from local information on an ad hoc sensor network. In *Proceedings of the International Workshop on Information Processing in Sensor Networks*, number 2634 in LNCS. Springer-Verlag, Palo Alto, California, USA, 2003.

106. F. De Paoli and G. Vizzari. Context dependent management of field diffusion: an experimental framewrok. In *Proceedings of the Workshop from Object to Agents, WOA 2003*. Piagora Editrice, Cagliari, Italy, 2003.

107. V. Parunak. Go to the ant: Engineering principles from natural multi-agent systems. *Annals of Operations Research*, 75(1):69 – 101, 1997.

108. V. Parunak, S. Brueckner, and J Sauter. Erim's approach to fine-grained agents. In *Proceedings of the Workshop on Radical Agent Concepts*. NASA Goddard Space Flight Center, Greenbelt, Maryland, USA, 2002.

109. V. Parunak, M. Purcell, and R. O'Connell. Digital pheromones for autonomous coordination of swarming uav's. In *Proceedings of the Unmanned Aerospace Vehicles, Systems, Technologies, and Operations Conference*. American Institute of Aeronautics and Astronautics, Norfolk, Virginia, USA, 2002.

110. M. Paskin and C. Guestrin. A robust architecture for distributed inference in sensor network. In *Proceedings of the International Symposium on Information*

Processing in Sensor Networks. ACM Press, Los Angeles, California, USA, 2005.

111. T. Payne, R. Singh, and K. Sycara. Facilitating message exchange through middle agents. In *Proceedings of the International Conference on Autonomous Agents and Multi-Agent Systems*. ACM Press, Bologna, Italy, 2002.

112. G. Picco, A. Murphy, and G. Roman. Lime: a middleware for logical and physical mobility. In *Proceedings of the International Conference on Distributed Computing Systems*. IEEE CS Press, Providence, Rhode Island, USA, 2001.

113. W. Piekarski and B. Thomas. Arquake: the outdoor augmented reality gaming system. *Communications of the ACM*, 45(1):36 – 38, 2002.

114. K. Pister. On the limits and applicability of mems technology, 2000. Defense Science Study Group Report.

115. K. Pister. Invited plenary talk, 2003. International Conference on Distributed Computing Systems.

116. R. Poor. Embedded networks: Pervasive, low-power, wireless connectivity, 2001. PhD Thesis, MIT.

117. Quake iii arena. http://www.idsoftware.com/games/quake/quake3-arena.

118. A. Rao, C. Papadimitriou, S. Ratnasamy, S. Shenker, and I. Stoica. Geographic routing without location information. In *Proceedings of the International Conference on Mobile Computing and Networking*. ACM Press, San Diego, California, USA, 2003.

119. S. Ratsanamy and al. Ght: A geographic hash table for data-centric storage. In *Proceedings of the International Workshop on Wireless Sensor Networks and Applications*. ACM Press, Atlanta, Georgia, USA, 2002.

120. S. Ratsanamy, P. Francis, M. Handley, and R. Karp. A scalable content-addressable network. In *Proceedings of the SIGCOMM Conference*. ACM Press, San Diego, California, USA, 2001.

121. A. Ricci, M. Viroli, and A. Omicini. Agent coordination context: From theory to practice. In *Proceedings of the Cybernetics and Systems Conference*. Austrian Society for Cybernetic Studies, Vienna, Austria, 2004.

122. M. Ripeani, A. Iamnitchi, and I. Foster. Mapping the gnutella network. *IEEE Internet Computing*, 6(1):50 – 57, 2002.

123. Robocode. http://robocode.alphaworks.ibm.com.

124. Robocup official site. http://www.robocup.org.

125. G.C. Roman, C. Julien, and Q. Huang. Network abstractions for context-aware mobile computing. In *Proceedings of the International Conference on Software Engineering*. ACM Press, Orlando, Florida, USA, 2002.

126. M. Roman and al. Gaia : A middleware infrastructure for active spaces. *IEEE Pervasive Computing*, 1(4):74 – 83, 2002.

127. K. Romer. Tracking real-world phenomena with smart dust. In *Proceedings of the European Workshop on Wireless Sensor Networks*, volume 2920 of *LNCS*. Springer-Verlag, Berlin, Germany, 2004.

128. S. Roundy, D. Steingart, L. Frechette, P. Wright, and J. Rabaey. Power sources for wireless sensor networks. In *Proceedings of the European Workshop on Wireless Sensor Networks*, volume 2920 of *LNCS*, Berlin, Germany, 2004. Springer-Verlag.

129. A. Rowstron and P. Druschel. Pastry: Scalable, decentralized object location and routing for large-scale peer-to-peer systems. In *Proceedings of the Con-*

ference on Distributed Systems Platforms. ACM Press, Heidelberg, Germany, 2001.

130. J. Scholtz. Ubiquitous computing in the military environment. In *AeroSense Symposium.* SPIE Publisher, Orlando, Florida, USA, 2001.

131. S. Seidel and T. Rapport. 914 mhz path loss prediction model for indoor wireless communications in multifloored buildigns. *IEEE Transactions on Antennas and Propagation*, 40(2):207 – 217, 1992.

132. D. Servat and A. Drogoul. Combining amorphous computing and reactive agent-based systems: a paradigm for pervasive intelligence? In *Proceedings of the International Conference on Autonomous Agents and Multi-Agent Systems*, pages 441 – 448. ACM Press, Bologna, Italy, 2002.

133. W. Shen, B. Salemi, and P. Will. Hormone-inspired adaptive communication and distributed control for conro self-reconfigurable robots. *IEEE Transactions on Robotics and Automation*, 18(5):1 – 12, 2002.

134. F. Sparacino. Sto(ry)chastics: a bayesian network architecture for user modeling and computational storytelling for interactive spaces. In *Proceedings of the International Conference on Ubiquitous Computing*, number 2864 in LNCS. Springer-Verlag, Seattle, Washington, USA, 2003.

135. W. Spears and D. Gordon. Using artificial physics to control agents. In *International Conference on Information, Intelligence, and Systems.* IEEE CS Press, Rockville, Maryland, USA, 1999.

136. Spec. http://www.coe.berkeley.edu/labnotes/0403/spec.html.

137. M. Spivak. *A Comprehensive Introduction to Differential Geometry.* Publish or Perish, 1979.

138. M. Srivastava, R. Muntz, and M. Potkonjak. Smart kindergarten: Sensor-based wireless network for smart developmental problem-solving environments. In *Proceedings of the Conference on Mobile Computing and Networking.* ACM Press, Rome, Italy, 2001.

139. D. Steere and al. Research challenges in environmental observation and forecasting systems. In *Proceedings of the Conference on Mobile Computing and Networking.* ACM Press, Boston, Massachusetts, USA, 2001.

140. I. Stoica, R. Morris, D. Karger, M. Kaashoek, and H. Balakrishnan. Chord: A scalable peer-to-peer lookup service for internet applications. In *Proceedings of the SIGCOMM Conference.* ACM Press, San Deigo, CA, 2001.

141. K. Stoy and R. Nagpal. Self-reconfiguration using directed growth. In *7th International Symposium on Distributed Autonomous Robotic Systems.* Springer-Verlag, Toulouse, France, 2004.

142. K. Sugihara and I. Suzuki. Distributed motion coordination of multiple mobile robots. In *Proceedings of the International Symposium on Intelligent Control*, pages 138 – 143. IEEE Press, 1990.

143. R. Szewczyk, J. Polastre, A. Mainwaring, and D. Culler. Lessons from a sensor network expedition. In *Proceedings of the European Workshop on Wireless Sensor Networks*, volume 2920 of *LNCS.* Springer-Verlag, Berlin, Germany, 2004.

144. The semantic web. http://www.w3.org/2001/sw/.

145. The sims. http://thesims.ea.com.

146. The social superorganism and its global brain. http://pespmc1.vub.ac.be/SUPORGLI.html.

147. The swarm simulation toolkit. http://www.swarm.org.

148. O.C. Thorpe. Computing curvature using amorphous computing, 1998. Technical report, MIT.

149. K. Tsukada and M. Yasumrua. Activebelt: Belt-type wearable tactile display for directional navigation. In *Proceedings of the International Conference on Ubiquitous Computing*, number 3205 in LNCS. Springer-Verlag, Nottingham, United Kingdom, 2004.

150. Universal plug and play. http://www.upnp.org.

151. C. Unsal and J. Bay. Spatial self-organization in large populations of mobile robots. In *Proceedings of the International Symposium on Intelligent Control*. IEEE CS Press, Columbus, Ohio, USA, 1994.

152. B. Warneke, M. Last, B. Leibowiz, and K. Pister. Smart dust: Communicating with a cubic-millimeter computer. *Computer*, 34(1):44 – 51, 2001.

153. R. Weiss, S. Basu, S. Hooshangi, A. Kalmbach, D. Karig, R. Mehreja, and I. Netravali. Genetic circuit building blocks for cellular computation, communications, and signal processing. *Natural Computing*, 2(1):47 – 84, 2003.

154. S. Wolfram. *A New Kind Of Science*. Wolfram Media, 2002.

155. D. Wolpert, K. R. Wheeler, and K. Tumer. General principles of learning-based multi-agent systems. In *Proceedings of the International Conference on Autonomous Agents*. ACM Press, Seattle, Washington, USA, 1999.

156. L. Wolpert. *Principles of Development*. Oxford University Press, 1998.

157. H. Wong and K. Sycara. A taxonomy of middle-agents for the internet. In *Proceedings of the International Conference on MultiAgent Systems*. IEEE CS Press, Boston, Massachusetts, USA, 2000.

158. World wide web consortium. http://www.w3.org.

159. M. Yim, K. Roufas, D. Duff, Y. Zhang, C. Eldershaw, and S. Homans. Modular reconfigurable robots in space applications. *Autonomous Robots*, 14(2):225 – 237, 2003.

160. M. Yim, Y. Zhang, and D. Duff. Modular robots. *IEEE Spectrum*, 2002.

161. F. Zambonelli, M.P. Gleizes, M. Mamei, and R. Tolksdorf. Spray computers: Explorations in self-organization. *Pervasive and Mobile Computing*, 1(1):1 – 20, 2005.

162. F. Zambonelli, N. R. Jennings, and M. Wooldridge. Developing multiagent systems: the gaia methodology. *ACM Transactions on Software Engineering and Methodology*, 12(3):417 – 470, 2003.

163. F. Zambonelli and M. Mamei. The cloak of invisibility: Challenges and applications. *IEEE Pervasive Computing*, 1(4):62 – 70, 2002.

164. F. Zambonelli, M. Mamei, and A. Roli. What can cellular automata tell us about the behaviour of large multiagent systems? In *Proceedings of the International Workshop Software Engineering for Large Multi-Agent Systems*, number 2603 in LNCS. Springer-Verlag, Orlando, Florida, USA, 2002.

165. F. Zambonelli and V. Parunak. From design to intentions: Sign of a revolution. In *Proceedings of the Workshop Engineering Societies in the Agents World*, number 2577 in LNAI, pages 13 – 28. Springer-Verlag, Madrid, Spain, 2002.

Index

Printing: Krips bv, Meppel
Binding: Stürtz, Würzburg